My Brother, Roy

**Family & Friends Remember Leonard Franklin Slye,
the Boy Who Grew Up to Be
Roy Rogers**

To order more copies of this book, contact:
John R. Simon
8721 Pond Creek Road
West Portsmouth, Ohio 45663
(740) 259-6 337

My Brother, Roy

**Family & Friends Remember Leonard Franklin Slye,
the Boy Who Grew Up to Be
Roy Rogers**

By
Cleda Slye Willoughby
and
John Roger Simon

With a Foreword by
Dodie Rogers

London
Books
2014

Cover and book design by

813 Rogers Court
Ashland, Kentucky 41101
designs-on-you.net

TABLE of CONTENTS

For my sister Mary Kathleen Simon, Ph.D.,
her husband, Gary Gemmer,
and their boy, Edward Simon Gemmer

FOREWORD

Many books have been written about my parents, Roy Rogers and Dale Evans. Their lives affected people around the world, both on- and off-screen. As entertainers, they worked hard and invested long hours but enjoyed the opportunity to perform. As "regular folk" (as they referred to themselves), they appreciated the chance to give back, helping others however they could, but never forgetting their roots.

They led extraordinary lives while always staying true to their beliefs and character, qualities shaped from childhood. Throughout their lives, they experienced many joys and were challenged by much heartache.

My father often told stories of his adventures growing up in Ohio. Although there were lean times, he accepted these hardships as a normal part of life. As time went by, I forgot many of Dad's stories. I forgot that the past has a strange way of bringing us around to what inspires us today. I find it hard to think of life before cell phones, computers, the Internet, big screen TVs, and walking for any reason except to improve one's health.

My dad was the only boy among three girls. He had two older sisters, Mary and Cleda, and one younger, Kathleen.

I was surprised and excited to learn that my Aunt Cleda had

written her account of their childhood and given another insight into my father's life.

After reading a few pages, I was anxious to read more. Cleda's story brought back memories of my grandparents that I had filed away. Though his children called my grandfather Pop, we also called him Pop. There was no mistaking who was being addressed.

As long as I can remember, my dad hunted, an activity born from self preservation when he was a young boy. The challenge of hunting stayed with him throughout his life. Although it may have seemed to conflict with his love of animals, it did not. Being part Native-American, he believed one must respect all animals, even those whose lives were taken. We always had pets at our home, at times more than most people. Dad and Trigger had a synergy that fans felt and recognized.

I was adopted in 1952 when I was seven-months old. We lived in Chatsworth, California, until 1964 when we moved to the high desert, Apple Valley. Aunt Cleda and Aunt Kathleen and their families moved also. Dad and his sisters enjoyed getting together to spend time singing, strumming, and sharing memories.

When my parents went out on tours, Cleda would often stay with me. She was stern which meant I couldn't get away with much. Often times, my cousin Roger, Aunt Kathleen's son, would visit. He was only a year older than I was and we could come up with adventures of our own, although Aunt Cleda was not always amused by our behavior. However, even with her no-nonsense attitude, there was no doubting her protectiveness and love for us all.

Aunt Cleda eventually moved back to Ohio. She became close friends with John Simon to whom she expressed her intent to write her story. Unfortunately, Cleda passed away before she could finish her book, but not before requesting that John complete it for her. It is because of this closeness with her that he is able to fulfill her wish. I am so thankful for the opportunity to read the account of her life with my father, Roy Rogers.

Dodie Rogers at the Roy Rogers Festival, Ramada Inn, Portsmouth, Ohio, June 2009. *Image courtesy of Ginny Harness.*

Dodie Rogers at the Roy Rogers Festival, Ramada Inn, Portsmouth, Ohio, June 2010. With western stars who were honored on U.S. Stamps Roy Rogers, Tom Mix, William S. Hart, and Gene Autry. *Image courtesy of Ginny Harness.*

Tues –

Dear John –

Thank you, so much, for sending the tape of Cleda – We love it & when she is gone from us, we shall treasure it – She's a great person – and such an honest, loving person –

It hurts to know she has hope to go thru this' cancer thing – I pray the Lord will call her Home before her suffering in worse – It is good for her to be with Marion in Florida, where the weather is always temperate –

Thank you, again, for the video & may God richly bless your life –

Sincerely
Dale E. Rogers

When Cleda died, the author sent Roy and Dale a video. He received a thank you signed "Dale E. Rogers." Circa 1996. *Image courtesy of John Roger Simon.*

INTRODUCTION

It's nice to write about people who grew up in this area, a place we hold so dear. We traveled the same Happy Trails. My mother Clara Walsh Simon and father Edward Louis Simon allowed for my love of home and they along with my sister Mary Kathleen Simon recognized how music guided my direction.

The cowboy Westerns promoted all that and somehow I recognized their value. At first it was Red Ryder, Roy Rogers and the others followed.

Cleda Mae Slye Willoughby and her brother, Leonard Franklin Slye, who became known as Roy Rogers, never got over their love of home. They appreciated this area for numerous reasons: the music, geography, friends, and other aspects of our culture here in Scioto County, Ohio.

Their family was a warm and close one. Cleda grew up with sisters Mary and Kathleen and brother Leonard. Their parents were Mattie and Andrew.

The family went from Portsmouth, Ohio, to Cincinnati for work about 1909. They soon tired of big city living so they built a houseboat and towed it to Portsmouth where they lived on the river for a few years. While there, the children attended the old Union Street School. They were living on the river during the vicious 1913 flood.

In 1919 Andrew bought fifty-seven acres in the area known as Duck Run, about seventeen miles from Portsmouth. Other roads feed into Duck Run. Inskeep Road and Allen Hollow were two of those. The Slye family moved from town to a home at the head of Allen Hollow which is now Sly Road. The house was the last one up the hollow and sat up on the left bank. It's no longer standing.

For the next two years the family worked together under Andy's direction and built another house down at the point where Allen Hollow and Inskeep Road joined. It is known as the home place. Mattie liked the new location because she could see and visit with those coming and going on both sides of the house.

Andrew built the house by himself and taught the rest of the family his skills as he went so they could help. Cleda often told me, "You would have liked my pop. He was such an interesting man. He worked his entire life providing for his family, and he could pick that mandolin."

The Slyes lived a rich family life. They worked hard as they farmed, canned, hunted, swam, pulled taffy, and made sorghum. Family music was their most precious luxury. Both parents played and sang and so did the children. Neighbors, too, were musical. Leonard learned to play musical instruments, and to sing and yodel.

Yodeling is an outgrowth of hollering which was a technique the Europeans brought when they settled this land. People who lived in the hills often communicated by hollering and it developed into a form of music known as mouth sounds.

Everyone loved to dance and Leonard became a good dance caller, an art he demonstrated in several of his movies. All those skills proved valuable assets for Leonard when he worked at Republic Pictures.

At home, Leonard, best friend Charlie Hiles, and other neighborhood boys sometimes got into trouble over an occasional missing chicken or other boyish pranks.

The children attended the Duck Run one room school which consisted of eight grades. One teacher, Guy Bumgarner, made each child feel special. Roy said, "Charlie Hiles and I would have been in reform school if it wasn't for Guy Bumgarner. He related school to our life—music, 4H, sports—and he mixed with our people."

Others lived on Duck Run who became famous too. Branch Rickey, was a pioneer in America's favorite pastime, baseball. His father was Cleda's "no nonsense" choir leader at Duck Run Church. A short distance down Inskeep Road, between the homes of Slye and Rickey, lived the Strickland family who produced the sixty-eighth Governor of Ohio, Ted Strickland.

The Slye family members formed lasting friendships. Hubert Crabtree said he and his brothers, along with Leonard and the Hiles boys, had paths worn between their houses. The boys were like brothers. Hubert recalled walking to Duck Run School with Leonard, Norman Crabtree, Strauther Hiles, and brothers Ellis and Riley DeLong. The families of Jordan, Slye, DeLong, Strickland, Hiles, and Crabtree were close.

Mary Slye wed and moved to Lawndale, California, in the late 1920s. The rest of the family visited her one summer and found the place to their liking, so they soon followed in their old Dodge. In the autumn of 1930 the Slyes returned to Ohio and sold the home place. The next spring the Dodge made the trip west again, this time permanently. Cleda said the journeys were like two long picnics.

The Slye home place still stands to this day and is owned by Mary Lou Crabtree, Charlie Hiles' daughter.

In California the Slyes found various jobs. From a young age Leonard always said, "Everybody is equal but with a gift." He sang with several local groups and with the help of Bob Nolan, eventually formed the Sons of the Pioneers. They practiced at the Slye home and Cleda told me they invited her to sing on the radio with them a few times.

When an opening for a singing cowboy came at Republic Pictures, Leonard auditioned and won the part. They called him Dick Weston and he starred in his first film in 1937. After further consideration they changed his name to Roy Rogers. With the help of his exceptional horse, Trigger, Dale Evans, and George "Gabby" Hayes, his popularity grew quickly and he became King of the Cowboys.

Cleda remained in California and worked with Roy for fifty years. However, she often thought of her origins and old friends. So, in 1981 Cleda came home to southern Ohio.

Cleda told me once, "I have a fondness for home and for this town, and longed for these hills and creeks. I was always fascinated by Appalachia and would have spent the rest of my life in the country, but had to settle in town near people."

Soon after Cleda returned, she and I got acquainted through music. She loved dance music and frequently came to square dances to hear the fiddle and to dance. She and I were often partners. The dances were usually held at the McDermott fire station or the Pond Creek Community Hall, built by Father

Patrick O'Donnell. Square dances have been held there since 1955.

Cleda sometimes came to the Simon farm with Bill Sanders and his wife for Sunday fiddle music played under the sweet gum tree that had been planted in 1961. At her home she would usually get out her vintage little Martin guitar to play and sing in her gentle manner. One day Cleda and I went to the home of John and Bea Hollback in South Webster, Ohio, and renewed childhood behaviors of having a big taffy pull (sorghum taffy). After the taffy, we all played and sang together.

Cleda admired her father's lifelong effort to provide for his family. She also appreciated how he played his mandolin with those work worn hands so used to physical labor. She also knew that her pop liked a little mischief and enjoyed a drink from time to time. Sometimes she helped him with that. She said, "I remember a funny experience. He was working in the garden one day and kept coming over to the little bedroom window. He had a half gallon jug of moonshine whiskey in there and I'd hand it to him. He'd take a nip and go back to work. Mom wondered how he was getting tipsy. I was a little girl, but I didn't tell."

Cleda thought highly of her father and admired the life of her brother as well—except for one thing. She loved animals and treated them accordingly. Roy was a big game hunter and she often admonished him for that.

It was said that Cleda held their family together.

Cleda had read and heard many stories about both her dad and brother that were not accurate. She was driven to write her own book but lacked confidence for she thought her formal education was inadequate. At the time, there had not been a book written by a family member and she realized that she knew the Slye family better than anyone. She especially wanted to tell the true story, to provide her own perspective. As memories came to her, she wrote them down and her book developed gradually.

In 1996 Cleda became ill, entrusted her story to me, and asked me to complete it. Since there had been no book written about Roy by anyone from his home community, I decided my part of the book would develop from interviews with local people and a few others who had special personal experiences with him.

Help came from my sister, Mary Kathleen Simon, Jamie Williams, disc jockey James A. Perry, Harry Johnson, Grand Ole Opry photographer Les Leverett, Gary Hurn, Mary Lou Crabtree, and fellow author Ruth White. Dodie Rogers wrote a sensitive forward.

Gene Arms had a special story about eating head cheese, Chris Copp helped in acquainting me with the home and property of his great uncle, Branch Rickey and Georgia Furr gave the most help of all.

Suzanna and Tony Stephens made me welcome in their classic home and helped edit and publish the book. Their sparkling granddaughter, Marie, sang to me; they made me feel comfortable. Many other locals encouraged and helped, and it was so pleasant meeting such interesting people like ninety-seven-year-old Ray Boldman.

Special days were spent with Cleda and two meetings with Roy made this even more meaningful. In 1989 a breakfast was held for him, a gathering of his chums from Union Street, Duck Run, and McDermott School days. They included me and I was to present him with one of his favorites, a jar of sorghum. After breakfast I was alone in the back of the room and found him standing next to me. I said, "Roy, I'm a square dance caller and in several of your movies you were calling a square dance. They were the same tunes and calls we use."

He said, "That's 'cause I learned to dance and call when I lived here." He asked what calls I used, the tunes we played, and where the dances were held. I told him that Cleda often attended the dances. I added that we were having a dance at Pond Creek that evening and invited him to attend. He replied, "I have to go to a banquet but I'd rather come to the dance."

In her final days, I often went to Cleda's home, sat beside her bed, and took notes as we talked. Her niece, Diane, was staying with her and the three of us usually sang at some time during the visit. Cleda liked that best. Cleda's favorite was "Four Walls," Jim Reeves' signature song. She sang a beautiful soft harmony.

Cleda gave me her beautiful calico cat, Josephine. The cat lived a long time out at the museum here on the farm.

When Cleda was confined to the hospital, Roy and I met again. I was working on my farm and thinking about Cleda. It was late springtime. Her favorite flowers were those that grow wild in Roosevelt Game Preserve. I picked up a pint Mason jar, went to the forest, and selected a variety. Arriving at the hospital I went to her room. Her door was closed. A man was standing there in the hall with no hat, no Western attire, and no smile. I knew it was Roy but didn't want to intrude. He said the medical staff was attending to Cleda. I told him she and I were friends and that we sent him a jar of sorghum each year. He said no more and never smiled. I stayed back. Soon a door down the hall opened. Several nursing students emerged, followed by their instructor, Sharon Scott. She walked down to us and gave me a hug and a peck on the cheek. At that Roy straightened up, smiled brightly, and said, "Do you send her sorghum, too?"

Roy was called into the room and soon I followed. I spoke to Cleda, her student nurse, and Sharon. Cleda was pleased with the flowers. At the end of her bed sat Roy Rogers and Dale Evans. Cleda introduced us. What a striking scene! Dale said, "May I see the flowers?" I knelt beside her and held the jar. She went over each of them and Cleda told her their names. Dale was most taken by the white dogwood. She said, "I've never seen one before."

Roy said, "Aw, everybody knows the dogwood story. Both the Maddox Brothers & Rose and Wilma Lee & Stoney Cooper

John Roger Simon presenting Roy Rogers a quart of sorghum at a breakfast for Roy's childhood chums held at Shawnee State Park Lodge. June 1989. *Photo courtesy of Pat Crabtree.*

have famous songs about the dogwood legend." Cleda told Dale how the tree was tall, straight, and strong until it was used as the timber for the old wooden cross. God blighted the dogwood so it would never be tall and straight again, but always small and crooked. Its four, delicate white blossoms were marked with stains of where the blood-covered nails pierced the hands and feet of Jesus. The center of the flower resembles the crown of thorns placed on the head of Jesus. The flowers were the topic of a long conversation and Cleda seemed happy we were there.

In researching the life of Leonard Franklin Slye, it strikes clearly that the strongest influence his family had on him was their passion for music. He was also shaped by the dancing, singing, playing, and yodeling in his community as well as the wisdom of his teacher, Guy Bumgarner, who had the good sense to include music in his daily classroom experience.

Upon arrival in California, Leonard and his dad became migrant workers. At night they lifted everyone's spirits by providing music to those with whom they worked. He sang with several groups through the years and helped form the Sons of the Pioneers.

Timing was right and Republic Pictures fit his musical talents perfectly into his movie character. He played the music he loved and became King of the Cowboys. He was the people for whom he played.

Leonard Slye lived one of the strongest values known to our Appalachian culture; "Whose boy are you?" After success came to him, when he met someone from home, he wanted to know their heritage and their knowledge of home—who are you connected to and where do you live?

His smile wrinkles were permanent reminders of his pleasantness and his legacy "Happy Trails."

When Roy died in 1998, a memorial was arranged by Shirley Adams. It was held in front of his handsome mural, painted by Robert Dafford on the Front Street flood wall in Portsmouth. Our band, consisting of Jack Strickland, Bea and John Hollback, Tommi Stanley, Sharon Scott, and I, participated. It was a pleasure and honor to give Roy our music.

Cleda was not a professional writer but her story is a true and

Tommie Stanley, John Hollback, Bea Hollback, John Roger Simon, and Sharon Scott sing "The National Anthem" in the memorial for Roy Rogers at his mural in Portsmouth, Ohio. July 1998. *Photo courtesy of John Roger Simon.*

interesting account of the Slye family. With slight editing her portion is presented in her voice, just as she wrote it.

—John Roger Simon

Chapter One
CLEDA'S STORY

The Ohio River had been in flood for several weeks now. Though it was returning to its channel, it was muddy and swift in the middle. The houseboat was tied to the willows. When the water receded it would be put up on blocks. A gangplank reached from the deck to the bank. A small boy standing on the deck was trying to see the water. He had just thrown another piece of kitchen cutlery overboard so he could hear the *ker-plunk* as it hit the water. He was two-years-old with white hair, bobbed "Buster Brown" style. His eyes were blue and shining with mischief. He had almost emptied the drawer of spoons, knives, and forks. When the water finally receded, they were found sticking in the sand. The time was the spring of 1913. The boy was Leonard Franklin Slye. He was to become *Roy Rogers, King of Cowboys*, much loved by thousands over the world.

This is the story of his early childhood in Portsmouth, Ohio, later on the farm on Inskeep Road at Duck Run, Ohio, and through his adult life in California. A good many books and countless magazine articles have been written about his life. I am Cleda, his sister, and for a long time I have wanted to write the true story of our childhood. I wish to set straight some of the things written. Some of them implied that our father was a kind of "guitar-playing, ne'er-do-well, and did not work. Some indicated that Roy had no shoes until he could buy his own, or that he was the one who provided for us. This is not true. Our father was one of the most hard-working men ever. As I look back, I wonder how he accomplished so much, working in the shoe factory all week and then running a farm, raising a crop, and doing all things required.

I will start at the beginning. Our father, Andrew, was the third son of six boys born to Alonzo and Mary Rebecca Slye. They raised their family in a cottage at the corner of Front and Waller Streets in Portsmouth, Ohio. There was little education for the Slye boys and they all quit school to go to work early in their lives. William, the eldest, was blind from the age of five- or six-years-old. A playmate threw sand at his eyes which contained pieces of glass that blinded him. He was sent to the Institute for the Blind and received a more formal education than the others.

All of the brothers had natural musical talent. They sang, played mandolin, guitar, and the violin.

Their playground was the bank of the Ohio River. They fished, swam, and camped. They gathered coal that dropped from the barges that plied the river.

The barges carried products such as sand, gravel, scrap metal, large machinery, and tanks of petroleum in later years. The river was a means of keeping in touch with the world in the early days when there were few roads. Flat bottomed barges following the current brought household furnishings, medicine, and clothing from the large cities to the settlers in the valleys. After steamboats were invented, there were circuses, minstrel shows, and traveling evangelists. The show boats were very beautiful, glistening white with gay bright trimming. The calliope played and everyone went down to see the boats, sometimes going to see the shows. The *Delta Queen* was one of the boats. She traveled from Pittsburgh to New Orleans on summer cruises.

Houseboats still anchor in the shade of the trees along the bank.

The Slye brothers enjoyed long summer days fishing and swimming. Sometimes they would take a tent and camp. They made nets for fishing and in those days there were no locks and dams in the river. In winter, the river sometimes froze over and a horse drawn wagon could be driven across the ice. Such a winter was 1917 when we walked across to Kentucky on the ice. I was seven-years-old and World War I was on.

Our father was exempt since he had four children. He served by making shoes for the army. Uncle Will had married a widow with three children. Their son Elmer went to France, was wounded, and died from the effects of mustard gas.

There were many Liberty Bond drives, and the movie stars of the day, such as Mary Pickford and Douglas Fairbanks, traveled the country raising money for the war effort. We heard stories of atrocities by the Kaiser and the Huns. Our aunt was always worried and grieving about her son and son-in-law, in the thick of the battle in France. It was a great day when it was over. There was a big parade with bands and flags flying. We were proud of our sister Mary, marching in her replica of the Red Cross uniform. She was almost twelve-years-old. It was an exciting time, but everyone was glad when the war was over.

Mary, Leonard, and I went to the Union Street School. Mary was an excellent student. She was very humiliated on young

Leonard's first day of school. He did not understand what the teacher wanted him to write on his paper, so he wrote nothing. He proudly showed a large "goose egg" the teacher had given him and Mary cried.

Leonard had a few adventures. One day, he and a friend Bob Stevenson hopped on the back of an ice wagon to get the small pieces of ice. The deliveries were being made and the driver whipped up the horses. They were powerful draft beasts. The wagon was going too fast for the little six-year-olds to get off. So, to the police station they went. When Bob's mother got there they were crying and scared. Their faces were dirty and smeared with tears. Bob's hair was as red as Leonard's was white, and all messed up. They never hopped on another wagon.

Our houseboat had three rooms: front room, bedroom, and kitchen. There was blue and white linoleum on the kitchen floor and brussels carpets in the other rooms. It was kept immaculately clean. There were curtains at every window. My mother was proud of her home and would not let anyone call it a "shanty boat." It was a houseboat. "Shanty boat people" were looked down on as lazy and their boats were not well kept.

The 1913 flood was a time to be remembered and talked about frequently by the whole family. My father, Andy's, boat saved the day as it was caulked and made ready when the river began to rise. The water covered most of Portsmouth and we floated along, picking up our uncles' families and some of their belongings. It was fun for all the kids, but an anxious time for parents. We watched all kinds of things floating by, household items and even a small building. I was three-years-old and remember some, but not all, of the things our parents talked about later on.

Once after the water receded and the boat was tied up to the willows, I attempted to cross the gangplank, following Mary. I slipped and fell, but hung on to the plank guardrail. Pop heard Mary's screams and jumped off the boat roof he was repairing and caught me. They said I would've drowned if I'd let go. The waters ran swiftly and the currents would have carried me under the boat.

Pop and his brothers were all strong swimmers. Even though he was blind, Uncle Will would dive over the paddle wheel of the ferryboat that they sometimes sneaked on.

We all liked the river. The water was clean and clear when not in flood and we had many pleasant times swimming and playing in the shallow part under the shade of the willow trees.

We raised all kinds of vegetables on the riverbank. The soil was rich and black loam. It was a small lot but we had room for a woodshed and we kept a few chickens and had our own fresh eggs. Berries were plentiful across the river in Kentucky. My father picked and my mother canned blackberries and huckleberries. We stayed there until we moved to the country about 1919.

Leonard was born, on November 5, 1911. The year before that we moved to Cincinnati. There my father worked in a shoe factory. He did not like city living, so he and Uncle Will built the boat, and decided to sail back to Portsmouth. They made a sail out of bed sheets, but it just didn't work. They had to be towed.

Along the way, they caught fish, swam, and had music in the evenings. My father playing the mandolin, my mother, the guitar, and Uncle Will, with his violin, made a fine trio. They loved to sing. Mom and Pop met at a music party. My father and his brothers were well known for their beautiful singing and harmony. My mother also came from a family with musical talent. She and her sister, Dixie, sang in churches. Her brother Egbert and Grandfather Womack played violin, so I believe my brother, Leonard, came by his talent naturally.

When my father decided to move to the country he found a farm of fifty-seven acres about seventeen miles northwest from Portsmouth. It was the winter of 1919. He wanted to get out of the houseboat in time to plant a garden, so it was February when we moved. The roads were poor to begin with, but by the time the house came into view they had grown even rougher and narrower. The last stretch was only a wagon's width, so if we met another team it took some maneuvering to get past each other. However, there was a small chance of meeting another wagon as our house was the very last in the hollow.

In February, everything was cold and dreary looking. The house was a two-bedroom clapboard with a front porch the width of the house. There were outbuildings, a cellar, an orchard, and a long grape arbor. There were several ponds and the creek ran in front of the place. Sometimes the water rose to the front porch when a storm came up. There was a good well.

My father wasted no time clearing underbrush and getting the garden patches ready. He kept his job at the shoe factory, boarded in Portsmouth, and came home on weekends to cut wood and do the dozens of other things that had to be done.

I often think now about my mother living at the head of the "holler" with four children under twelve. There were wildcats and wolves then, even bear. Mom had a gun and sometimes fired at a suspicious noise. We also had a fine watchdog. He was big, white, and long-haired, and was named Rover. He could

(L to R) Zeke Mullins, Cleda Willoughby, and Elmer Sword at the homeplace. *Photo courtesy of Don Brooks.*

hear people coming up the road miles away and stormed up and down the barnyard growling and barking. When visitors came, we tied or fastened him in one of the out buildings. We had visitors often on weekends.

People soon learned of our parents' music making and singing. We also had one of the first Victrolas, with records of "Uncle Josh" who performed on the talking records. My father enjoyed good music, John Phillips Sousa marches, and he bought us Enrico Caruso records.

My mother made taffy and popcorn for us. My brother, Leonard, was a natural comedian and kept the big boys laughing at his songs—some of them "off-color" but funny. He was nicknamed *Funny* and always had a crowd surrounding him. My parents made music for square dancing and Leonard called long before his voice changed.

We went to a one-room school about a mile from where we lived. In winter it was nearly dark before we got home and we would still have wood to bring in, a cow to milk, and chickens to feed. Everyone had work to do.

On Saturdays we cut wood, dragging the trees down to the wood lot, then sawing and splitting them into lengths for our heater and cook stove. Leonard and I were the sawyers each on the end of the crosscut saw. We'd sometimes disagree on the length and we'd jerk the saw back and forth and have the stick cut off—almost—in two places. When we had these rare disagreements, and if our father didn't settle it, we'd end up laughing at each other.

We were glad when winter was over. There was still plenty of work to do, but a different kind. The hills and trees were beautiful and wildflowers were everywhere. The creek ran full, young chickens were hatched, and a new calf was born. We planted every kind of vegetable. There also were blackberries, raspberries, huckleberries, and dewberries on our place, as well as plums, grapes, peaches, and several different kinds of apples. We canned and preserved everything.

My mother made sure we had time to play, too. She often walked with us to the Henry Springs place beyond the school, where there was a nice swimming hole. The creeks close to us were shallow, sometimes dry, but the Henry Springs place (sulfur springs used by the Indians as a curative and healing power) was where everyone went to swim. It was also used when people were getting baptized.

Our first teacher at Duck Run was Miss Mildred Tracy. She was crippled, as was our mother. She limped, though not as badly as Mom.

The school was divided with boys on the teacher's right and girls on the left. Her desk was a platform with a long recitation bench for the students to come forward and recite their lesson. Every grade from first to eighth attended this school. Books were few and sometimes had to be shared. The teachers of that time should be admired and respected having thirty to thirty-five students all in different grades, and few books to share. They did a fine job teaching the 3 Rs: reading, writing, and arithmetic. We also had history, English, and hygiene. Often, there would be just one or two come forward when this class was called. A big pot-bellied stove was in the center of the room. The kids nearest to the stove got too warm, while those the farthest away were too cold and had to wear sweaters and coats. The playground was a field between the church (also one room) and the school. The creek at the back was part of the playground, too. In winter, there were stretches of ice to skate on. There were no balls and bats provided, so we made our own. (Since the county did not even provide books, why would they provide play equipment?) Our young people today cannot imagine this, yet, we got a better education than some of our kids today with all of the "extras" provided.

The boys got into all kinds of mischief. Some of them hated school and the teacher. One teacher in particular was the object of some of their boyish pranks. He believed in using the switch and always had a bunch ready, standing in the corner. The boys often got these switches and would ring them, cutting them nearly through in several places, so when the teacher would begin switching one of them across the legs, the switches would fly apart.

How that man became a teacher, we'll never know. He must have hated his work. I don't believe anyone learned much from him. He gave me my first and only switching. It was more of a humiliation to my brother, Leonard, than to me. I was a big girl, in the eighth grade. My hated enemy had pulled my hair and ran. I picked up a rock and threw it. The bell rang for us to go back to school and I couldn't believe that I had actually hit this boy, but I did—in the head! I had never been able to hit anything. Leonard, on the other hand, was a crack shot, and could, and did, kill all kinds of things with a slingshot and rocks. The teacher called us to the front of the class, my enemy, bleeding from the blow from my rock. We were both switched. That was another mark against the teacher, in Leonard's book.

Looking back, teachers of that day had a hard time, all poorly paid and few books for their students. Many times students were almost grown by the time they reached eighth grade. Teachers needed to earn their respect.

After I was out of school, one special teacher came along, Guy Bumgarner. I believe he saved some of those boys from getting into serious trouble. I know his coming into my brother's life when he did turned his life around. He was a smiling, cheerful bachelor who gained the boys' goodwill. He got out on the playground with them. He also acquired some bats and balls and other equipment. He organized games and a 4-H Pig Club. For the first time in their lives, a teacher was genuinely interested in these young men. He lived at Haverhill, with a bachelor uncle, and went home on the weekends. He often took some of the boys with him. Leonard was one who enjoyed some of these times. Haverhill was only twenty or thirty miles away, but in those days, it was quite a trip. Guy played guitar and had a fine singing voice. He sang with the boys and encouraged them to develop their talents.

One year the school put on a Christmas play and Leonard was Santa Claus. I believe Guy could see Leonard's talent in singing and acting even then. A well known artist, George Little, was one of Guy's students. He could see his potential and urged him to develop and pursue it, which he did, in spite of parental objection. His paintings are well known in this part of the country.

Guy also encouraged the boys when, under his direction, each of them bought a pig and took care of it, according to 4-H club rules. They fed them regularly and tended them. Guy came to their homes each Saturday to check on them. He often landed at our house at lunchtime, so we got to know him well. He was genuinely interested in the boys. What a lift for these boys! They responded by feeding their animals regularly at 6:00 a.m., 12:00 noon, and 6:00 p.m.

When the Scioto County Fair came, the pigs were shown. Leonard's sow, Evangeline, took the blue ribbon. The following year she was bred and sent to Columbus, sow and litter, to the State Fair, as part of the prize he had won the year before. She didn't win there, but Leonard spent a fine week at the fair. There's a story that he spent much of his time riding the elevator in the hotel. It supposedly was the first one he'd ever seen.

IT'S A BASEBALL TEAM. Roy Rogers (with hands behind head) played on the eight-man Duck Run Orioles in the 1927-28 era. The team did not have uniforms, but some of the lads managed to get sweat shirts and sewed the letter "O" on them. There is no won-lost record on the books for the Orioles. The team included (back row, left to right) Rogers, Leslie Colley, Homer Boldman and Lawrence Wiseman and (front row, left to right) Charles Hiles, Leroy Colley, Clyde Cyrus and Strauther Hiles. Guy Bumgarner, a Lucasville teacher, coached the team. *Image courtesy of Ruth Adkins.*

We lived up the hollow for about two years. My father bought ten acres down on the point. Our houses at Duck Run were always thought of as up the holler and down on the point. The land was between two creeks and two roads, where Allen Hollow and Inskeep Roads came together, thus creating a point. It was wooded so it had to be cleared. We left a few nice oak trees standing for shade.

There were so many rocks that Pop used them in the forms for the cement foundation for the house and two cellars. Later, we learned that the house was sitting on layer after layer of sandstone. A large stone quarry is there now. My mother became very indignant when a visitor from Portsmouth said to my dad, "Well, Andy, it looks like about all you could raise here is a fight… there are plenty of rocks."

Mom knapped plenty of those rocks into small pieces as she sat on the ground with a small hammer, making small pieces out of large rocks. These were put in the forms for the foundation. The cement and sand mixture was poured around them, and tamped down as the cement was mixed by hand.

The house was strong and sturdy and still stands in use today. My mother was so proud of her house and also was glad to be closer to neighbors and where she could see people going by. We had a large barn, a long chicken house, a cow, a mule team, and pigs. We sold eggs and chickens for frying. We dug a well and learned about the layers of rock. It took a lot of dynamite to blast through the rock. The cold and sweet water was called hard water. There were no water softeners so we carried water from the creek to wash our clothes, unless we could catch rainwater.

The family and the children were very busy growing up. Mary had married while we were still living in the holler. Leonard hunted and fished when he wasn't at school or working. There were square dances on Saturday night, taffy pullings, and always music.

In the summertime, our father came home every night from his job in Portsmouth. My mother's sister Dixie and her daughter Lillian worked in the shoe factory, also. On weekends our place was a favorite for young ones to gather. Around the neighborhood someone would have a dance. One of the boys,

Lowell Crabtree, was an expert caller. My brother learned calls from him. People went as families to these dances and a room was cleared of furniture. Babies and the smaller children were placed on beds to watch the dancing or to sleep. Sometimes the lady of the house collected ten cents from the boys who danced to pay musicians, but my parents played for free because they loved it.

Both square dances and taffy pullings were very popular with the young people. At the taffy pullings, my mother was the chief taffy maker. The boys brought the sugar and everyone got into the pulling. Sometimes it was a mess, with taffy and stickiness everywhere.

My brother was quite a carpenter and learned to drive a nail straight at a very young age, so he was Pop's right hand, sawing and hammering along with him to build the house. Our evenings were spent at "the point" after Pop came home from Portsmouth and supper was over. We'd all walk down and work until after dark. It was a satisfying time of accomplishment for our parents.

We owned a two-story house, three bedrooms upstairs, a downstairs living room, a large kitchen, a small hall, and porches across the front and back. From the porches, we could see the roads and creeks on either side in the winter when the trees were bare. My mother liked living there where she could see people passing.

Pop was the only one of the brothers who had moved to the country and there were plenty of visitors. With no telephones, Mom never knew for whom she was cooking, but every weekend there were guests. We always had fried chicken, vegetables, and fruit from our garden and orchard. Mom made many batches of biscuits. Summer brought one or two of our cousins to stay all summer. My father would let them know they would have to work along with us but they came, as the freedom of the country was so different from city living.

Grandmother Slye came for a week each summer at berry picking time. She'd come to McDermott on the train and sometimes Mary would meet her with horse and wagon. It was about five miles to McDermott. The journey on the train for a week in the country was her vacation. Grandma picked berries and Mom helped her make them into preserves and jelly to take home.

Grandma was a little woman weighing less than one hundred pounds. She picked up firewood, tiny sticks that burnt up in a flash, but she loved doing it. During the rest of the year she did housework for people out on the hill.

Grandpa Slye always worked for the City Water Co., but there was never enough money that Grandma could stop working. Grandpa was an alcoholic and that is where all the money went. I think of him as a short sturdy man with a brush-like sandy mustache, with never much to say to us children. Their little house on the corner of Front and Waller streets was jammed with boxes of things people gave to Grandma. Grandma's house was a gathering place for the brothers and families.

Many played and sang and the men drank beer, but the women did not drink. We had good food and the kids played outside or sat and listened, as I did. The voices blended in the old tunes of the day and my mother was the only one of the wives who sang, but they all loved music. A friend, Earl Phillips, who played beautiful guitar, often joined us, as did the Bostwick family. Two of my cousins became gifted guitar players. They were Chester, Uncle Hono's (Alonzo) son, and Stanley, Uncle Brownie's (Russell) son. Stan and Leonard much later formed a duet and tried their luck as entertainers in California. They called themselves the "O-H-TEN Boys," but did not have much success during the depression of the 1930s.

While living in the country, Leonard loved to hunt and fish and Pop gave him a shotgun as soon as he was old enough to handle and care for one. Before that time he'd go along with the big boys to carry the game or help dig the rabbits out of holes. When the season for rabbit hunting came, he was always alert to the gunshots. If he wasn't out with the hunters, he'd rush to the porch upon hearing the shot and yell, "Did you get him, Ed?" Ed was a neighbor just down the hill from us, who later became part of our family. Leonard always said Ed, rather than Lloyd or Lowell, or many of the other hunters it could have been. Our family thought this was funny and cute, one of the endearing things that we remember.

During these years, Pop bought a beautiful black mare named Babe. She had been a sulky racer and could really travel! She was Leonard's pride and joy. He rode her everywhere and sometimes even to school. There was no place to shelter her there, so he didn't ride her to school often. Pop bought Babe from Mr. Wiseman who lived out on McCullough. A piece written by Helen Wiseman in the magazine, Reminisce, mentioned this many years later, pointing out Leonard had become Roy Rogers and owned a famous horse named, Trigger.

Lawrence Wiseman was one of Roy's good friends and a picture of the two boys and Ol' Babe is now in the Roy Rogers Museum in Victorville, California. Laurence was a member of the

4-H Pig Club and a part of the bunch of boys that Guy Bumgarner taught and helped. He married Ester Allen who played the part of Mrs. Claus in the Christmas play when Leonard played Santa.

In one Christmas program Leonard recited a piece that goes:

Father calls me "William," sister calls me "Will,"
Mother calls me "Willie," but the fellers call me "Bill."
Mighty glad I ain't a girl, rather be a boy,
With all them curls and fancy things, that's worn by Fauntleroy.
Love to eat green apples, and go swimming in the lake.
Hate to take the 'castorile' Ma gives for belly aches.
Most all the time the whole year round, there ain't no flies
 on me.
But just before Christmas, I'm as good as I can be.

Leonard did a great job and the audience loved it. After he started to high school, he'd once in a while ride Babe, but most times he walked to the pike where Pauline Burcham, a schoolmate who had a car, picked him up.

In 1928 - 1929 Pop decided to go to Cincinnati to work. By this time, Mary and I had married. Mary's husband was Joseph Odell who lived for a while in McDermott, then moved to Colorado, and later to California. She was very young and my mother worried and grieved that she was so far from home and family. She was able to come home in 1927 for a visit. She liked living out west and probably that was when Pop began to think of a trip to that part of the country.

During the winter of 1929 - 1930, Pop and Leonard worked in the shoe factory in Cincinnati and Leonard tried to go to

(L to R) The Slye children, Mary, Cleda, Leonard, and Kathleen stand behind their mother, Mattie Slye, on the front porch of the homeplace on the point. Thier pop, Andy, can be partially seen to the far right. *Photo courtesy of Bill Sanders.*

night school to get his high school diploma. He also got his first guitar in a second hand shop for $20.00. Before that he played our mother's guitar. It wasn't easy working days and going to school at night.

Cincinnati was a great city to us, about 100 miles from

Portsmouth on the Ohio River. My husband and I had stayed on the farm taking care of cows and chickens, but we visited them and marveled at the tall buildings and long rows of steps that served for sidewalks in some places. The family got tired of the city, especially Leonard and Pop. It was getting to be impossible for Leonard to hold a day job and attend school at night.

By this time Mary had moved to California and wrote glowing letters of the mild climate. She sent photos of the orange groves, palm trees, and ocean. Leonard, more than any of us, wanted to go for a visit to see the Golden Land of California. There was much talk and plans were made. Mom and Pop had a 1929 Dodge sedan, so in the spring of 1930 they came to the farm, ready for the trip to California.

By this time, I had two little boys, Andy and Richard. We stayed and kept the farm going and wished them a good trip. Roads were not very good in 1930 and cars were not very dependable. There were flat tires and trouble with the engine. Pop was a good mechanic, though, and Leonard learned from him. They made it to California, camping along the way with hundreds of others who were looking for a job and a better place to live.

Mary and her family were so happy to see them. They lived in Lawndale and Josie, Mary's husband, owned some trucks. Leonard went to work for him hauling gravel. They all loved the sunny weather and the beaches. They stayed all summer, coming back to Ohio in the fall with plans to sell the farm and go back to California. On the return trip they had engine trouble and bought another car which they towed back for the spare parts. From the two cars my Dad built the truck that carried all of us to California in May 1931.

(L to R) Ol' Blue, Leonard, Mattie, and Andy Slye with the old Dodge heading to California. *Photo courtesy of Mary Lou Crabtree.*

Their talk was all about how great it was in California, everything was better. My mother especially liked the warm weather and cool nights.

Lawndale was in the Los Angeles area, about three miles from the ocean. The days were sunny with a cool ocean breeze. Mary's father-in-law was in Ohio at this time and was going to California so Leonard went with him. He was too restless and eager to get back out west to wait and go with the family in the spring of 1931.

He had been doing some singing with groups, but without pay. There was a talent show and contest in nearby Inglewood at the radio station. Mary made him a colorful Western style shirt and almost pushed him onto the stage. He sang "Haidy-Brown" and yodeled. The audience liked him but he didn't win. The next day he got a call from the leader of a group, The Rocky Mountaineers. They had heard him sing and asked him to come join their group. That was when he and Bob Nolan met. It was the beginning of the much loved and later famous Sons of the Pioneers.

My father had worked and planned all winter for our departure in May. He sold the farm and all of their possessions except bedding, clothing, and cooking utensils. The truck was loaded with seven passengers: Mom, Pop, Kathleen, cousin Egbert Johnson, my two boys, and me. We looked like pioneers with the sides of the truck covered with canvas. I think we were a kind of pioneer and there were many others on the road. You could see them camping along, cooking and sleeping.

Mom cooked on a two-burner stove. Pop unloaded and got it going. Mom sat on the ground, peeled potatoes, and cooked eggs and bacon while making coffee. It smelled and tasted wonderful. It was easy to find places to camp in those days. Often we'd find a nice creek where we could wash our clothes and the kids could swim and play in the water.

In 1931 a cabin could be rented for $1.00 or $1.50 with outside community showers. You could see them all along the highways. We traveled on Route 66 most of the way. Sometimes the cabins were shaped like tee-pees or little log cabins, or other imaginative shapes to attract the travelers' dollars. Travelers like us saved our money for food and necessities, because we could easily sleep out. Mom spent many nights in the truck where she had a nice comfortable bed, not sleeping on the ground with a bedroll. We were young and healthy and my boys liked the adventure. My mother just wanted to get to California and settle down in one place. She was a good traveler and her cooking was something we all enjoyed, it was kind of like a long picnic. I don't think we ever ate in a restaurant. For one thing, we needed to save money to buy the lots so we could build our house in California. I marvel today at how my father was able to do this. Land was cheap but money was scarce. Somehow they saved enough to buy the lots. The way some books were written pictured my father all wrong. My mother rarely had to live in a rented house.

On the way, we rented a cabin only if it rained. We found fruit and vegetable stands all along the country roads, sometimes picking tomatoes and corn. It was early for ripe fruit, but there was always plenty to eat. We went to grocery stores. Sometimes we'd treat ourselves to a hamburger that cost about fifteen cents. It was a change for us and a break for Mom from cooking. In Tucson, Arizona, a drive shaft broke on the truck while we were in the outskirts of town in a Mexican section. We stayed there for two nights until Pop and Egbert repaired the truck. There was never any thought of taking it to a garage. My father could fix anything.

I have always resented the first book written about Roy and Dale. In it, Pop was pictured as neglecting his family and allowing the burden to rest on my brother to provide food for us. That is a lie. We always had plenty to eat. It might have been beans and potatoes, after the fruit in the cellar had been used and the hogs we butchered were gone, and before the gardens came in again. Leonard worked no more than the rest of us. Why do people write such things when the truth is just as interesting? When the book came out, my sisters and I spoke to Art Rush, Roy's manager, about the picture it gave of our hard-working father. It hurt us and it hurt him. Art said it was too late. Whether it sold more copies for that woman, I don't know. Maybe people like to read such things. The tabloids and trashy papers and magazines that keep going on scandal and gossip about famous people are a negative mark on our society and I deplore them!

My mother, being crippled, slept in the truck on our journey to California. She also cooked for us. The weather was pleasant, the heat of the summer not yet on us. We went into California and saw the ocean for the first time in San Diego. My boys loved it, as we all did. Beaches were clean and uncrowded. We found a sheltered spot and bathed and played in the wonderful Pacific Ocean. I made the mistake of trying to wash my hair in the salt water, we carried fresh water with us, so we rinsed the salt water out of our hair.

We crossed the Rio Grande border into Old Mexico. The bridge was narrow and not many people crossed in those days. My father, Kathleen, my two boys, and I walked across to buy a few souvenirs and postcards. My mother and Egbert stayed with the truck.

We drove the rest of the way to Lawndale in sight of the ocean on the Pacific Coast Highway. We were all glad to get to Mary's. We hadn't seen her since 1927 so it was a very happy occasion for all.

After a time, we rented a house and everyone looked for jobs which were almost non-existent. My Dad, Leonard, and cousin Stan drove the truck north to the fruit orchards. They picked apricots, peaches, and grapes. They met many families who followed the fruit-picking season. All were migrant workers, most with small children to be fed. My brother remembers giving the children who were standing around the campfires the bacon and eggs they had cooked for their supper.

As cheap as food was during the depression, there was still no money to buy many groceries. John Steinbeck's novel, *The Grapes of Wrath*, was based on these people and this time of the Great Depression. Leonard and Pop had their guitars and mandolin and made music after work around their campfire. There were always plenty of listeners, some joining in with harmonica or banjo or singing along. It was a bright spot in the dreary lives of the workers. These were homeless work-weary people and they forgot their misery for a while. They would sing and listen and, sometimes, Leonard would call a square dance for them. They danced on the dirt around the campfire and forgot the cares of the day. Leonard always remembered those times.

Our small house in Lawndale was crowded as my father's brother, Brownie (Russell), and his family had come to California. This made five more people to cook for and bed down, but Mom was always able to have food for a couple more of Roy's (or Leonard's—he had not yet become Roy Rogers), friends and fellow musicians. The Pioneers Trio practiced many times at our house: Bob Nolan, Bill Nichols, Slumber, (before Tim Spencer), and Leonard. They found a few jobs, but most were non-paying except for food and tips from their kitty. Kathleen and I sang and one time they allowed us to sing on their radio show. There were not many girl country singers then. It was even before Patsy Montana or Patsy Cline.

Mary was a fan of Stuart Hamblen, a cowboy singer who wrote many songs and became popular. A couple of well-loved ballads were "It is No Secret," and "This Ol' House." They became very famous.

There were numerous groups trying to make it. One of the

groups the boys joined for a while was the Texas Outlaws. A columnist gave them a lift in his "Best Bets of the Day," column in the L.A. Examiner which was widely read. The radio station KFWB decided if they were good enough to be mentioned in that column, they were worth a salary of $35.00 per week and put them on as staff musicians. They worked out unusual arrangements of "Tumbling Tumbleweeds" and "Cool Water," both Bob Nolan songs. They added a fiddle player, Hugh Farr. Later his brother Karl Farr joined them. By 1935 they had a radio sponsor and some exciting things began to happen. They had guest shots on big radio programs and appeared in a movie now and then. They played Salvation Army benefits and one time they were on the same program with Will Rogers. Leonard had long been a Will Rogers fan, so he and his co-workers were surprised and pleased to learn that Will Rogers was a fan of The Sons of the Pioneers. After the program was over and Will Rogers shook hands all around, he told them he would not see them for a while, he was taking off the next day for Alaska with Wiley Post. They had worked with Will in his last performance.

After Leonard became Roy Rogers he was sometimes mistaken for that great American humorist's son. Leonard had the same kind of homespun qualities and his love for people and grassroots language was the same. He did not know he would adopt the same last name at that time. After Will Rogers was killed in Alaska, Roy visited his museum in Oklahoma. There was so little to show for this great man's work, that Roy decided he was going to save everything, which he did, filling house and storage room until he opened his world-famous museum in Victorville, California, many years later.

The Slye family in California. (L to R) Front row: Kathleen, Mattie, Andrew, Leonard. Back row: Mary and Cleda. *Photo courtesy of Georgia Furr.*

In 1936 after Leonard met and courted Arlene Wilkins, they were married. Then one day, as it has been written many times, Leonard was in a dry cleaning shop and a young man came in and told the clerk about Republic Studios auditioning for a "singing cowboy." Gene Autry had threatened to quit if he didn't get a raise in salary, so Republic wanted to be ready for this. Roy was at the studio the next morning bright and early. Leonard was finally able to audition for Republic and he was signed to a contract. They changed his name to Dick Weston for a while. He was later renamed Roy Rogers. His first picture was an immediate smash hit at the box office and voted Best Western of the Year.

He traveled with the picture, and on and off the screen he was sensational. Young girls fell in love with him, women went for his boyish appeal, and men agreed that he was handsome but no sissy! He was the hero of countless boys and girls all over the world. The critics liked his music.

When he finished the tour, Republic showed him a room full of fan mail. He was stunned and said he felt like a shooting star. Right from the start he insisted on all mail being answered. Mail came in from all over the world. At one time six people were employed just in the fan mail office. In England, there were 50,000 members in the Roy Rogers Fan Club, the largest in the world.

Before his big break, it was a constant struggle to earn enough money to even live. In those days everyone was in the same boat, looking for jobs. The many groups of country and Western singers competed with each other and the Slye family supported the Rocky Mountaineers, the Texas Outlaws, and for a short time, The International Cowboys. There was rarely a cash prize for the winners of these contests, just a chance to play and to meet others hoping to make a living doing something they loved to do. We'd go and clap and scream ourselves hoarse for the Mountaineers or whatever group Roy/Leonard was a member. Before the Pioneer group was formed the boys, especially Bob Nolan and Bill Nichols frequented our home. This was before Tim Spencer joined them. They practiced their harmony and Mom was able to always have enough for them to eat with us. She could really make a pound of hamburger go a long way.

Sometimes we'd go to the beach for a wienie roast and they'd take their guitars. Soon after they began to sing, groups of people gathered around. Bob worked as a lifeguard at Santa Monica beach part of the time. Beaches were very different then—clean and uncrowded. We never had to search for a place to park or to put our blankets and picnic baskets down.

I had no skills and only an eighth grade education, so I did housework and babysitting when I could. That meant I was away from my children at night. I was lucky to have such good and loving parents who were like mother and father to my boys. Leonard finally collected enough money to pay my tuition at The Paramount College of Beauty. It was in Los Angeles on Broadway, between Seventh and Eighth Streets. It took me eight months—six days a week, eight hours a day—to complete the program. Pop worked at Fern Shoe Company on Thirtieth Street and South Grand and had to be at work at 7:00 a.m. I didn't have to be in class until 9:00 a.m. so I rode with him to work, then walked to school.

For a time, two other students and I rented an apartment on Twelfth Street for $12.00 per month and divided the rent. We'd take food from home and we cooked too. The Big Grand Central Market was within walking distance, so we were able to save money there on food. Our uniforms were white cotton and had to be starched and ironed. When I got through there and passed the state board, jobs were still scarce, but I found one near home and I could be home nights. I was so grateful my brother helped me in this way.

It was 1934 and he was still working where he could, playing and singing. If he found himself in downtown L.A. anytime, he'd come to the Beauty School to see me. It would be easier for us to talk if he got a manicure, which he did. The manicure tables were all in the front of the building so while he was there, most of the girls slipped up to get a look at him. He was handsome and I was proud. He was doing his singing on the radio and getting some fans. He was unmarried at the time, too. This made the girls more interested. He dressed in his cowboy outfit with a white hat. Although Hollywood was not far away and they were making Westerns—many of them—it was still unusual to see a cowboy dressed in Western regalia in downtown Los Angeles, so he drew a lot of attention.

Around this time Pop began to build another house. He bought four lots near Prairie Avenue on 165th Street (DePew). We moved in as soon as possible and he finished the inside while we lived in it. At first, there was no indoor plumbing, but there was city water, so a piece at a time, we acquired an indoor bath. The house was surrounded by open fields. We got a cow and staked her out each day. We had chickens and fruit trees.

The soil was adobe that made it hard as rock when dry. When it rained it was a sticky heavy clay, like mud. Sometimes the boys would begin walking across a wet field and their feet would get heavier and heavier as the black mud stuck to them. It was almost more than they could do to get across the field.

There were six rooms in that house; three bedrooms, a living room, a dining room, a kitchen, and a bath. We also had front and back porches. The winds swept across the nearby empty fields so Pop planted a honeysuckle vine to break the wind from our little backyard. Neighbors were not close. There was bus service on nearby Hawthorne Boulevard; the bus connected with the #5 car at the end of its line in Hawthorne.

There were two movies in Hawthorne, the nearest town. We could go to the Rex for a dime and the Plaza was fifteen to twenty-five cents. If my little boys could have twenty-five cents on Saturday they could see the double feature Western, the news, the previews, the Saturday serial, and a cartoon—and also buy a bag of popcorn. From our house to the movies was a good mile, so Saturday afternoon saw them walking to the theater. My sister, Mary, lived a few blocks from us, and her two little girls and my boys often spent Saturday afternoons at the movies. They saw their Uncle Roy, in *Under Western Stars*, which came out in 1937. After that, his movies came out so fast we could barely keep up with them. By that time there were movie houses all over within short driving distance of us.

After Republic Studio realized how much the public loved Roy, they lost no time making one film after another, as fast as possible to cash in on the new star. We, living near the beach saw little of Roy. He was so busy making movies and personal appearances. He always kept in close contact with our parents calling them from all parts of the country. He bought a chicken ranch in the San Fernando Valley for them later on. It was stocked with chickens and ready to go. There were walnut trees and grape vines, peach and apricot trees. We, the girls, lived near the beaches and we had many family gatherings at the Havenhurst House. Mother's Day, Father's Day, and our parents' birthdays were times for us to celebrate together. There was always Mom's fried chicken along with our families' favorite dishes.

Early in Roy's career, he and The Sons of the Pioneers were invited to San Simeon by William Randolph Hearst, the owner of the Los Angeles Examiner newspaper. I believe this attention was brought to the Pioneers by Louella Parsons, a movie gossip columnist of the day—perhaps I should say THE movie gossip columnist. Hearst liked the boys' harmony, so they were invited to the fabulous ranch to entertain. At that time there was no road into San Simeon and the last lap of the trip was by pack mules. What an adventure for these boys trying to get a start in the world of entertainment!

San Simeon is world renowned as a tourist attraction. I have been there a couple of times and it's impossible for me to describe the grandeur of it—artwork and paintings from all over the world. Hearst was so fabulously rich he could, and did, have all of these great works shipped in. One time there was work being done on a tapestry of great value, people were on scaffolds cleaning and mending this valuable work of art. William R. Hearst is probably remembered as being creator of San Simeon, the fabulous castle, which he imported from different parts of the world and reassembled on the coast, inland of California. Marion Davies was at the castle when Roy and the Pioneers were there. I can imagine how these boys, who were struggling along, trying to get a foothold in the entertainment field, reacted to the wealth of this man and his castle. To their eyes, San Simeon was like a fairy tale with its towers and spires and countless rooms, swimming pools, and beautiful gardens. I am not sure if it helped them further their career, though. I am sorry I did not hear them talk of it.

My last trip to San Simeon was in 1989. It is a beautiful and fascinating place. One cannot help wondering why this wealthy man created this castle. It is, I'm certain, A MUST among California's tourist attractions.

Back at home, there would be our usual music with Uncle Frank playing bass with the broom handle. He could draw the broom over his thumb resting on the table and it was an excellent bass. There was a big yard there which we needed since the house was so tiny. Roy wanted to build a larger house for our parents on his Chatsworth ranch, but Mom liked her little house. As she grew older and it became more difficult for her to get around, a bigger house wouldn't do.

She had been crippled since she was a year old. Her sister dropped her and for years they believed that was why she was crippled. She sat in a chair for a year. She was born in 1882, and in those days and times they knew little, if anything, about polio. After Roy and Dale were married she was x-rayed and fitted for a brace. Then they learned she had had polio. Mom always wished her sister Ann could have known that the fall from her back had not been the reason for her being lame. Ann had died at age seventeen. We did not think of our mother as being a cripple or handicapped in any way. She worked, bore four children, and did all the things a farm wife had to do.

One year while we were still living up the holler, Pop planted a steep hillside of corn. We all worked, hoeing and weeding that corn. Mom always came along with us.

Sometimes Pop hired a neighbor to hoe and cut weeds. He cut wood for us sometimes, too. He was a widower with several grown children. He would often be at our house at mealtime. Mom would invite him to eat. He'd say, "Well Mrs. Slye, I'm not very hungry, but I will have a cup of coffee." He'd then sit down and eat everything on the table. It was kind of fun for us kids, as we knew what would happen.

He cut cords of wood out in the woods and ricked them up. A cord is eight feet long, four feet wide, and four feet high. We'd sometimes find the ricks knocked over and we suspected that he had shorted us on the size. He'd say, "Well Andy, the wind must have blown the rick over!" He knew Pop would not rick it up again to prove that it was a short cord.

He was a kindly man and many evenings we walked by the light of his lantern to prayer meeting.

After we left Duck Run he built a log cabin as close as he could to the line fence of our old place. The land belonged to his father. His father and mother were a couple who had raised their family and all of them had families of their own. They were our nearest neighbors when we moved out from Portsmouth. He was a big, heavy man who worked for the county, building roads such as they were. When he was plowing, he could be heard for miles hollering at his team. On Saturdays he'd go to Portsmouth to deal with the road commissioners and often his team had to bring him home. He would have a few too many drinks.

His wife was a little woman who made beautiful quilts—such intricate patterns with small pieces no larger than a quarter. They are no doubt, today valued heirlooms for some of their descendants.

When we made Christmas decorations, stringing popcorn for the tree, these neighbors came and listened to the music either played by Mom and Pop or on the Victrola. Pop was a lover of good music, too. I remember Enrico Caruso records and also the Sousa band records. Young people liked Uncle Josh's talking records.

Our neighbors had two yellow, mongrel dogs named Jack and Peeler. They never did get used to us passing the house. They'd rush out bearing their teeth, growling, and barking. Our big dog Rover avoided them by circling up through the woods. One day I guess he just got tired of the pesky animals. He stood his ground when they came rushing out. He whipped both of them and they went whimpering into the house. Our neighbor complained to the other neighbors that Rover had tried to kill her dogs.

When Mary got married and moved to McDermott, Rover went, too. He would not stay home, so we decided he believed Mary was his owner. After bringing him back several times, we finally gave up and let him stay with Mary.

Leonard always had a hound or two on hand, Redbone and Blue Tick hunters and fox and opossum hounds. One time Mom let him raise a whole litter in the kitchen behind the stove, four of them, I believe. He kept them until they were old enough to sleep in the barn.

His love for dogs and animals has been a lifetime thing for him. When he lived in Hollywood he always had dogs and once had to move because neighbors complained of the barking. He had Weimaraners, Lana and Joaquin, that had several pups and several times Roy gave my husband and me a whole litter. This was the start of the kennel we had in Gardena, California, in the early 1950s.

Another Ohioan who became well-known was Branch Rickey. His family lived in a big house on Duck Run. His father was the leader of the choir at our church. The choir was made up of anybody who wanted to sing. Mr. Rickey was a stern, no-foolishness man when he was teaching a song or practicing. He could read music and tried to teach the young people to read also. One of the favorite hymns was, "In the Sweet By and By."

Leonard would get the kids to laugh by singing "in the sweet," then softly so Mr. Rickey couldn't hear him say "gimme some pie to eat…we will meet on that beautiful shore, gimme some more." Mr. Rickey would wonder why the kids were laughing, but I suspect he finally caught on.

Most of the young people and their parents went to church and to Sunday school. There sometimes would be a picnic with tablecloths spread on the ground and all sharing their good home-cooked food. Mrs. Rickey, a sweet faced lady, was our Sunday school teacher. A Rickey son was sheriff for Scioto County. Branch was the first one to bring an African American, Jackie Robinson, into the all-white major league baseball. The Rickey house is still in use by some of the family.

After we left Portsmouth to move to Duck Run, our trips to town were for shopping and, now and then, a movie. These movies were "silent," before talkies. Portsmouth was a booming town with about five movie houses. The LaRoy sometimes had live stage shows. My cowboy hero was Tom Mix. Leonard's was Hoot Gibson. We had pictures of them the size of playing cards. They were our treasures. We also had Kathleen Williams (for whom my sister Kathleen was named), M.P. & D.F., The Farnham, Dustin and Williams, and other actors.

Chillicothe, Gallia, and Second Streets were the shopping centers. Shoe factories and the steel mill were busy. Pop's Aunt Liz Wessel and Uncle Harv lived on Third Street, just around the corner from the Hurth Hotel, which to us was a grand hotel. It still stands and is a home for retired folks. It was a good place for us to rest and leave our packages if we had more shopping to do.

Aunt Liz was my Grandma Slye's sister. She was fat and

spoke broken English. The family came from Germany. One of our Christmas treats was to see Aunt Liz's Christmas tree. She filled one corner of her little used parlor full of ornaments, tinsel, and popcorn. Some of the ornaments came from Germany. There was a beautiful nativity scene that we all loved. Pop would take us down to see the tree and she always gave us cookies of every shape—stars and half moons and every kind of animal. We'd put a string through them and hang them on our tree. Aunt Liz never married, but she mothered her sister's family. My dad was her favorite and he sometimes helped her ice the cookies.

At night Chillicothe Street was exciting to our country eyes with blazing marquees on all the movie theaters. Market Street, was fun for us, too. As farmers, we brought produce into town to sell on Saturday in summer. Wagons and teams would be lined up along the street with all kinds of fruits and vegetables, chickens, eggs and freshly churned butter. We had our own fruit and vegetables so we didn't have to buy those, but the store, Schaeffer's, was a busy place. It was run by a family,

t focused on family, religion

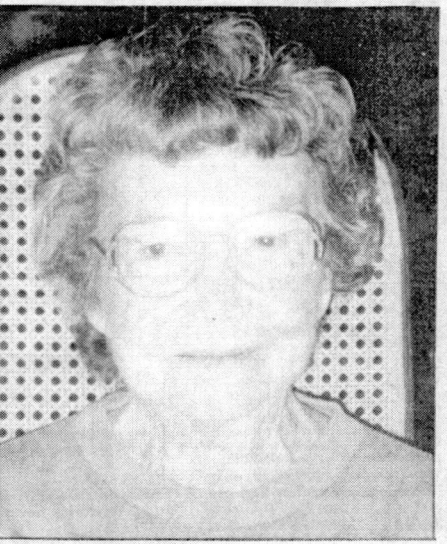

NISCING — Cleda Willoughby, 83, tells the story of achian Christmases past.

And Santa used to an-
his arrival in another
certain households.
ry room had a door, to
he heat in," Simon said.
'hristmas tree would be
n a room with a fire-
If the fire was built,
neant that Santa had
here. Children couldn't
until they could see the
coming from under the

e children would write

Santa first. And some would
put the letters in the fire and
let the smoke carry their
words to the North Pole."
Even the animals were in-
cluded in Christmas tradi-
tions, Simon said. Some Appalachian people believed animals were given the gift of
speech every Christmas night,
since they were the first to see
the newborn Jesus.
Christmas dinner included
turkey, wild goose, canned

fruit, and pumpkin, berry and
apple pies, Willoughby said.
Another Christmas treat
were "springerlies," hard cookies with raised designs in the
center, Simon said.
Almost all ingredients for
the meal were grown on the
farm or hunted or caught in
the woods.
Often, families would set an
empty place at the table, saying that whoever came to the
door that night looking for
food would represent Jesus.
Some families would begin
their butchering on Christmas,
while the weather was cold,
Simon said. And it was a fine
time for ice cream — a winter
treat, since that was the only
time families could get ice
from the creeks to use in their
ice cream machines.
At school and church, children would be given treats of
candy, oranges and nuts.
"Some of those kids didn't
get anything for Christmas except that," Willoughby said. "I
don't know where the money
came from."
Simon said the food was a
welcome change from the pork
families regularly ate.
For entertainment, Wil-
loughby remembered, the
whole family, including her father's five brothers and their
families, would come to her
parents farm. They would
bring their own instruments to
play, or listen to the Victrola
play Sousa bands.
Outside, the children would
slide across the ice on the
creeks, using their shoes instead of ice skates. Or they
might play Fox and Goose, a
sort of modified game of tag,
where players were confined
to the rim and spokes of a

"wheel" trampled out in the
snow.
But most important, the two
friends agreed, were the
church and school plays and
services.
"We always had church programs," Willoughby remem-
bered. "One year, Roy played
Santa Claus. I think his
teacher at the school on Duck
Run realized he had acting
talent.
"I remember one year, I was
supposed to recite "Twas the
Night Before Christmas," and
I forgot it. There was no one
behind the curtain to cue me.
I just forgot part of it.
"I still remember a lot of it
now, though I wouldn't want
to try to recite it."
During Christmas time, families would hitch up the horse
and sleigh, complete with
bells, get comforters and
straw, and head to church, Simon said.
The ground would be so
slick, the horses' shoes would
be equipped with spikes at the
toe and at the horseshoe ends.
"The Protestants would attend daytime services," Simon
said. "But we were Catholics,
so it was imperative we go to
midnight Mass. Afterwards, on
Christmas Eve, we would open
our presents.
"I have an Appalachian music class, and we were discuss-
ing this. One of my students,
an older woman, said,
'Because we didn't have anything then, church meant
more to us.'
"It was a good time for kids,"
Willoughby agreed, nodding,
"We didn't have much, but we
had what counted. We had
family, and we loved each other. That's what counts."

Cleda Willoughby speaks of Appalachian Christmas' in a newspaper article written by
Susan Schwartz from the *Portsmouth Daily Times*, December 1993. *Newspaper clipping
courtesy of Ruth Adkins.*

the Schaeffer's, and each customer had a clerk waiting on him,
weighing out coffee, flour, sugar, etc. They sold nails, building
supplies, clothing, and yard goods. What a busy place! Pop always

bought stick candy in pound packages—peppermint, lemon, orange, cinnamon, and horehound. Often, if Mr. Schaeffer waited on Pop, he'd give us a treat, a sack of assorted sticks when Pop paid the bill. We had very little candy from the store, but Mom made taffy and Mary sometimes made fudge or "sea-foam," which I believe is like divinity fudge, made with egg whites.

Pop always took us to buy our shoes and most times the sturdy ones were chosen over the pretty ones. At Easter, Mom made us pretty dresses of voile of dimity with flowers. We'd have baby doll pumps or Mary-Jane's, black patent leather with a strap and button on the side. Our school shoes were high top with buckles, strong and sturdy, which we needed for the muddy, snowy roads, usually we'd have overshoes or artics with side buckles. Mom made most of our clothes, dresses for us girls and shirts for Leonard. However, our parents bought denim overalls.

Aunt Liz Wessel was a fine tailor. Pop had her make a coat for me one winter. It was black caracul (lamb's wool), warm, and satin-lined. I'd rather have had a red or blue coat, but as I look back, it was beautiful, such fine woolen material. It was the only new coat I ever had as a child. Mary got the new ones, and I got the hand-me-downs. Then they went to Kathleen, when I outgrew them, then through the Hiles family, who had several girls and were our neighbors.

Another good memory is coming to town to visit two aunts who had player pianos with lots of rolls of good old songs. They'd let us sit and pump the piano as long as we wanted. They also usually had babies that we could push up and down the sidewalks in their buggies. These two families lived together, Uncle Brown's and Uncle Dave's family. They made homebrew and sold it and their house was nearly always filled with laughter and friends drinking beer. I remember the big cup with a handle on either side that held a quart. They'd fill it and pass it around. There would be music and singing and fun. One time, they had a poolroom on the first floor and lived in the upstairs. They were always happy to turn over their babies to me for a few hours.

Uncle Brownie (Russell) was Pop's youngest brother. He married Stella Kellem and they had three boys: Stanley, Herman, and Garland. They moved to California about a year after we did and lived with us for a while. Everyone was very busy making a living or trying to.

We were lucky that we had a roof over our heads. So many did not in the Great Depression years. I remember how my mother was always sorry for her sister Dixie having to work most of the time in a shoe factory. I am grateful to my father for providing a home for us. We all worked to help with food and bills but Mom never had to move around from one rented place to another.

Mom and Dixie were so different. Mom was the practical one, always thinking about getting the bills paid and food on the table. Aunt Dixie liked pretty clothes, getting her hair marcelled, and dancing and having a good time. Mom was fun loving, too, but necessary things came first, like wood for the stove and food. We always took food, especially coffee, when we visited Aunt Dixie. It was really fun and I remember how these sisters laughed together, and then maybe cry, remembering Poor Ol' Pa.

Some of Mom's stories of their childhood are very dear to me. She told about her brother Egbert's trip to Oregon in 1906. There were eight children and Grandpa's youngest brother, Dick. One son, Harold, was born in Oregon. We have always been sorry that Mom never saw her beloved brother again. They wrote letters and, after we moved to California, we hoped they could see each other. When Leonard became Roy Rogers and was making some money, he wanted to fly Mom to Oregon. She wouldn't fly. She said if she could keep one foot on the ground she'd go. Sister Mary visited Uncle Bud, also Aunt Dixie. We all regret that we didn't somehow get Mom to go to Oregon to see her brother before he died.

We made a trip back to Ohio in 1936, after we'd been in California for five years. Pop and I both had jobs then and we decided to save our money for a trip back to Ohio. When my boys got out of school in June, we started out. We had a 1929 Ford Model sedan. It had a big trunk on the back for our good clothes. I had been working in a beauty shop, my first really good job. We'd been able to save money. The depression was barely over and jobs were getting easier to find. I had hopes of coming back to the same job after our trip but I couldn't blame Mary, the owner of the shop for taking another operator after I quit and left.

Kathleen was married and had a family so it helped her to be able to live in our house that summer.

Pop always had itchy feet, I think, as I did, wanting to travel and see new, different things and places. Our first stop was in Azuza to see Aunt Dixie and stay overnight. Azuza was perhaps fifty miles from where we lived in Lawndale. We, as always, had food with us when we visited Aunt Dixie. Mom could never get going without her coffee. The sisters did not see each other often as Aunt Dixie always had to work. Their reunions were always such fun, talking of old times of and catching up on everything that was happening.

We saw the Grand Canyon and the Petrified Forest on our way east. Traffic was not heavy then and there were lots of side roads and places to camp. One night we traveled late and put our bedrolls out beside our car. We woke up to find we were right in front of a house and nearly in their yard. The folks were looking at us rather suspiciously.

We did not take Pop's mandolin or Mom's guitar on that trip. With five of us, there was no room. The Ford had a running board so Pop built a box to keep our cooking utensils and groceries in. We camped on this trip too, to save money. We had a gallon jar of pickled eggs that we ate all across the country. Before we got to our people in Cincinnati, we emptied the jar and dumped what was left of the eggs. We got tired of them and they got tough after being in vinegar for a long time. We often wondered if anyone saw them and wondered how pickled eggs got there.

We stopped in Cincinnati to see "Spec" and Ella. Spec (Ernest) was Pop's cousin, a fun-loving man we enjoyed visiting. Then we drove along the Ohio River to Portsmouth. The road is now State Highway 52. In June it's so beautiful and green with lots of blooming wild flowers.

We stayed with Pop's brother, Uncle Dave, and Aunt Lula for a while. Then we went to Gallipolis where the Hiles family was living then. While visiting them we went to Duck Run one weekend. We stayed in the barnyard of the old place up the holler, spread out our blankets, and camped there. The Hiles family lived near the Ohio River in Gallipolis, so we walked to the river to swim and fish.

After we'd been there for a while, we went on to Detroit where Uncle Frank and Aunt Cassie lived. It was really hot and there was no air conditioning in those days. They had a nice house with a basement all fixed for cooking and eating. The bedrooms upstairs were hot and like ovens, but we had a good visit swimming in Lake Erie that felt like it had been heated, it was so warm.

We took a trip to Windsor, Canada. We went to movies and I cut Aunt Cassie's long, beautiful, warm, brown hair. The doctor had told her to have it cut as it was the cause of her headaches. It was such beautiful hair and my experience as a beautician served me well there. Aunt Cassie was such a lovely person, and she and Mom were like sisters. We stayed with them a few weeks, then returned to Ohio.

Charles Hiles went back to California with us to look for a job. I will always remember what he said when he saw the Pacific Ocean for the first time, "Big, ain't it?" He cared nothing for the beach and was unhappy away from Ohio. He didn't find a job and was so glad when his mother sent him a bus ticket to come home. He was like a fish out of water and, except for a few years in the Army, he lived all his life in the state of Ohio.

His daughter, Mary Lou, and her husband, Ferrell Crabtree, own our old homeplace now. I feel as if they are family and we feel free to visit our old home and take friends. They have kept it up very well, also.

During the summer we spent in the east, Roy had married Arlene Wilkins in June 1936. He had not yet made his first picture, which started him on his rise to stardom and fame as King of the Cowboys.

On our way back to California we visited the Wilkins family in Roswell, New Mexico. They were lovely, hospitable people.

(L to R) Mary Lou Crabtree, Cleda Willoughby, and Ferrell Crabtree at the homplace on the day the road sign was changed from Allen Hollow to Sly Road (notice the missing "E").. *Photo courtesy of Georgia Furr.*

We stayed several days and had a trip to Carlsbad Caverns. There was a swimming pool just across the road from the Wilkins' beautiful big house and everyday Mrs. Wilkins gave my little boys the money to go to the pool. There were six of us, counting our passenger, Charles Hiles. I'm sure it was a job to bed us and feed us. I have only pleasant memories of that time and their lovely hospitality.

Don Wilkins, Arlene's brother, worked for the paper and one evening he took us out to a fire caused by a haystack that spontaneously combusted.

Mrs. Wilkins was a fine cook and the meals were delicious to us who had camped across the country. She sent us on our way with a picnic lunch, enough to last us for two days.

Mr. Wilkins had a nursery. Later on they all moved to California, where he also had a nursery. After I was married, he gave us two nice trees for our backyard. At that time, we couldn't afford to buy them. We had many pleasant times with the Wilkins family.

Our grandfather, Archer Womack, was a Confederate soldier, a cavalry man in the Third Virginia. Mom told us many stories about him. I remember him as tall and stern with a long gray beard.

When he was young his beard was black and long enough to fasten under his belt. Mom said he always had a beard, as the one time he shaved it off, his children didn't know him.

Kentucky was a divided state during the Civil War. Even families were divided, as Grandpa's was. His brother Dick fought on the Union side. Grandpa never acknowledged that the Confederacy lost. He always wore a gray suit and kept a fine saddle horse.

He had been in the battles of Gettysburg and Bull Run. He met my grandmother while he was in the hospital after being wounded. She was the daughter of a plantation owner in Virginia. Her name was Patty Hatchett. She was young and doing volunteer work in the hospital. Grandpa was nearly forty-years-old when they were married. After the war, she went to Kentucky with him and raised a family: one boy, Egbert, and five girls, Lee, Mattie, Dixie, Ann, and Fanny. Ann died at age seventeen. Fanny died in infancy.

I try to think of how it must have been for this girl, having slaves before the war, moving to this poor Kentucky tobacco farm. Large plantations were no more and what a change for those used to having everything done for them, now having to work with their hands.

Grandpa suffered from the results of his wounds for the rest of his life and did very little work. He received a small pension that my mother always said was used for patent medicine. There were many drummers (salesman) going around the country, preying on such people.

Mom's brother, Egbert, had the adjoining farm, so he worked both farms. Mom's mother died at age fifty-two from cancer, a small pimple on her cheek grew into fatal cancer. Mom took care of her and was seventeen when she died. I am sorry I did not learn more about my grandmother's family, the Hatchetts of Virginia.

Mom told us stories, and she had a way of making things come alive for us. She could talk and imitate anyone, she could have been a great actress! My mother's stories were of their day-to-day living and visits with aunts and cousins, many of whom lived close.

I think of our times after we had eaten and Mom told us of her friends and things that happened in her childhood. Grandpa was one of ten children, so there were aunts, uncles, and many cousins. Grandpa died at age eighty-two while we still lived up the holler. I remember when he died and a letter was sent to Mom. In it was Grandpa's handwritten last will and testament. He asked to be buried in a homemade coffin and shroud with no shoes. He did not want an undertaker to touch his body. Uncle Albert and Aunt Dixie carried out his wishes as best they could. The letter and will was kept in our family Bible, along with a braid of Grandma Womack's hair. I remember seeing these things when I was little. I can well remember my Mom's grief. Where he lived in Kentucky with Aunt Dixie at the time was not far from us but my mother was unable to go. We do not know where he is buried, but hope that his grave is marked as a soldier who served his country.

Grandpa wrote Mary a few times and there is one letter still in the Bible in Roy's museum. This past summer, 1994, I thought there might be some family names in the Bible, so we looked and found the will and the letter which we had forgotten about.

The Bible was not really our family Bible, but one given to my father during the 1913 flood. One side is inscribed "Richard" in gold and the other name is "Ella." I can remember my father getting out that big heavy Bible and reading from it every night at the kitchen table. Pop was not a "church-goer" but he was religious man in his way. He allowed us to attend Sunday school even though Sundays were work days for him.

I marvel at what he accomplished. As I look back, I wonder how he could build houses, repair cars, and provide the countless things we needed. He sent to Sears & Roebuck for items such as an apple peeler and a huge grind stone that you could turn by sitting on a seat and pumping with your feet rather than turning the wheel by hand. Neighbors often used that stone to sharpen axes and knives. We also had an easy-to-push cultivator and a corn dropping machine. We probably were the only family in Duck Run who had these "modern" tools to help make our work a little easier and faster.

Grandpa Womack visited Mom when they lived in Cincinnati and when he'd go out, being southern gentlemen, he'd always speak to people and tip his hat to the ladies. One day after walking he asked Mom, "Baby," (he called all his girls Baby) "what's the matter with these people around here? I speak to them and I get no answer." To his way of thinking, country-bred and being a gentleman, he could not understand city people, especially Yankees! I'm sure there were many like him. Mom said he rode his horse so proudly in parades and revered Robert E. Lee. He visited Uncle Bud when he got settled in Oregon. The trip to Oregon was by train and on the stops to take on wood, they sometimes found a cow to milk. Uncle Dick was with them, a young unmarried man, so he helped with the children. They were pioneers, too, on a slow train instead of a covered wagon. They tried to carry along as much food as possible, and it would take a great lot for that many.

After Grandma died he didn't try to keep a house but lived with Uncle Bud. It was a large busy household, with eight children and Grandpa's family, too.

I have been fortunate to go with Roy and Dale to state fairs, rodeos, and other events where they've made personal appearances.

The summer of 1959, Pearl Wright, who came along, got sick. She looked after the little girls, Dodie and Debbie. She washed their hair and kept them neat and clean, and watched them when Roy and Dale were busy. They needed a great deal of care. Five of the children were in the show that year. Roy and Dale were making movies and personal appearances at that time and had to be away from the children so much. When summer came and they were out of school, they took them along. One year all seven were in the show.

This year, 1959, after Mrs. Wright couldn't go and they needed someone they could trust who knew the children, I went, along with Pop. Mom had died in 1958 and Pop was very lonely so Roy took him along on these trips whenever possible. The kids carried along so much stuff, we made quite a crowd in the airports. Dusty had a beat-up old rabbit, Peter Cottontail, he always carried along, but by this time he was twelve- or thirteen-years-old, a little old for stuffed animals, so he made Dodie carry Peter. What a sight we made, often, the kids were very loud, talking and yelling at each other and dropping their stuff. Pop, being very quiet, would be embarrassed and pretend not to be a part of our crowd which included manager, secretary, Republic Pictures men, and all the family.

We needed two Chevys to carry us to the hotels. Chevrolet was their sponsor then. I remember Pop kind of edging away from such a noisy group and Dale and I riding herd on the kids. Dale had never been one to hold her voice down if one of them needed to be reprimanded. She felt you have to do it now, not wait until it's too late and ineffective. I quite agree. We need more old-fashioned discipline.

We went to Portland in June to the Rose Festival. We have relatives there. My mothers' brother had a large family, nine children and they all had families.

When we arrived at the hotel and got settled in our rooms, Roy and Dale were caught up in interviews. Our family came for Pop and he stayed with them. I got busy settling the little girls and trying to quiet Dusty and Sandy in their room. The plane ride and having to sit quietly was over. Their energy had to be let out somehow, and it was with wrestling and roughhousing. I look back fondly at that summer and think about these kids, how they were envied by so many thousands. All have grown to be fine citizens. I believe it was their parents' determination to keep them away from modern life pitfalls, especially as the children of movie stars and famous people are so susceptible to making bad decisions.

We always went to church as at that time there were no shows on Sunday, or very few. I believe this religious training was a very important factor. Crowds were every place and I marvel at the near worship of so many thousands. Roy and Dale never allowed this to go to their own heads, much less, the children. There was little privacy even at mealtimes. Waitresses brought papers and books to be autographed. Today, I understand these autographs are sometimes sold and money hungry people make big bucks, often making a living.

One afternoon we had a boat ride on the beautiful Columbia River with lunch. We were supposed to have a private room but even as we ate lunch, people had their faces pressed against the window. A celebrity's life is very hard work and even if they try to be a part of the crowd, wearing dark sunglasses and jeans and ordinary clothes, they rarely can. Someone always recognizes them, so it's no wonder the children of these stars get caught up in drugs and alcohol, and their story often ends tragically.

We were five days in Portland and ended up at a family dinner at the Womacks, my mother's people. It was impossible to keep it quiet so the yard and street were full of people other than our family. The crowds along the parade route were pressing and even with a police escort, I'd nearly get claustrophobic when people grabbed at the car and tried to touch Roy and Dale. What is this magic? I have often wondered, as they have, perhaps.

It is not hard for me to believe God has given them their mission. They reach so many thousands and make them happy. Their message to kids that it's not sissy to go to Sunday school had real punch and carried a lot of weight, and the kids really listen! There are people of middle-aged now who still love Roy and Dale. Today there are no heroes for kids to look up to, heroes who wear white hats and ride handsome horses, and always fight for right and win.

One year Roy had a real struggle with management and powers that be to keep a religious number in their program. They finally said we'll do the number or we won't go on. The number was "Peace in the Valley." Roy rode out in a white suit sparkling with sequins. Trigger was so beautiful, golden and shining with his flowing white mane and tail. The lights formed a cross and it was so quiet, the song so beautifully done by Roy backed up by the Sons of the Pioneers with their unique and incomparable harmony. The applause, after a moment of silence was deafening and prolonged. Roy and Dale then both rode around the arena shaking as many hands as they could reach. Sometimes the foreground of the arena was filled with wheelchairs and their little crippled occupants. They made it a point to have a show for these handicapped children. They visited the wards of sick and handicapped, also. Roy was allowing them to touch and hold his guns. It was heart rending to see a blind child touching the fringe on his shirt and Roy telling him, as best he could, him how it looked. It was very touching.

A well-known singer has written a book called *Rhinestone Cowboy*. Roy is really the original rhinestone cowboy. He began wearing bright, colorful outfits in the huge stadiums that had thousands of seats. Nudie, the tailor who made Roy's suits, became famous, too, as other singing cowboys had suits made. These outfits became popular with country-Western singers who never made a movie. The brighter they were and the more sequins and rhinestones, the better. Actually, Roy's outfits were rather dull compared to some you see presently. They were heavy and fitted. I used to help Roy between his acts when he'd change. He'd come in wet with perspiration and the fitted zippered shirts were not easy to pull off. Some made of wool and gabardine, heavy with shiny stones and fringe. The song "Rhinestone Cowboy" became popular long after Roy had been appearing in such outfits. As the years went by the clothing tamed down somewhat. Roy and Dale have many colorful outfits in the museum from his shows in Madison Square Garden, the Rose Parade and many more.

Trigger was the most admired horse in the world. One time a rumor got started that Roy was going to sell him. He did have an unheard of amount of money offered by a Texas millionaire for the horse. He never had a thought of selling him, but the fan mail rolled in from children all over the country asking him not to sell Trigger. Many sent in money, thinking that was why he was selling him. Roy issued a statement that Trigger was not for sale for any amount of money and that he belonged to the children of America. Trigger received 269,000 letters in three months. Roy and Trigger have their imprints in cement in the Grauman's Chinese Theater along with countless other Hollywood legends. Roy's hand and boot print are right next to Trigger's hoof print.

A World War II Air Force bomber was named Trigger after the famous horse. When Roy reenacted Paul Revere's ride for a war bond drive, schools were closed along the fifteen-mile route, so the children could see their hero and his beautiful horse. At one time, the fans almost stripped Trigger of his tail, pulling out hairs, one at a time for souvenirs. He had to start wearing a switch. Roy was obliged to use soldiers to guard him along a parade route. Sometimes the city police did this. Trigger was so popular he received an invitation to appear, at one time, without Roy. Roy was delighted, Trigger took it all in stride. Roy retired him to a beautiful ranch in the San Fernando Valley, where he lived to be thirty-three-years-old. He is now beautifully mounted, rearing on his hind legs, the most familiar of his poses, along with Buttermilk (Dale's horse), Trigger, Jr. (Roy's next horse), and Bullet (Roy's German shepherd), all there to see at the Roy Rogers Museum.

Many thousands visit the museum in Victorville each year to look at the mementos of the Rogers' career. If Roy is in town, he comes to the museum each day to put on his white Stetson and play "Ol' Roy," as he says. Middle-aged people are now sometimes teary-eyed when they see him and can shake his hand, their childhood hero. They spent countless Saturday afternoons riding the range in pursuit of conquering the "Bad Guy," good always winning over evil. Roy often says he was a babysitter for these kids. Mothers could drop their kids off at the local theater and know they would be safe for several hours while they watched their hero.

There were quite a number of cowboys making these movies at that time. Gene Autry was the first singing cowboy, then Roy. Other cowboys were Tex Ritter, Rex Allen, Johnny Mack Brown, Eddie Dean, Hopalong Cassidy, Lash LaRue, Sunset Carson, Bob Steele, Red Ryder, and more. None reached the height of popularity that Roy did. He often wondered why, as he didn't think he was all that good-looking nor, in his opinion, could he sing well. But he had a certain magic that drew people.

After he and Arlene were married for a few years and there were no children, they adopted Cheryl from an orphanage in Texas, Hope Cottage. She was a beautiful, blonde baby with dark eyes. She looked very much like Shirley Temple. As often happens, it wasn't long until Linda Lou was born then, in 1946. "Dusty," Roy Rogers, Jr., came along next. Roy was so happy to have a son. Soon tragedy struck as Arlene died from an embolism a few days after Dusty was born. We did not see much of Roy in this extra busy time of his life, but we all knew and felt his grief. Once in a while, he would invite us to come on the set at Republic Studios. We enjoyed these rare times, meeting members of the cast and watching them work. There was plenty of time between takes to visit.

It was on one of these occasions we met Dale for the first time. She was warm, friendly, and outgoing—a country girl. We all liked her at once. She had worked in Chicago and New York singing on the radio and in nightclubs. As soon as she was cast in a picture with Roy, the fans loved them together. I believe she tried to work again in pictures other than Westerns with little success.

Roy had worked with a succession of leading ladies, but none caused the fans to want their hero to have a steady partner as Dale did. Little boys decided if Roy had to have a girl in his movies, let it be Dale. Fan mail came in by the hundreds of thousands. Little girls liked Dale's short-fringed shirts and fancy white boots. Also, the songs they did together and with the Pioneers pleased the kids as well as the parents. At that time heroes did not marry and there were no love scenes. It was said that instead of kissing the girl, he kissed his horse.

For a long time Dale's name was second to Trigger. Dale has said that Roy did not need her. He already was number one in Westerns but after her experiences in movies other than Roy's, and the clamor the fans put up for her to be in his movies, she decided she could do worse, I believe. However it was, the more movies they made together, the more the fans wanted. Herbert Yates realized what a box office draw they were together, so he offered her a contract. Their days were long and filled with hard work, making one movie after another as well as personal appearances. They also worked for the war effort, appearing at camps and hospitals.

Dale had married very young and had a son, Tom. She had been unable to acknowledge him as her son because of studio rules. This really bothered her. At his graduation from high school she disguised herself to go, wearing dark glasses and no make-up. As it happened when people are well-known, they can't conceal anything for long—especially a son. Dale was relieved when a columnist wrote of it. She felt she'd been living a lie.

She had joined a church when she was young and been baptized, but her work in movies and on stage took precedence over her personal beliefs. She went along with the wishes of the studios to be a young star, or whatever they were called. She was unhappy about it. Tom was raised in Texas by Dale's parents. They gave him a stable Christian home and they influenced his whole life. He grew to be a very fine man with a lovely wife and three daughters who were all in Christian work. One daughter and her husband have been missionaries in Holland for years.

Dale has written many books. The first one, *Angel Unaware*, has been a best seller and helped untold numbers of parents of special needs children. She has written about Debbie, their adopted Korean daughter, *Dearest Debbie*. *Salute to Sandy* was about their adopted son Sandy. The proceeds from these books have helped many parents and children.

Debbie was adopted when she was three-years-old through World Vision. She could not speak a word of English, but she learned quickly. She was a beautiful twelve-year-old when she was killed in a bus accident while on the way from Tijuana where they had visited and taken gifts to an orphanage with their church. Debbie was Roy's little girl, always happy to see him come home, getting his slippers and letting him know she loved him. It was a tragedy for them all. The Chatsworth Ranch came to be a sad place. The other victims in the bus crash had been best friends with Debbie and lived nearby. One father, unable to cope with the death of his daughter, drove his car into an empty building on Roy's ranch that was some distance from the house and died there from carbon monoxide poisoning. He was discovered days later. This added tragedy was one more reason for Roy and Dale to make a change.

The family moved to the high desert in June of 1965. They bought the Apple Valley Inn, a place that had been a popular spot for movie stars of the 1930s and 1940s. It was far enough from Hollywood to be private and away from the business of the city and movie making, but not too far away. The desert air and quiet had proven a tonic for stars such as Clark Gable, Carole Lombard, and Wallace Beery. Apple Valley had been discovered and promoted by Newt Bass. The property was sold, mostly one acre at a time and it was fenced with white railing. The posts of railroad ties were purchased through Bass, a very enterprising man whose salesmen frequented the Apple Valley Inn looking for people who came there. The building across the highway from the Inn had been a bowling alley. Roy purchased it and turned it into the museum.

I had been working in Roy's fan mail in Hollywood along with a lady who handled the business letters. I did the regular fan mail and sent out photos. They had been trying to cut down on mail, but they were never able to cut it off completely. If folks take the time to write to him, Roy still believes the letters should be answered. I believe he feels its only good manners to reply. Rather like speaking to someone if they speak to you. Some days there was only a dribble of mail compared to the floods that came in earlier times, but it required an answer according to Roy's way of thinking. I was doing this job, working three days a week, when my brother-in-law, Ted, came in and said, "Honey, get ready. Roy and Dale want everything moved out to Apple

Valley." I was living in Gardena, making the trip to Hollywood on the very congested freeways, sometimes bumper-to-bumper traffic going home on the Santa Monica and Harbor freeways. It was a welcome change. The desert is very beautiful and I had a little office in the Inn for the fan mail, three days a week.

My sister, Kathleen, had a little gift shop called Dale's Pantry in a room at the right of the entry. She sold preserves and jelly made by a friend of Roy and Dale's who lived in Chatsworth. Ted made regular trips to get the preserves. The jars were labeled Roy Rogers Inn. They sold well and they soon added other gifts and souvenir items, all labeled Roy Rogers. I helped Kathleen in the shop on the weekends, the busiest time. There was another shop there that sold jewelry and luxury items, and also a nice restaurant and bar. It was a restful place for weekend guests. A swimming pool and tennis court served the guests. They had stables with horses to ride, and an outdoor steak fry was very popular along with a hayride.

People came for visits and many bought lots and houses. Apple Valley Village was a little desert town, quiet with very little traffic. Through the years this has changed, and it has grown and spread out over the desert.

Big Bear and Lake Arrowhead are in the mountains about forty-five miles from Apple Valley. Snow falls nearly every winter in Apple Valley as it is over 3000 feet above sea level. It is called the High Desert. One winter a heavy snow fell and we had to close the museum for a few days. The Cajun Pass closes to traffic sometimes as cars can slide off the road. There are so many big trucks traveling Highway 15 to San Bernardino freeway that it is very hazardous when there is a heavy snow and ice. Most of the year the weather is clear with no smog and the winds blow most of the time.

Roy and Dale suffered another tragedy when Sandy died right after they moved to the desert. I will always remember Roy's grief when he got the phone call. I stayed with them when Dale had to be out of town, so I could cook for Roy. This was an occasion when Dale was not there, when word came about Sandy. They were still shocked and grieving about Debbie. Roy was stunned and we all wondered what else could happen. The family got together to meet Dale's plane and she knew instantly that something had happened.

Sandy was in the army and stationed in Germany. He so very much wanted to be a soldier. He had been battered and abused by alcoholic parents. He'd been abandoned and was in an orphanage in Kentucky when they found him. He was five-years-old, a pale malnourished little boy with big blue eyes and a big smile. It was rather by accident that they got him. They were going to pick up Dodie, a Native American baby, at Hope Cottage after returning from several state fairs and personal appearances, including Madison Square Garden. A lady called to see if her daughter, Penny, who had been crippled with cerebral palsy could meet Roy and see Trigger. Roy asked, "Do you have any boys adoptable there?" At that time, Dusty was the only boy among three girls. Roy believed he needed a boy for Dusty to play with. So they brought Sandy along and Roy and Dale were won over by his big smile and, in spite of his physical defects, they were able to take him home with them. It was not difficult to arrange the adoption since five-year-olds with physical and mental trouble are not on the preferred list for adoption. Roy and

Dale talked long into the night about Sandy. Roy finally said, "Everyone wants a perfect, healthy child, but what happens to these little guys with all kinds of problems? Let's take him." So they did.

They bought clothes for him to travel on the plane. He got sick and vomited all over Helen, the secretary, who traveled with them. He probably had never before in his short life had enough to eat, so he ate too much. He grew into a fine looking young man, but he was never able to do many of the things boys do. His coordination was poor and he had breathing problems due to a closed nostril. They believed this was the result of an injury as an infant. After extensive testing it was found that Sandy had slight brain damage. Doctors at Los Angeles Children's Hospital informed them that Sandy would have plateaus of learning. He was not mentally retarded, but his mental and emotional development would be slow and often difficult. It would take him longer to do his lessons or learn a new skill.

Sandy gave everything he had to the task at hand and his satisfaction when he did accomplish anything was great. Dusty made allowances for him as he recognized his difficulties in games. If anyone gave Sandy a bad time about striking out or missing a ball, he had Dusty to deal with. So this young man who had tried so hard to be a good soldier was brought home and buried at Chatsworth. His commanding officer told them he'd been one of the hardest workers he'd ever seen. His death was caused from drinking several different kinds of alcoholic drinks. He was celebrating a promotion. He was not used to drinking any kind of strong drink, but to be one of the boys, he went along with what they did when being promoted. They carried him to his quarters and he choked on his own vomit, unable to turn over. What a waste!

Dale wrote the book, *Salute to Sandy*, about his short life. Later they went to visit Vietnam in tribute to Sandy. He had volunteered to go to Vietnam, but didn't make it. They entertained the boys there and in every young face they could see their son. Sometimes they were almost within sight of the enemy. A band from Apple Valley went along, and a cousin, Dick Slye, was a guitarist in the band. The war was such a waste of young lives. My son Andy was in the Air Force at the time, flying fighter planes and later the big cargo planes that took equipment to the troops and returned with the bodies of our young men who gave their lives for their country.

In 1965, the big move to get out of cities had not started, so Victorville and Apple Valley were quiet desert towns. We all enjoyed a few years there until things began to grow and people flocked to the mountains and deserts. There was a delightful creek, or river, Deep Creek, a few miles from where we lived. It was the headwaters of the Mojave River, rushing water in some places and deep pools in others—wonderful places to relax. We often went there for a wiener roast or just to wade and sit on the banks and enjoy the quietness. It was not long until hippies discovered it and they flocked in. Their motorcycles and shattering noises ruined it for us. We no longer wanted to take our kids there. A sheltered spot where there was a nice pool and shade was no longer a safe place for one to be alone. I enjoyed taking my writing there and reading for a few hours until it was invaded by these unlawful people. Their bikes cut up the desert and it was no longer a haven for those hoping to get away from big city traffic and business. The local people soon stopped going to Deep Creek. My grandchildren were young and their favorite spot was Deep Creek when they came to visit me.

In 1968, Roy had been on a round of personal appearance at state fairs. The last one of the season was at Columbus, Ohio. Dale and the children flew home when it was over but Roy wanted to visit Duck Run. Our sister Kathleen had not been back to Ohio since she left for California in 1931. Roy wanted us to come to Duck Run to be there when he got there. So Kathleen, her husband Ted, and I started out to drive to Ohio. It was much different than our previous trips in 1931 and 1936. Roads were much better and Ted's car was newer. We decided we could take two weeks from our little gift shop in the museum. We left it in the care of Pat, Kathleen's daughter-in-law. It was a good trip, but we drove long hours. Ted liked to drive. He had been a bus driver when he and Kathleen met. We did not camp out this time, as our time was limited.

We got to our old home a day or so before Roy came. Ethel Hiles was still living in our house. She had alerted our friends and the house and yard were full of people. On Saturday they wanted to have a barn dance. Word got out that Roy was going to be there. Long before the dance was to start, the road was lined on both sides with parked cars. By the time Roy arrived the police were there to control the crowd. There was no way Roy could visit his old friends. He had just finished a long week with fans and this visit was intended to spend a few hours with us, his old school friends, and people we all grew up with. It was not to be. He was so tired, he slipped away and went to the Hurth Hotel in Portsmouth. The crowd finally dispersed after they found Roy was not there. The next morning, he came out to Duck Run and spent a few hours. I believe one of his most endearing traits is that he genuinely likes to be with old friends, people who want to be with him because he is Leonard to them, not Roy Rogers.

A couple of people still ask, "How's Leonard?" We could attract his attention when he'd be riding on a float in a big parade, like the Rose Parade by yelling, "Hey Leonard!" He'd know it was some of his family or old friends.

The Rose Parade draws thousands of viewers and attractions from all over the world. Roy and Dale were frequently asked to be a part of the Rose Parade. They have ridden their horses in it and been on floats. I believe the last time they were in the parade, the theme was The Good Life. It is a long and grueling experience to sit there, waving and smiling to thousands for hours. Sometimes it's cold and has rained, but the parade goes on. It is an honor to be chosen Grand Marshall for this parade, a New Year's Day great event. People start gathering on New Year's Eve all along the parade route to get a good place to see it. They have blankets and sleeping bags, food and hot coffee. Some bring campers and motor homes. The Tournament of Roses is a special event on New Year's Day. A few times I have taken my family, starting out at 2:00 a.m. to drive to Pasadena from Hawthorne, in order to get a place close enough to see.

One year my cousins came from Washington state for the parade and Rose Bowl game. (Washington State played that year in the Rose Bowl.) Roy was in the stands at the game. Roy was always so good to do such things for family and friends. My two boys, Andy and Richard, were in the Air Force and tried to see him if he came anywhere near where they were stationed. They'd go to his hotel and he was always so glad to see them. He would call to relatives or old friends to stand up if he knew they were in the audience. He'd then invite them to come along backstage. Early in his career he went to Portland and had Uncle Bud up on stage with him. This was a delight to all the Womack family. We have cousins in Texas he has acknowledged when he was doing the fat stock show in Houston. Mom's sister, Lee, had three daughters who moved and settled in Texas.

There are quite a number of Womacks in Kentucky, as my grandfather Archer was one of ten brothers and sisters raised there. My mother had many delightful stories of his childhood as well as her cousins, aunts, and

(Top to Bottom) Roy Rogers, Cleda's two sons: Andy Henry and Richard Henry in California. *Photo courtesy of Georgia Furr.*

uncles. Uncle Mose had several sons and when there was a job to be done they all helped, like chopping down and hauling trees or plowing or whatever it was. He did not assign a different job to each, but they all worked on the same job. My mother who had only one brother thought this a very strange way to do and thought of how much more work could be done if each one or even two of the boys were allotted a separate job, but that was Uncle Mose's way. Mom said he would sell anything on the place and sometimes his wife would protest this. He would say, "You'd better watch out or I'll sell you!" Aunt Nan would say, "I'd expect I'd go like hotcakes!" and laugh.

My mother always emphasized the fun and laughter. There were many hard times raising large families on small farms with very little money. Nearly all food had to be grown on the farm. Clothing was homemade, some people even had looms to weave cloth. All girls were taught to sew and quilt. Sometimes quilting frames were standing if folks were lucky to have the space for the frames. Often these frames were drawn up to the ceiling to be out of the way if they were not in use. Not many families had an extra room.

Quilts were shown at the county fairs as were canned fruit and vegetables and baked goods. There were 4-H clubs for girls to show their skills at sewing, cooking, canning, and baking. Blue ribbons were much prized possessions and competition was keen.

The fair was a great event in our lives. We had to save our money for it, but all the rides, sideshows, games, hot dogs, popcorn, and lemonade were real treats for country kids. One year right after we moved to the country my father gave me a dollar to spend, and I thought I was rich. I went in a wagon with neighbors whose granddaughter was my friend. When we got there, the team was unhitched and allowed to graze near the wagon. We had a big picnic basket full of food. I came home with my dollar as our neighbor would not let me spend it.

I believe most farm people went to the fair to look at the food displays and livestock, the quilts and handmade things and visit and catch up on any news. Often families would see certain people only at fair time. The sideshows and games were of little interest to them. We liked the merry-go-round and Ferris wheel, but could ride only if our parents or someone older was with us. My friend and I tagged along looking at pigs, cows, and chickens, along with jars of all kinds of fruits and vegetables, and, of course, quilts. To our thinking it would have been more fun to be on the midway and see the bearded lady, the fat lady, or the baby with two heads, but we had to stay with our elders. As I look back it was a really good time when crops were in and the summer's work was over, a time to catch up on all the happenings of the year.

When Leonard was a baby, still in diapers, he was stricken with spasms they called convulsions. It was very frightening with his arms and legs stiffening, head thrown back, and eyes rolling. Mom would panic and call for Aunt Cassie, a natural born nurse who lived close. She always seemed to know what to do, putting him in alternate hot and cold baths. They gave babies grown-up food as soon as they were old enough to sit on their laps at the table. They'd eat bites of mashed potatoes and gravy, even though they were still nursing. Baby Leonard always loved fresh corn, roastin' ears—still does—and sometimes he'd eat more than Mom realized. Having no teeth, it went through him whole, we do not know if this caused the frightening spasms or not. I remember Mom crying and wringing her hands and I was certain my little brother was dying. I'd crawl under the bed crying. The seizures always happened while Pop was at work and they'd be over before the doctor got there. As Leonard grew older, they faded away and stopped, but we never forgot the terror we felt.

In the winter of 1918, there was a flu epidemic and many people died. We were all sick at the same time. The doctor came and later we all were vaccinated. This was after the worst was over. Chicken pox, measles, and whooping cough were all a part of childhood and growing up.

Pleasant times to remember were of the camping trip we had. On the Fourth of July we'd take tents and a hammock and plenty of food. They'd catch fish for frying, mostly catfish. The river had many sand bars then and the willows grew thick along the banks.

The Slye brothers had a good many adventures on the river, some very dangerous. One time two or three of the brothers went fishing for a day or two. They were camped after dark, frying bacon for their supper, and they heard a blood curdling scream that kept getting closer and louder. They were not sure what it was. It sounded like a woman screaming, but there were many wild beasts then: bears, panthers, and wolves They decided they'd better cross the river as the fearful cries got closer. They picked up the pan of bacon, stepped into their boat, and rowed across. When they got to the other side, they soon saw a huge panther, circling the fire. They were glad to have the river between them. They had heard stories of these fierce beasts attacking men if they were hungry.

The family remembered happy coal gathering times. The barges that hauled coal from the mines of Kentucky, West Virginia, and Pennsylvania, dropped some of this coal. People gathered it when the river was low. Pop would take us and sometimes Mom would go along sitting in the boat and watching us. The coal would be smooth and round from the flow and action of the water. We would feel it with our feet and be pleased when we could reach down and with a little digging, we could put a big lump in the boat. It was fun for us, as well as getting our winter's coal. Pop and Uncle Will most often went on these trips without us, as it was serious business. The water was deep and they'd dive for the coal. Sometimes the lumps were huge. They'd come home with the boat low in the water. It took many trips to see the family through the severe winters. Most times Pop had to buy coal, also. This coal gathering was done before locks and dams were in the river and the water was clean and clear.

In Kentucky, paw-paws grew and Pop brought them home, large green oblong fruit that would ripen like bananas. When we lived on the houseboat Pop put them under the boat in a bed of grass and leaves to ripen. They were delicious with large brown seeds that looked like brown butter beans. Mom was very fond of paw-paws. We saved the seed because they were pretty, the color of our Ohio buckeyes.

The river is now polluted and there are many locks and dams between Pittsburgh and Portsmouth. At Pittsburgh, the Allegheny and the Monongahela Rivers form the Ohio River. The *Delta Queen* and *Mississippi Queen* made regular trips on the river and people came from all over for these trips.

Our first car was a Maxwell touring car. I remember the huge lights that had to be lit with a match. There were side curtains that were kept under the seats until it rained. Then they had to be buttoned on. In the winter they helped some to keep out the cold, wind, and snow. Our trips to the country just for a ride were always interrupted by a flat tire—sometimes two or three. I can still see my dad sitting on the running board patching the tube. We would occupy ourselves gathering berries or flowers.

Our farm up the holler had all kinds of nut trees (walnuts, hickory nuts, hazelnuts, and chestnuts) that we gathered in the horse driven sled sometimes. Walnuts kept our fingers stained. The outer shell had to be taken off first. The liquid, or juice, was said to be used by the Indians to make dye. Mom made us put on the same old dress to hull the walnuts as the stain never came out of our clothes and took a long time to wear off of our hands. After the outer shell came off, the nuts were left to dry, then cracked with a hammer. I don't wonder nowadays at how expensive black walnuts are in the markets. But when I was a little girl we could not buy them. Living most of my life in California I got used to English walnuts, different in flavor and much easier to hull with thinner shells.

Other times to remember are apple butter and sorghum making. There would be an apple peeling when neighbors came to help peel the bushels of apples needed to fill the huge copper kettle. Every neighborhood had one of these copper kettles, which was reserved for the day. In our neighborhood I don't think anyone knew who owned the kettle. It was used by all. The fire was started early and it was an all day job. We all hoped for a good sunny day as when the apples were peeled, they had to be cooked, rain or shine. I can remember one day when it rained and Pop had to erect a canopy over the kettle and stirrer. The kettle was filled with apples and was stirred with a long handled stirrer with a paddle with holes in it. Once the apples began to cook, the stirring was constant. Everyone took a turn with the stirring. The fire could not be too hot or there would be scorching. Sugar and cinnamon were added toward the last, which made the stirring even more important as it was likely to stick and scorch. When thick enough, it was put into half-gallon stone jars and sealed with a metal top and sealing wax. This wax was melted over the fire and poured on the caps. It solidified to a rock-like hardness and a hammer had to be used to crack it, being careful not to crack the jar. When I think of the pints and smaller size jars we have now, I wonder what we did with all that apple butter, so delicious and thick.

I know Mom never went to visit a neighbor without taking something to them. The same way neighbors brought things to her. Even a couple of eggs in an apron pocket was welcome if hens were moulting.

Sorghum molasses was made in the fall, too. People grew patches of sorghum cane. The stalks of the cane were fed into two large stone wheels, which crushed the juices out of them. The mule that turned the wheels went round and round in the same track. Nowadays a tractor power motor is used to crush the cane. A man who owned a pan in which sorghum molasses was made could be hired. The kids always knew where this was being done and they'd go after school and were allowed to get a piece of the sweet sugar cane and dip it into the foam where the molasses was ready to be run into the jugs. The long pan was divided into maybe six or seven sections into which the juice was run one at a time. It was green and clear, the consistency of water. The juice would enter a section and be cooked for a certain length of time. There were little gates the molasses maker would open to allow the juice into the next section. As it progressed along and became thicker, it was finally put into jugs—delicious thick sorghum molasses.

A man in our neighborhood made and sold moonshine. Some called it white lightning among other names. One night when Leonard was about twelve or thirteen a bunch of his friends and he stole a gallon jug out of the trunk of the moonshiner's car parked outside the church while revival meeting was going on. They drank the liquor and were carried home by older boys who knew they'd surely be in big trouble if they were caught either by the owner or the police. I can remember a young friend carrying Leonard upstairs as limp as a rag. He was so sick the next day he could barely move. My parents were really troubled about this. They thanked the boys who brought Leonard home and I believe it was a good lesson, learned the hard way. Leonard never drank nor could he stand the smell of moonshine the rest of his life.

Boys tried everything, I'm sure, that often got them into trouble. As I look back it was all a part of growing up. Leonard was no angel and he has often talked about why he became the idol of so many kids. Some families had no father, and mothers could leave their children at the local movie, knowing they were safe and in good hands for a few hours. The movies they saw were clean with a story that a boy or a girl could relate to or at least understand. Little boys all could imagine riding to the rescue of a troubled family about to lose their ranch, or the pretty girl heroine on a runaway horse. There are no cowboy heroes today, but the middle-aged men and women whose heroes were Roy and many others, wearing white hats and always standing for good and right, have not forgotten them. Not only did these movies give boys and girls many afternoons of pleasure, but they gave them a good set of values. There was right and wrong, good and bad, and their heroes instilled in them to always choose good over evil.

I have heard that even today these grown-up cowboys ask themselves when a problem arises, "What would Roy do?" I have seen the rules of the Roy Rogers Riders Club that have been reprinted and I expect there are those who still hold and treasure their original membership cards.

THE ROY ROGERS RIDERS CLUB RULES
- Be neat and clean
- Be courteous and polite
- Always obey your parents
- Protect the weak and help them
- Be brave, but never take chances
- Study hard and learn all you can
- Be kind to animals and learn to care for them
- Eat all your food and never waste any
- Love God and go to Sunday school regularly
- Always respect our flag and our country

Today some might think they are outdated and corny, but I believe the people who follow these rules are the backbone of our country. It's rather like the Boy Scouts, when boys learn things that carry them through their lives and make them better citizens. It's also like going to Sunday school or church.

Roy told the children that it was not sissy to go to Sunday school. He had received a letter or two that a boy had been teased and his friends told him only sissies go to Sunday school. So Roy would tell the kids it was not sissy. He made it a point to do this especially in his personal appearances in the huge stadiums and arenas.

If today children learned these rules and lived by them, how much better it would be. It seems that good manners and common courtesy are no longer taught to children. I don't say all children are not taught, but it looks like many parents leave too much up to teachers. I suspect the kids who learned from the old cowboy heroes in the '40s and '50s who are parents and grandparents now, are teaching their children those same values.

Here is a prayer that was supposed to be read at the beginning of the Roy Rogers Riders Club meetings which were held in theaters before the movie started:

> O, Lord, I reckon I'm not much just by myself
> I fail to do a lot of things I ought to do
> But Lord when trails are steep and passes high
> Help me to ride it straight the whole way through
> And when in the falling dusk, I get the final call
> I do not care how many flowers they send
> Above all else the happiest trail would be
> For you to say to me, Let's ride my friend,
>
> > Amen.

A very enduring memory of my mother is how she played the "French harp" (harmonica). She kept it beside the phone on a little shelf. She'd pick it up several times a day and play "Anglin Curve," a catchy toe-tapping tune. Her favorite hymn was "The Old Rugged Cross." Christmas was a favorite time and she would join in singing "Silent Night" when she heard it on the radio or TV. She'd begin thinking of Christmas in October. We'd take her to Penney's and Sears and she'd buy all of the grandsons pretty flannel shirts. We would wrap them for her as she loved to see the brightly wrapped gifts. In her later years she let us take her shopping in her wheelchair that Roy got for her. The year she died, she did not talk of Christmas or shopping. We later remembered this and feel that she had a premonition. She was a true child of God although she did not attend church. She treasured weekly visits with Bible readings from a religious group.

She died November 2, 1958, after a stroke. All of her life she prayed that she would "never get so she couldn't get around." We heard her say these words many times. The dear Lord heard her too and answered. She was ironing when she was stricken and died within a few hours. She was seventy-six years old.

My two sisters and I used to go to her grave and place flowers and talk and remember so many of her endearing ways. We would laugh and cry, remembering.

One memory dear to me was how sometimes in the middle of a busy day Pop would say, "Mommy, let's play a piece." So they would get mandolin and guitar out and sit down and play. When I think of the work they had to do, especially Pop with the shoe factory job during the week, then all the work of a farm, I wonder how he did it. Maybe the music gave him strength and courage to go on. I think of these times now and feel that the music somehow renewed them or inspired them.

A mandolin played by itself is not nearly as beautiful as when accompanied by a guitar. My mother and father would have made a big hit in Bluegrass music today, I believe. They knew many old tunes, "Birdie," "Walking Down Broadway," "Arkansas Traveler," and many others. My mother did not like the Carter family. She said they were *sagerly*. This word was her own and meant, I believe, the twangy sound that Bluegrass singers today use. Mom would not have liked Bill Monroe, Father of Bluegrass. His high voice, as he says his high lonesome sound would have been sagerly to Mom. She didn't like Hank Williams, either.

She was outspoken and I believe her opinion was highly valued. Spade Cooley and his first wife, Ann, were friends of Roy and Mom. As Spade became more popular and had different girl singers, he would always ask Mom how she liked them. As he became well known he got caught up in drink, dope, and had more money than he could handle. He was full-blooded Indian, as was Ann. He had a beautiful ranch in the San Fernando Valley. It had a good many acres and was remote from neighbors. One night he killed his wife Ella Mae. She was his current girl singer. He was sent to prison for years and he was getting out on parole when he died. What a waste of life due to drugs and alcohol.

Mom had died before this happened. She and Ann were friends until Mom died. She would have been grieved about it all. Spade was always welcome at her house. He valued Mom's opinion.

I think of when Bob Nolan had his nose fixed. He was a handsome Canadian and his nose was Roman-like and suited him. I guess he didn't like it so he had an operation to straighten it. The first time he went to see my folks my mom said, "My God, Bob, you are ruined." It was her outspoken way to say exactly how she felt. She did not mean to hurt anyone, but she felt compelled to speak her mind. Bob was not offended.

Roy has some loyal fans who are now grown-up, some even grandparents. One couple I'm thinking of come faithfully to the Roy Rogers Festival held in Portsmouth, Ohio, each June. One lives in Canada. He was born and raised in England, a member of the 50,000-member fan club. His father, an alcoholic was kind of replaced by Roy, as was the case with many kids who had no fathers or had abusive ones. He migrated to Canada and made his way to Duck Run to Roy's old home. He got acquainted with the lady living in our old home place. She was a family friend who was delighted to tell him what she knew of Roy and our family. Later he went to California to Apple Valley. He finally met up with his hero at the bowling alley in Victorville. My sister Kathleen and I also became acquainted with this ardent, young fan. He came to the gift shop each day hoping to meet Roy and we were so glad when he finally did.

Another fan from Canada, a member of the Royal Canadian Mounted Police, was a lifelong admirer and collector of Roy Rogers memorabilia. These two came to Portsmouth together to the Roy Rogers Festival. The first man works for Lloyd's of London and travels extensively in his work and when in California goes to see Roy and Dale and the Museum at Victorville. The Royal Canadian Mounted Policeman died young of a brain tumor. These two had such loyalty, love, and admiration for Roy, their childhood hero. This can rarely be found nowadays.

In my opinion, I doubt if Dale would have reached the height of popularity she did, had she not married Roy. Her desire to become a musical comedy star and be on Broadway had not gone far when she was cast as Roy's leading lady. She made such a hit, it gave her a real lift, career wise. She has said that Roy did not need her in pictures. He was already number one in Westerns on the charts, but after her first picture with Roy, his fans accepted her and it seemed they were destined to be together. At the same time I wonder if Roy would have retained his popularity without Dale.

God saw fit to take Arlene who was in perfect health. Dusty had been a Caesarian baby and often, when surgery is done, an embolism—a blood clot or bubble—forms. If one hits the brain it is instant death. Arlene had eaten breakfast and was sitting up in bed when this happened. In those days, patients did not get up and walk right after surgery as they do now.

Then he sent Robin to Roy and Dale. I have no trouble believing Robin was an angel sent to help thousands of troubled parents and their children with Downs Syndrome. Dale's book, Angel Unaware, was an inspiration from God and countless parents have been helped to love and care for these children and not hide or be ashamed of them. They are sent from God and no one can know how far reaching the little book has gone to help.

A woman who worked for Roy Rogers Enterprises took the thousands of letters that flooded the offices and wrote a book called *The Angel Spreads Her Wings*. So it goes on and on. All of these proceeds from the book went to the National Association for Retarded Children (NARC) and Roy and Dale together have made countless appearances for crippled and sick children in hospitals and orphanages. Their museum has cases of awards given for their humanitarian efforts.

If Roy had not married Dale and become a Christian, he might have gotten into the wrong crowd in picture making, although he was never a party-goer. He felt out of place at parties and would rather go with two or three good buddies hunting or fishing. His career might have faded out. The combination of Roy and Dale was such a sure-fire winner at the box office. Their lives were so busy there was little time for their family, which was growing. With the death of Robin, they adopted Dodie, a Native American baby, and Sandy at the same time. Their children were in their shows—at one time seven of them. Having them in the show worked well in two ways. The children could be with their parents and the shows were much loved by thousands of kids and parents as well.

Cleda Willoughby and versatile local historian and friend, Bill Glockner attend the Murals Banquet in 2002. *Photo courtesy of Bill Glockner.*

Roy Rogers loved Zeke Mullins' rural humor and unpretentious intellect. Zeke once said to me, "When you perform, it's not so important how good you are. People want to laugh so I've always made that most important." Since this book is part local flavor, I've chosen to honor that lesson taught by Zeke, and put a Zeke Mullins' or other local story at the beginning of each person's tale.

Zeke and his wife, Doris, enjoyed taking drives. One particular day they had been down in Kentucky and were returning home. It had been a long trip and Doris developed persistent hiccups. Because of the heat and the fact he had been sitting for such a long time, Zeke was galded.

They came to a general store and Zeke went in. A fellow was there all bent over and mopping the floor. Zeke says, "Hey buddy, do you have anything for hiccups?" The man didn't respond, but kept on mopping. Zeke spoke again, a little louder this time. "Say, do you have anything for the hiccups?" The clerk stood up and hit Zeke right in the face with the mop. Zeke said, "Gee whiz, what'd you do that for? All I said was 'do you have anything for the hiccups'."

The fellow answered, "Well you don't have the hiccups anymore do you?"

Zeke said, "I never had them in the first place. It's for the woman out in the car. But since I have your attention, would you have any talcum powder?"

The clerk replied, " Yes I do. Walk this way."

Zeke answered, "If I could walk that way, I wouldn't need the talcum powder!"

Zeke and Doris Mullins on their sixtieth wedding anniversary. *Photo courtesy of Zeke and Doris Mullins.*

Chapter Two
ZEKE and DORIS MULLINS

Doris Liles, who married Zeke Mullins, was born at Third and Jefferson Streets in Portsmouth, Ohio, to Frances Belle Scott Liles when Frances was sixteen. Her father was Granger Liles. The family soon moved to Lewis County, Kentucky, where Doris was raised.

Earcel "Zeke" Mullins was born in 1921 in Burdine, Kentucky, to Millie Alma Clay Mullins and John David Mullins. Earcel's mother ran a boarding house. His dad was a barber.

Burdine is a coal camp near Jenkins in Letcher County. Kenny Baker, the great fiddler, lived in Burdine, too.

Earcel's dad was from Olive Hill, Kentucky, and when Earcel was young they moved there. Earcel ran with a group of boys there who called each other nicknames such as Eif and Zeke. Zeke stuck with Earcel. When Zeke's pop drove the car, he always chewed tobacco. The kids learned not to sit behind him to avoid the flying tobacco juice.

Soon the family moved again, this time to Portsmouth, Ohio, where Zeke finished growing up.

So Doris was born in Ohio and raised in Kentucky. And Zeke was born in Kentucky and raised in Ohio.

Zeke says he never liked the name Earcel. It sounds like a

girl's name. Once the area Girl Scouts sent him an invitation to join and that did it! Yet, Zeke's mother always called him Earcel and, to this day, when Doris becomes stern, she calls him Earcel and he snaps to.

Earcel dodged the Girl Scouts but he did join the Boy Scouts. Camp Oyo was the site for many Boy Scout activities in Scioto County. Zeke was a good swimmer. One day he was there competing in swim races. He was to race against Don Yuenger. Don's mother made each of them swim trunks and the race was on. They swam underwater to the far end of the pool. When Zeke bumped the end he came up to get out and his trunks came clear off—a memorable sight.

Zeke and the rest of the country knew hard times during the Great Panic. President Franklin D. Roosevelt created the Civilian Conservation Corps (CCC) to protect and improve our environment and to provide respectable work for Americans during that time. Zeke joined at age seventeen and was moved to Kellogg, Idaho. At first he worked in forest fire reduction. Using a crosscut saw, ax, and wedges, he and a workmate sawed down trees that had burn damage. Then he moved to food management, mostly making sandwiches, but worked up to managing the canteen.

His usual need for music was satisfied in the evenings. There was a fiddler and guitar player on site so Zeke seconded on piano while others danced and sang. Since he had not completed high school, he enrolled in night classes at Hollister, Idaho, and earned his high school diploma. The CCC program helped Zeke.

When the Japanese bombed Pearl Harbor, Zeke was eligible to serve in the military. He joined the Merchant Marines in 1942 and took training in Florida. Zeke had learned to type in the

CCC so he was made a clerk. Assigned on the ship, the Joseph S. Conrad, he served in both combat and non-combat missions. He survived air attacks while at his post in the crow's nest with bullets all around. Zeke's sea duty took him to both the Atlantic and Pacific Oceans. The Joseph S. Conrad now floats at Mystic Bay, Connecticut, at the Merchant Marine Hall of Fame. It is the ship that was used in the famous movie, Mutiny on the Bounty. Zeke returned home at war's end.

He found comfort in music so he formed a group and accepted work as a performer. There were many opportunities to play after the end of World War II. Dance halls and clubs were everywhere, full of people wanting to be entertained. In 1946, his group took an early morning job on WPAY radio in Portsmouth. The station was situated upstairs on Gallia Street where it is today. It provided little income, but a fan base was built and many community music jobs resulted. They played schoolhouses, play parties, round dances, Grange halls, clubs, taverns, corn schuckin's, weddings, sorghum makin's, and bean shellings.

Zeke's band was called The Western Melody Aces. The original members were band leader Zeke Mullins, playing rhythm guitar and singing, Al Mercer, a Kentuckian on steel guitar, Russ Hodge from Stout, Ohio, on fiddle, and Gib Charles playing lead guitar.

Their half hour radio show came on at 5:30 each morning, Monday through Friday. Southern Ohio listeners, and even more Kentucky fans just across the Ohio River, loved their brand of music. In 1947 Russ Hodge and Gib Charles left the band and Don Boots and Ansel "Red" Ruggles replaced them. Red and Zeke were sometimes introduced as "Ancel and Earcel." All four members were singers.

The Western Melody Aces 1947. (L to R) Zeke Mullins, Al Mercer, Don Boots, and Red Ruggles.*Photo courtesy of Zeke and Doris Mullins.*

Another group, The Rhythm Rascals, performed on WPAY at five in the morning before Zeke's band. In their band were Carl Poulin, lead guitar; Jimmy Smith, rhythm guitar, Tex Turner, fiddle, Lucky Boggs, rhythm guitar, Don Hancock, bass, and Kitty Henton, vocals.

The two bands played early morning radio and during the rest of the day they entertained at many locations in the geographic listening area. Don Hancock once recalled a trip to the west side of Portsmouth. They had his bass tied on top of the car but it fell off and the neck broke as they crossed the Tow Path. When they played the job, they tied the neck on as best they could and Don performed carefully.

One person who loved that music was Doris Liles. At age

seventeen Doris graduated from Lewis County High School in Kentucky and took a job at Williams Manufacturing in Ohio. She operated a perforating machine that cut shoes in such a way that she could put flowers on them. The shoe manufacturing business was a major employer in Portsmouth and the city was known nationally for shoe production. After a year and a half she got a better job at Selby Shoes as a service girl. She checked out materials to workers. When they put the shoes together they checked the boxes in to Doris. She recorded them and they were paid accordingly.

Early each morning Doris, Bill Lewis, and a group of women boarded the Blue Ribbon bus in Garrison, Kentucky, and rode to work. Selby Shoes was close to WPAY so the group walked from the bus stop to the WPAY Restaurant across the street from the radio station. Doris always bought a coffee, then strolled over to the radio studio to watch Zeke's five-thirty show for a short time. Doris began her shift at six so she left early enough to punch in on time. One morning she noticed the restaurant had donuts for sale. She bought a sack full. They were so good she ate the whole dozen and got sick enough to regret the entire event.

Her crowd all liked Zeke's band. Bill Lewis commented one morning, "That Zeke's the best one of the bunch, but he sure is ugly." Even so, the surrounding circumstances along with the lure of music brought Zeke and Doris together. There wasn't much chance for them to visit at the station but they had certainly noticed each other and decided to get better acquainted. Dating followed and Zeke pursued. "He just wouldn't stay away." In 1947, Zeke and Doris married, beginning a life together that has touched many through entertainment and friendship.

Their first two children, Bill and Judy, were born a year apart. The kids loved music and cowboys—especially local cowboy Roy Rogers who, by that time, had his own television show. When they watched the show, they sat on the arm rests at each end of their couch and rode their horses. Bill called his armrest Trigger and Judy's was Buttermilk.

Zeke developed as a versatile musician and made a living for his family that way. Driven by his popularity and humor, he had work on radio and made regional public appearances as well. Many business places wanted to advertise through his program. Doris liked that Zeke would work, she supported him in it.

On September 3, 1965, Zeke found a new and lasting identity. He became a radio disc jockey at WPAY. He had to learn to "run the board," make the machinery work, and project the message to area listeners. When he sat in front of the microphone he was so busy he appeared to have five arms. Because of his relaxed approach, humor, and love of traditional music he succeeded from the start. In the beginning, he hardly had enough appropriate records to do a two-hour show but they started to come in and he soon had plenty.

Zeke was required to be on the job early and he was always in a hurry, wanting to be on time. One morning on his way to work he stepped it up a little. The police had been looking for a car like Zeke's. They followed him and pulled him over. When they shined their light through the window one said, "Oh, hell… we caught Zeke!"

When Zeke came on the air each morning, he needed an opening. He appropriately chose a real country sound; a hound barking and Ol' Roho the Rooster, crowing in the background as Zeke's voice announced:

> Well a great big howdy to you neighbors. This is your old cornbread-eatin' buddy, Zeke Mullins, from way out in the country, where the corn grows tall and everybody says you all. Yes sir, where them taters grow big, the little boys strong, the little girls pretty, and the creeks are knee deep in the wintertime, and the mud's over your shoetops when you go out to slop them hogs and feed them dogs, where you'll find the prettiest women and the ugliest men in the whole U.S.A.

He'd sometimes add, "Aw shut up, Roho."

Everybody loved it except a few spoil sports who wanted him to take Roho away. He kept the rooster.

Families from all over became Zeke Mullins' fans. As a result, he had many and varied experiences. He even named a baby once.

The Glen and Mary Holbert family from Red Hot, Kentucky, had listened for years. Mary was with child and knew her time was due. On the trip to a Portsmouth hospital they crossed the Ohio River over the U.S. Grant Bridge. Halfway across Mary gave birth to their infant. They called Zeke that very morning at the station and told him the news. Zeke suggested to them a good name for the new baby girl would be Bridget Grant and it was so ordained. Years later Zeke and Doris attended Bridget's wedding in a Greenup County, Kentucky, church.

Zeke became a "movie star" about 1960. A weekly series was

planned about Route 66. Tryouts were held in Portsmouth for parts in the pilot film that was to precede the series. Zeke was cast as a rural roughneck; he and Tom Vetter had the only speaking parts of the Portsmouth actors. Zeke and Tom went to California and were on the set about a week. Zeke had touble getting home due to heavy snow. After the film was shown a weekly television program followed that was called Route 66. Each week featured a story about a different town along the famous highway.

The Portsmouth Recognition Society was formed to honor local citizens who had done well, and Zeke became a member. Certainly they wanted to honor Roy Rogers and through that, Zeke became personally acquainted with Roy. The nature of each man drew them together and they liked to talk and laugh.

In conjunction with disc jockey work, Zeke and Doris began a tour bus sideline that was very popular. People like being with Doris and Zeke. Everyone laughed a lot on the tours. The bus sometimes went cross country so far as Victorville, California, where Roy Rogers' museum was located. Roy loved having people from home visit.

When Roy came home he tried to steal some time for doing what he liked. One day Zeke was at his early morning radio job and Roy just showed up, sat down, and talked with Zeke about any and everything for two hours. Zeke postponed the commercials but finally said he had to put them on. Roy said he should go anyhow. Newsman Jim Huffard asked Roy to do a news spot but Roy replied, "I've already been here two hours."

After thirty-four years, Zeke left WPAY. He worked short stints at Waverly radio and W101 in Wheelersburg. Jan Morton became WNXT radio station manager in Portsmouth. She hired

Zeke's son, Larry Mullins, to be FM disc jockey and Zeke for the AM job. WNXT felt good to Zeke and the locals had him back.

Because of Zeke's and Roy's respect for one another, a difficult situation was corrected. Roy often stayed with his sister, Cleda, who lived on Williams Street. She had bought her home from local musician, Bill Odle.

One day Roy called Zeke and said he'd like to walk down to Mill Street and look at his family's old houseboat that was being used as a home. The city had promised Roy they would see to its upkeep. Zeke met Roy at Cleda's and the three of them walked down to the property. To go unnoticed Roy wore sunglasses, a ball cap, and tennis shoes. When they reached Mill Street and

Zeke Mullins presents Roy Rogers a photo of home at Victorville. 1981. *Photo courtesy of Don Brooks.*

Waller, they found the place unkempt and in disrepair. Roy was greatly bothered and proclaimed he would never return to Portsmouth. And for a long time, he didn't.

The city needed the good will of Roy Rogers and they turned to Zeke. They repaired and painted the houseboat. Booklets were placed at many area locations asking people to sign, saying Roy, please come home. Zeke promoted the effort on the radio and thousands of signatures were collected. They were nicely bound into books that Zeke and Doris took with them on another bus trip to Victorville. At the museum they presented the petitions to Roy, and Zeke asked him to come home. It touched Roy and he returned several times.

On one of Roy's visits home, the manger of WNXT made a request of Zeke. He loved Roy Rogers but had never met him. He gave Zeke a photo of Roy and asked him to get Roy to sign it. Zeke drove over to Cleda's and explained the request to Roy. Roy signed the picture and also told Zeke a story. When President Ronald Reagan was elected, Roy was invited to the Inauguration. He asked Roy to work the reception and sign autographs. It went on for hours, wore him out, and he missed the ceremony. Roy didn't like signing autographs anyway so he made a new policy after that: no more autographs. He would allow a picture to be made with him, though. He felt it was more personal and comfortable.

Because Portsmouth is situated on a flood plain, a strong concrete wall runs between the city and the Ohio River to give protection from the river. It is known as the Wall of Stars because large stars have been painted on the river side of the wall. Some successful locals are selected to sign the stars. When Roy was

Saturday, June 4, 1994

Stars blaze trails in Portsmouth

Stan Kokotajlo/Daily Times

Roy Rogers finally adds his signature to the star saved for him on Portsmouth flood-wall during a ceremony Friday when he was also presented with a proclamation and key to the city by Mayor Frank Gerlach.

Local boy Leonard "Roy Rogers" Slye signs the Wall of Stars in Portsmouth, Ohio, 1994. *Newspaper clipping courtesy of Ruth Adkins.*

chosen, he asked Zeke to accompany him. They met at Cleda's house and rode to the river in a rented convertible. Roy's signing brought the biggest attendance in history.

Not long after that, Zeke was asked to sign one of the stars. He did so in front of the second largest crowd ever. The audience included Doris, city manager Frank Gerlach, Jeff Horton, Zeke's brothers, Clarence and Orville Mullins, and the five children of Zeke and Doris. When Zeke went up in the bucket to sign, WNXT manager Jan Morton and Zeke's granddaughter, Chelsey Kate Mullins, were also in the bucket.

On the last bus trip Zeke and Doris took to Victorville, they found Roy's health had slipped a bit. He came to see them on an electric scooter. He called it Trigger Three. Roy had previously owned two Palominos, both named Trigger. Soon after that, Roy's death signaled the loss of a true friend for Zeke.

Zeke is a man of stamina and has weathered the storms. For a while, he and his friend Red Ruggles (Ancel and Earcel) were the only two surviving local musicians who were WWII veterans. Then Red died in 2012.

Zeke and Doris have traveled extensively both together and on their own. Doris is of French heritage and has visited Paris. She has been to all fifty states and seven foreign countries. Zeke says he likes an inch or two of being around the world.

Zeke is now ninety-two and has never wanted to stop being a DJ. He worked at that full-time occupation for fifty-one years and was once honored as Mister DJ USA. He also performed

(L to R) Red Ruggles, unidentified, unidentified, Doris Mullins, Bill Sanders, Zeke Mullins, and Don Hancock at Ray Litteral's Old Timers Days. *Photo courtesy of Zeke and Doris Mullins.*

as a humorist and musician before and during those years. He presently works as part-time DJ at WNXT. He and Doris go there once a week and record their weekly program together. His listeners wait for it eagerly.

Doris is capable in so many areas. It causes one to wonder who she would have become had she and Zeke not met. But they did. Zeke's cells are eaten up with music and he uses music to support his primary role, that of a humorist. The two of them perform together. "That way there are no other egos to feed," Zeke says.

Doris complements their show by singing harmony, adding to Zeke's stories and providing those of her own. Her singing developed in church and at home and together they can do most any sort of song. She can also play the straight for Zeke's humor. A good example is the song, "I Will Marry You. "

Both Zeke and Doris were raised in a traditional setting. She can perform as well as being wife and mother. Doris gave birth to their five wholesome children—Bill, Judy, Larry Dale, Scott, and Lisa—all of them musical in their own right.

Zeke says he never would have made it had it not been for his old friend Poncho, the station janitor who brought him a coffee and two donuts each morning. He bought them at Mrs. Renison's Crispie Creme Donut Shop that was originally at Eighth and Gallia Streets, but is now at Gallia and Waller.

Sometimes a fan wrote a song that Zeke would record and popularize such as "Guess I'll Be Eating Cheerios Again Tonight" about a fellow in the dog house.

But Zeke wrote his own songs about local happenings, too. He wrote "The Tuba Concert," about playing that instrument in public school. The recording included some attention getting notes. His "Selby Shoes" tells of the closing of the historic shoe manufacturing employer and the effects on our community. Another, "The Blue Cloud," was about a blue object erected at Roy Rogers Esplanade and the curiousity stimulated by it in our community. The U.S. Grant Bridge was closed for a good while. It greatly affected travel habits and daily convenience. Zeke was inspired to write "The Bridge Song" and it was highly requested.

Zeke enjoyed strong support from area business. He sang some of the ads. Originally, the radio station devised them but Zeke preferred to write and arrange his own, and his were an improvement. His "Take that Spot to Edwards" worked nicely for Edwards Cleaners.

Zeke's singing ads were popular. The Foodland markets ad is an example:

Zeke and Doris Mullins' family at Zeke's 80th birthday celebration. (L to R) Lisa, Scott, Larry, Dale, Judy, and Bill. *Photo courtesy of Zeke and Doris Mullins.*

Come in to Foodland,
Come in to Foodland,
Come in to Foodland,
Come out better every time.

Glick's Furniture Store was on Second Street. Upstairs over the store was a dance hall where Zeke Mullins and his band played for square dances. Zeke also did shows in Glick's window. A singing ad was written about Glick's that Zeke performed on the air.

Buy your furniture at Glick's on Second Street.
For the furniture at Glick's just can't be beat.
You can buy on easy credit, don't delay and don't
    forget it.
Buy your furniture at Glick's on Second Street.

Bill Questel and Mary Martha Welty went to work at Glick's the same day. When Mary Martha saw Bill she said, "That's the man I'm going to marry." She did and they're a special couple in our community today.

So many of us are more full from loving and laughing with Zeke and Doris Mullins. We will ever remember Zeke Mullins' stories and, if you get to visit their home, you'll find over the door a picture of Roho, the Rooster.

Georgia Furr (on left) and Nancy Horsley at Leonard Slye's grave. Apple Valley, California, July 1998. *Photo courtesy of Georgia Furr.*

Seamus Welsh from out in Otway moved to town. He was enrolled in one of those schools that had a football team. Seamus wasn't very big but he tried out for the team. It was a time when they wore old helmets with no face mask guards, though they did have ear pads with holes in them that hung down. Seamus was the smallest man on the team but he was so good he was put at fullback. In his junior and senior years in spite of his diminutive size and the small size of his school, he was the leading ground gainer in the whole state. When asked how he did it Seamus replied, "I turned my helmet sideways, looked through the ear hole, and they couldn't tell if I was coming or going."

Chapter Three
GEORGIA FURR

Georgia Furr, known to most as Georgie, was born on Inskeep Road a little above the Slye family home. Her parents were Loyd and Dorothy Jordan Crabtree. Their property bordered the Slyes'. Georgia's birth was assisted by community midwife Dorie Henry. She and her brother, Frank, lived near the Crabtrees.

In those days, Dorie and all the neighbors had outdoor toilets. She was a very inquisitive woman and didn't like to miss a thing. When she visited the outhouse, after she got situated, she would leave the door open so she wouldn't be left out of anything.

Georgie was one of four children, two boys and two girls. It was good to experience childhood in that closely knit neighborhood.

When Georgie came of school age she attended the

Dorothy Jordan Crabtree (Georgie's mom) and Roy Rogers. *Photo courtesy of Georgia Furr.*

new brick, two room building on Duck Run. It had replaced the old one room school. Marjorie Walker taught grades one through three, and Zelma Doll taught grades four through six. Georgie went to McDermott after sixth grade.

While in junior high Georgie's family did as so many other Appalachian families did. They moved to the city for work. Several people from Inskeep went to Cleveland to work in defense plants in the early '40s. They lived near one another there and held to that closeness they had felt at "home."

Leonard Slye had become famous by then. When he performed in Cleveland, he would visit the Hiles, Jordans, or Crabtrees at night to sing and visit.

After World War II the Crabtree family returned to Scioto County and, at age sixteen, Georgie went to work at Selby Shoes. She soon moved to Otway and earned her G.E.D. studying at Otway School. Georgie married Durward Chandler and they parented three children.

She studied to become a beautician, a profession she liked and was good at. She opened a shop in her home and was able to practice her artistry that way.

Otway has a storied history. It once had two large tie yards and was the largest tie yard center on the Norfolk and Western rail lines. Otway thrived with several service stations, blacksmith shops, a school, two restaurants, a hotel, a bank, a funeral home, a livery stable, two general stores, the George Ort and George Walsh saloons, and Methodist, Christian Union, and Catholic churches. Doctor Gordon was a very popular man and he cared for everyone.

Georgie liked all that history and became interested in the governance of her town. She was elected to town council and served for twenty five years. When Myron Miller resigned as mayor, Georgie was elected and spent twelve years in that position. She worked hard for the Otway community.

When Northwest District consolidated their schools, some wanted to save the school building that was going to be closed. Georgia became involved in the effort and the village was able to buy the school for ten dollars. Several people have worked together on the building's maintenance. Various community activities are held there.

Otway has the distinction of having the only covered bridge remaining in Scioto County. It spans Brush Creek on State Route 348. Georgie has helped to secure grants for repair, and prospects for additional funding look promising.

Cleda Willoughby herds her wagon at the Otway, Ohio, covered bridge, 1994. *Photo courtesy of Bill Sanders.*

Georgie further expanded her skills by going to work for AAA. She became a planner and escort for trips. Exploring the geography of America is a great responsibility and a wonderful experience.

Several years ago local Roy Rogers enthusiast Jim Wilson presented the idea of a Roy Rogers festival. He got that notion from attending other Western events around the country. He, AAA president John Irwin, writer and historian Elmer Sword, and others developed this event that continues today. Georgia was a member of the founding group. Also, she is the only one who knew both Cleda and Leonard Slye and their family. When the festival was being organized, Georgie and her daughter, Cheryl, attended a Western festival in Knoxville, Tennessee to get pointers on creating a successful event.

After Cleda worked for her brother, Roy, in the Victorville

(L to R) Hubert Crabtree, Georgie Furr, Mary Hiles Linegar, unidentified, Elmer Sword, unidentified, at Leonard's home place. *Courtesy Georgia Furr.*

museum for fifty years, she began to long for home. She was good friends with Georgie's mother, Dorothy. Through that relationship, Georgie got to know Cleda better and to become better acquainted with Roy. When Cleda returned to the area she had no house, so she lived with Georgie in Otway for a summer or so.

At an early Otway Farmer's Institute, Georgie was in charge. A camper was set up at the covered bridge in order to sell food. Cleda told Georgie that Roy was coming out to get a sausage sandwich. He was in civilian clothes and sat at a bench enjoying his two sandwiches. Singer Jim Evans' mother walked by, stopped, and asked, "Anyone ever tell you how you resemble Roy Rogers?"

He answered, "A few."

Later, she walked by again and said, "I bet you wish you had his money." Then she came by a third time and exclaimed, "You *are* Roy Rogers."

At the time, Georgie was running a music building across the tracks near Simon's Mill. Locals gathered there spontaneously to perform, visit, or listen to music. The following night Cleda and Roy showed up and he sang a couple of songs. No one knew he was coming. It must have been difficult for him to still find settings such as that!

Cleda's stay with Georgia afforded them time to recall life on Inskeep and where they attended both Duck Run school and church. Leonard went to church there, too. A special topic for them was resident Sade McFann, a great friend of Leonard's. Sade worked hard and valued her property. The layout of her place easily accommodated anyone who might want to steal a chicken—and Leonard was known for taking a few. Sade let him know she knew about it, though. Cleda remembered the

Daily Times file photo

Roy Rogers poses with other Charter Members of the West Side Pioneers 4-H Club in 1927, from left, Clyde Cyrus, Leslie Cooper, Lawrence Wiseman, Homer Boldman, Leroy Colley, Roy Rogers, Strauther Hiles, Guy Bumgarner, club advisor.

Guy Bumgarner and the 4-H Club he had including Leonard Slye. Duck Run School. *Newspaper clipping courtesy of Georgia Furr.*

family's hard work and that the home place had a screened in porch so they could keep out the flies and do their canning. It is now boxed in.

Cleda knew how special her brother was. She thought Dale was good for Roy, but it bothered her when Dale bossed him. He had a great ability to let it "slide off."

The Slye children thought highly of their parents. Mattie was quite efficient, though crippled. Andy was versatile and hard working. Originally employed in a shoe factory in Cincinnati, he went to Excelsior shoes after coming to Portsmouth. After the family's move to Inskeep, he worked in the shoe factory while most neighbors were busy in the local stone industry.

Cleda and Leonard were middle children in a family of four.

Cleda, who was older then Leonard, married Ed Henry and had two sons. Her youngest was killed in an automobile accident in England. Cleda later married Alfred Willoughby and they had a daughter, Gloria.

While staying with Georgie, Cleda became acquainted with several special people. The Bumgarners were such people. Guy had been a great influence on many of his students, including developing artist George Little.

Nell Bumgarner and her daughter, Laura Rachel, introduced Georgie to George. His father was a successful farmer and wanted his son to follow the path he had taken. He never saw the value of being an artist, but George persisted and became a success at it. Earlier in his life he had taken a job for the county engineer, painting road signs.

George and his family once stayed a week with Georgie. At the time he had a place in Chattanooga, Tennessee, called The Little Art Shop. While at Georgie's he painted the Freeman's old brick home next door, the covered bridge with people walking through to make it personal, and the new State Route 348 bridge. In it he put Georgie's grandchildren. George also gave her an autographed painting of the Slye home place.

Cleda returned to California. After a short while she called Georgie. The place was too noisy and the heavy traffic scared her so she wanted to come home to stay.

Cleda was encouraged to return to the area by her old friend Dorothy and Dorothy's brother Paul Jordan. A DVD has been made of an interview with Paul. In it he validated many stories that have circulated for years in the area. He grew up with Leonard, went to school with him, and knew him well as a boy

(L to R) Lowell Crabtree, Loyd Crabtree, and Cleda Willoughby. Music session at Georgie Furr's, Otway, Ohio. *Photo courtesy of Georgia Furr.*

and a man. Paul had an intense interest in and knowledge of nature and history and was known by many as The Mountain Man. Leonard shared that interest.

In the interview Paul emphasized, "I grew up with Leonard Slye, not Roy Rogers. All the boys loafed together, no matter age— especially Loyd Crabtree, Leonard Crabtree, Leonard Slye, and Paul Jordan. We followed paths not roads." Paul recalled that they all rolled their own cigarettes, but they were pretty uneven. He also mentioned that Leonard had a horse named Babe he used to ride to school. Sometimes he and Babe would race the old school bus.

Paul remembered that the first thing a teacher did at the start of the school year was cut ten hickory switches and set them in the corner for the kids to see. The boys got lots of lickins.

Several grades of students were taught in the same room and students would have recitation. An example of that was when one grade would sit on the recitation bench and have reading, spelling, writing, and arithmetic.

Paul and his friends shot slingshots, and hunted rabbits (and everything) by day, and opossums by night in Allen Hollow. They built eight feet by twelve feet caves for parties, and cooked wild game or "borrowed" chickens. Sometimes the caves were built in sawdust piles since there were lots of saw mills.

(L to R) Lillian Jordan, Short Noel (far right), Dean Jordan talking with Roy Rogers at the homeplace. *Photo courtesy of Georgia Furr.*

When they swam, it was usually down at the Henry Springs Hotel swimming hole. In the winter they went sleigh riding and Cleda always went along. She loved it! Pearl Allen took old bicycle rims and fixed them on sled runners to make them go smoother and faster.

Paul remembered the day the Slyes went to California. It was a loss to their community. Andy Slye got Ed Jordan to fix up the old Dodge sedan and off they went.

Everyone missed Leonard but he loved to come home and when he did, there was often a square dance. Dale seldom accompanied Roy on those trips, but one time when she did, they danced all night. Paul danced Dale off her feet!

Paul and the childhood gang consisted of Beecher Henry, Pat Jordan, Leonard Slye, Strauther and Charles Hiles, Lawrence Wiseman, Fred and Harry Matthews, Pearl Allen, and Paul. It was a fine group.

Paul married a Cleveland girl and she took this as her adopted area. They and their son, Wayne, had a good life.

Cleda again returned home and lived with Georgie for a while but soon found a comfortable home in Portsmouth on Williams

Leonard Slye's real chums at the homeplace. (L to R) Fred Matthews, Charlie Hiles, Paul Jordan, Lowell Crabtree, Loyd Crabtree, Clayton McFann, Orville Strickland, and Jasper Strickland. *Photo courtesy of Georgia Furr.*

Street. Roy usually stayed there when he visited the area. Cleda called Georgie one evening and invited her to supper because Roy was home. He had driven a rental car from Columbus. After supper he said, "I want to go to Duck Run." Cleda discouraged that for it was sort of late. Every now and then he'd stomp his foot and say, "I want to go to Duck Run!" Finally he put on a ball cap and tennis shoes and they walked down along the river where the Slyes once lived.

When time provided, they did go to the country. When they could get up a square dance, Roy was tickled and so were the folks there. Ed Henry often played fiddle and Leonard's cousin, Chester, played guitar. Leonard Slye did his part taking a place in the dance band.

Childhood memories were frequently recalled during these

events. They had all been square dancing in their earliest years, back before the coming of the automobile. Dances were held in homes with people dancing a set in each room; callers situated so everyone could hear. Some of the wooden bridges had good even floors where dances were held at night. Those kind of events can be traced back to Ireland and other countries where it was fashionable to hold cross road dances at midnight. Our square dancing evolved from the very traditional Irish set dance as well as other forms of dancing.

Dancing was so popular families built outside dance platforms. Neighbors were welcome and there were many available musicians. A bit west of Duck Run, two families had outside dance platforms on Bloody Run Hill. They were the Walshes and the Finns. Georgie's parents took her to a dance held at one of those places. It was down Duck Run, past Colley Road, a short distance on the left. A square log cabin that sold beer was located there. The platform was next to the cabin. The Slyes attended, too. Georgie has spirited memories of being seven or eight, sitting on the edge of that platform listening to the fiddle, and watching the dancers get to it.

Roy happened to be home when the wake for his old friend, Fred Matthews, was held at William McKinley Funeral Home in Lucasville. He and Cleda attended, after which Roy commented, "I saw more of my friends there than at any other visit home."

When Leonard Slye, the boy from Inskeep, died, a girl from Inskeep, Georgie Furr, went to his funeral as a representative of the people of Duck Run. Accompanying her was Nancy Horsley, a representative of the Roy Rogers Association. They flew to California and stayed a week in a motel. Also staying at the motel was Roy's niece, Eileen Kisling, from Maryland. She was the daughter of Roy's sister, Mary. Some special Roy Rogers fans were there, too. One who spent her life honoring Roy was Lois Sanders. (She may choose to be buried in the same cemetery as Roy.)

On the day of the funeral, Cleda's son, Andy Henry, picked up Georgie and Nancy and took them to Roy's and Dale's house. Dale had experienced a heart attack and was in a wheelchair. After their visit, Andy took them to the church for a noontime memorial service held before the funeral. They were treated as members of the family. Others who were allowed to attend had to have a pass, but not Georgie and Nancy. There was special singing done by an old, black man who was a friend of Roy's. He had a fine voice. Georgie later saw him on Dale's TV program. The Sons of the Pioneers also sang.

The funeral for Roy was held at the church he attended, The Presbyterian Church of the Valley. It was at 5:30 P.M. on Saturday, July 11, 1998. There were large crowds at all the services.

After the funeral, they rode to Sunset Hills Memorial Garden cemetery which was far out in the country. Along the road people lined up for miles, standing quietly and respectfully with their hands over their hearts. "Happy Trails" signs were everywhere.

When the procession reached the cemetery Roy was moved from the long black ambulance, placed in an antique horse drawn hearse, and taken to the burial area. At the grave his horse club, the Shriners, and several others spoke. Roy had specified that he wanted to be buried as the sun began to go down over the hill. Twelve white doves were released. They circled and flew away as Leonard Slye, the boy from Inskeep was laid to rest.

The hearse that carried Leonard Slye to rest. Apple Valley, California July 1998. *Photo courtesy of Georgia Furr.*

Afterward, three trucks a day hauled in piles of mail expressing sympathy or giving contributions for charity. Georgie and Nancy remained at the museum a few days to help before returning home.

Georgia considered it a blessing to have witnessed her rural neighbor reaching heights of color while remaining a man of simplicity.

Georgie Furr has always been involved in the history and betterment of her town. She deserves sincere thanks for being so completely willing to help with this book.

Leonard Slye and Hubert Crabtree at the home place. 1982. *Photo courtesy of Hubert Crabtree.*

The older the fiddler, the sweeter the tune

Chapter Four
HUBERT CRABTREE

Hubert Crabtree was ninety-two at the time of our visits. He and his wife, Tharlene, raised nine children. His parents, Elijah and Nancy, also raised nine: Loyd, Lowell, Francis, Alma, Sara Ellen, Thelma, Ora Lee, Anice, and Hubert. They raised Everett Meadows, too.

Portsmouth was the closest town of any size, but the Crabtrees did not go there often. Hubert's parents told their children that in Portsmouth streets were lit at night by gas light. Each day the lights were pumped up enough for them to burn all night.

The Crabtrees raised most of their food and got the remainder at local groceries. Clothes were usually made at home but they had the Sears mail order catalog for shoes and other necessities. Elijah measured their feet with a stick and was able to tell which size shoe to order for each of them. When the new catalog arrived, the old one became toilet paper.

Medicine was mostly old reliable home remedies. A common one was moonshine and honey. Something in the Crabtrees simple lifestyle must have worked well because Hubert never took any medicine in his life until he was eighty-eight years old.

Hubert's family lived close to six other families on Inskeep

Road. Those included the Rufus Crabtree family, the Ephram Crabtree family, midwife Dorie Henry, Jim Henry, and Andrew Slye. The Hiles family and Stricklands lived on the other side of Mohawk Drive.

At that time, Hubert remembers Inskeep to be a dirt horse path from the head of the hollow down to Route 348. When traveling on that road, walking or on a horse, there were five gates to open and close. The gates separated properties and kept the livestock in. Those families felt they were a part of each other's families. Hubert said he and Leonard felt that way their entire lives.

There were no buses so the community children walked to school. Elementary students went to Duck Run and high school kids to McDermott. Leonard Slye was in their group. At the time Hubert was beginning grade school, Leonard was finishing.

Hubert's early years were at the old grades-one-through-eight Duck Run School. On the lower side of the school was a driveway and a well with a pump. The school sat next to the pump. Inside, the children all gathered around the wood stove to keep warm.

The old one room school was torn down and replaced by a brick two room. Bert Hill was paid fifty dollars to tear down the old school and haul it away. The new brick school held grades one through four on the south side, and five through eight on the north side. It was later changed to grades one through three, and four through six. That building is still standing and used by the church nearby.

Hubert went two years to the old school, four to the new one, and then to McDermott for grades seven and eight. Andrew Slye, Leonard's dad, bought a horse named Babe from Elijah Crabtree. Leonard sometimes rode the horse to school and tied it outside.

Grades 1 through 8 Duck Run one room school is no longer there. Charlie Hiles is to the left of Leonard Slye, seated far right wearing a white shirt. *Photo courtesy of Nellie Delong Rossa.*

Duck Run School had a boy's and girl's toilet outside and they used newspaper for toilet paper.

When Hubert attended McDermott, the grade school was behind the high school. When the grade school was torn down, a new one was built beside the high school. At McDermott, Hubert learned a great portion of the Declaration of Independence by heart. His eighth grade teacher, Guy Bumgarner, taught him that.

At home, the Crabtrees learned self reliance and to help their neighbors. Most everyone raised cows for milk, smear case,

On the left is the brick Duck Run School, grades 1 through 6, that replaced the wooden building. Hubert Crabtree attended here. It is still standing. *Photo courtesy of John Roger Simon.*

cheese, and butter. Pigs provided bacon, ham, and other cuts of pork. Chickens offered eggs, meat, and a morning wake up call. Most everyone helped at bean stringings, corn shuckings, butchering time, sorghum cook offs, potato diggings, threshings, and apple butter makings.

Many tales are told to add conversational color to Leonard Slye stories. Several of them highlight chicken thieving. Hubert pointed out that everyone had chickens.

Taking chickens was so common it was not really considered thieving. Leonard and Loyd Crabtree snatched lots of chickens together. Hubert told that one day Leonard and Loyd thought there was going to be a bean stringing down the road. They wanted to join in so they lifted a couple of fryers to contribute. When they arrived, there was no bean stringing so they went home, returning the chickens on the way. On another day, Dorie Henry had a bean stringing. She told Leonard and Loyd that Cecil Hilderbrand had lots of young fryers, to get two of them so she could cook them. Leonard and Loyd went over in the creek and smoked until enough time had passed that they could have gone to Cecil Hilderbrand's place. Then they grabbed two of Dorie's own fryers and gave them to her. While cleaning them she remarked, "They look a lot like mine."

Curt Bush, who lived on Slate Run, had fifteen acres of blackberries. Hubert, his parents, Sara Ellen, Alma, and Francis were berry pickers. They carried their lunch, walked the ridge to the Bush place, and picked all day. If they picked four crates, Mr. Bush kept three and the Crabtrees got one. They had to tote the berries home, but with them they made pies, jam, jelly, and even canned some of them. The rest were traded or given away.

As the boys aged and became young men they began leaving home to find work. Hubert spent a spell in Columbus at Fisher Body. Musical tastes from home went with him. His union was quite a social group and they held Western style square dances.

Dances at home were traditional, with two couples in a set of four dancing at the same time. In Columbus, all four couples danced at the same time.

A blow came to the Inskeep community when Andrew Slye moved his family to California. However, they often felt a need to come home and always stayed at the homeplace with Clell and Ethel Hiles when they did. Andy loved music and when he got the urge, he sent for Hubert to bring over his guitar and mandolin and they played, sang, and talked.

At the time, there were many fans of B Western movies with singing cowboys. Imagine the surprise of the locals when their chum, Leonard, became Roy Rogers, King of the Cowboys.

It was around this period that several of the young men from Inskeep began to find work in Cleveland. Loyd Crabtree and his daughter, Georgia, went there as did Frank, Strauther, and Marion Hiles, Paul and Ralph Jordan, and Hubert Crabtree. Hubert was a molder at Alcoa, making noses and propellers for airplanes.

When they came back for visits, it took thirteen and one half hours, one way. Roads were poor, crooked, and two lanes wide with lots of farmers, low speed limits, and other bad conditions. Hubert wondered how traveling musicians found it possible to make their dates.

Roy sometimes performed in Cleveland. One evening the boys went to Roy's Rodeo. Afterward, Strauther Hiles picked him up and brought him to their hotel. They talked, laughed, and sang the rest of the night. Another night Roy came over late and found they were all in bed. As he came up the stairs, he hit the walls on both sides with the palms of his hands. He went to Hubert's bedroom, took him by the foot, and pulled him out of bed onto the floor.

Eventually, most of the group returned home to work and live, but Roy remained in California.

Hubert was staying with his son, and daughter-in-law, Michael and Diane, when we first visited. Diane made references to Roy's lifelong desire to return and spend time with "home people."

Mike noticed that Roy especially liked to visit with Frank and Thelma Jordan.

Mike was young when he first began to pay attention to Roy. He appeared to be a quiet man. Roy liked to walk the road alone and Mike wondered what he thought about. He dressed plainly and walked by himself from the homeplace down Inskeep to Duck Run, and then on down to Whitaker's Grocery. Roy sometimes bought a shirt there, ate sardines and crackers, and sat and talked with the locals. Mike himself was walking Inskeep one day and came upon Rolly DeLong and Roy. Rolly was riding his bike and had stopped to talk with Roy.

Dale Slye and Cleda Willoughby in front of Whitaker's Duck Run Market, a store Leonard often visited. *Photo courtesy of Georgia Furr.*

One time Roy had been over to Hubert's, talking with Tharlene. Other family members dropped by and Roy visited with them a while. There was an outdoor toilet on the left side of the house. Roy asked Mike to take a picture of him coming out of it. Roy went inside and closed the door. Then he opened the door and stepped out with a big grin on his face and tipped his hat. Mike got a good shot of Roy in the toilet doorway but didn't keep a copy of it.

Hubert Crabtree sings Johnny Cash with the help of Georgia Furr and Linda Crabtree at Mike Crabtree's home. *Photo courtesy of John Roger Simon.*

Leonard Slye and Hubert Crabtree knew one another in their home setting, at school, through Leonard's transition to Roy Rogers, and the rest of their lives. Hubert said, "You'd never know him to be a star. He was as common as anyone."

If there was a force that drew them to one another it was "the heaven sent gift of music." They played music together in childhood and throughout their lives. When Roy came home he always wanted to have "a doin's" up at the barn—to sing, play, and dance. When Leonard tried out for the role of a singing cowboy at Republic Pictures, his ability to sing, play guitar, yodel, and call square dances went a long way.

During our last visit, Hubert had his guitar close-by. On request he couldn't resist picking it up to play and sing a Johnny Cash number.

Bill Sanders and Roy Rogers at the home of Cleda Willoughby.
Photo courtesy of Bill Sanders.

Joe hadn't seen the old fellow, Charlie, who lived down the road a piece, and was surprised to meet him one day. "How are you, Charlie? Haven't seen you for a spell."

"I been busy."

"What have you been doing, Charlie?"

"Well, I shingled the house, cut the weeds, dug the potatoes, and…oh, yeah…I got married."

"Well, what's your new wife like? Is she nice?"

"Yes, she's nice."

"Will she work?"

"She's a good worker."

"Can she sing?"

"Like a songbird."

"How old are you, Charlie?"

"I'm eighty-two."

"And how old is she?"

"Twenty."

"You're eighty-two and she's twenty? That could be fatal, Charlie!"

"If she dies, she dies."

Chapter Five
BILL SANDERS

Bill Sanders works as a plumber. He, too, is a performer and has often appeared at Portsmouth's Little Theater where they know him as Portsmouth's Passionate Plumber.

In the early 1930s, Bill lived with his family on Eleventh Street across from where OSCO (Ohio Stove Company) stands today. Two blocks east sat Four Pound Brown's house of prostitution. Three doors west was Kate's Brothel. Kate sat in her window in order to see approaching customers. Bill and the boys would tap on her window and run.

Bill's family was poor but happy. In some ways, they were better off than many. One of those was the fact that they had a water closet toilet. Families who had no city water hook up had no choice but to dig a hole and build a toilet over it; an outdoor toilet. Those with city water could have a "water closet." The seat was made of cold cast iron and behind it, elevated a bit, was a water tank. When the patron sat down the tank filled with water and since there was no vent, when you got up the water pressure flushed into the sewer.

Their neighborhood consisted of a healthy mix of black and white families. It hurt Bill when his black friends suffered discrimination.

The Lyric was the only theater in town to allow black customers and they had to climb an outdoor staircase between Fowler's Camera Shop and the theater up to the balcony. At Kresge's soda fountain, African Americans were not allowed to sit or be served food, but they could stand and have a drink from a glass with a purple ring around the top. They could not swim in the city pool, drink at the Kinney spring, be written about in the newspaper, or have upright cemetery monuments.

Bill was ten years of age and still on Eleventh Street when the Ohio River flooded Portsmouth in 1937. The water came into their house and they moved upstairs, but the flood kept rising so soon the Sanders family boarded a rescue boat. As they headed east, Bill could reach up and touch the traffic light at the intersection of Eleventh and Chillicothe Streets. Lincoln School was packed with flood refugees so they stayed in Roosevelt School a few days. After that Bill went to his grandfather George Bragg in Franklin Furnace.

At age twelve, Bill and his parents, brother, and sister returned to Portsmouth, making 1129 Mill Street their home. There was no levy there, so they could see the Ohio River. It was a poor section of town and an incinerator that burned city trash was next to their house. Air was foul and rats as big as opossums were everywhere. The incinerator stands today on Shawnee State University property.

The Sanders' neighbors included Bob Craft, Bob Bell, Melissa Green, bootlegger Ruby Bell, and her father Gump Bell. Kids amused themselves playing ball and marbles, shooting rats with slingshots, fishing, and going to the show. Cowboy movies that were accompanied by comedies, news, and serials cost a dime. They were shown at Portsmouth's theaters: the Lyric on Gallia

Street, the Eastland on Eleventh, the Westland on Second, and the Garden, built in 1925 at 718 Chillicothe Street.

The Garden was the easiest to slip into. One boy would buy a ticket, then let the others in through an alley door. Roy Rogers performed on that stage in 1939. It closed in the late '50s.

The Empress at Seventh and Chillicothe Streets showed Westerns for just a nickel. The toilets were not clean, however, and it was known as "The Potsie."

The LaRoy Theater at Gallia and Gay Streets was built in 1923 and named after the owners, Simon Labold and Dan Conroy. It did not show Westerns.

ST 19, 1959   THE PORTSMOUTH TI?

ROGERS' FIRST HOME in Portsmouth was on a houseboat shown after it was converted into a permanent home on Mill St. east of Waller. Bill Slye (on porch), Roy's uncle, along with Roy's father, Andrew Slye, built the boat in Cincinnati and had it towed here in 1914. Uncle Bill still occupies the residence.

The Slye houseboat was remodeled and moved to Mill Street and Waller. Roy's uncle Bill Slye sits on the porch. Bill Sanders lived close-by. *Photo courtesy of Ruth Adkins.*

Bill Sanders points to the general direction where the Slye family houseboat sat along the Ohio River in Portsmouth, Ohio. *Photo courtesy of Bill Sanders.*

The houseboat that Cleda's and Roy's family lived in had been moved between 1915 and 1920 and secured in place right across Waller Street in sight of Bill Sanders' home. Cleda's uncle Bill Slye lived there for years. Though he was blind, he made his way about the neighborhood. His favorite stop was Doc Price's pool hall at the corner of Front and Sinton Streets where you could get a beer and a sandwich. Uncle Bill loafed around there every evening, chewed tobacco, drank beer, and talked to everyone. Bill Slye's nephew Leonard was, by then, in Hollywood and known as Roy Rogers. Bill liked to brag of his progress.

As Roy's career grew, so did his enterprise. Cleda worked for her brother, mostly at the Victorville Museum for fifty years. In 1981 she did what so many Appalachians have done; she returned to the hills of southern Ohio. Cleda bought a home from Bill Odle on Williams Street and began making friends and attending musical events. Bill Sanders' wife, Betty, became her closest friend, so Bill got to know her and drove Cleda and Betty to Florida to visit Cleda's daughter, Gloria.

After Cleda moved, Roy was more inclined to come home to see her and his Duck Run friends. Roy and Bill were musical and they sang together at Cleda's house. Roy was comfortable to be with: "If he was at your house you would have no idea he was a movie star. He never pushed it."

Roy had known Bill's dad, also named Bill Sanders, and recalled that he "rolled his own" with Bugler tobacco. He played rhythm guitar at community square dances with fiddlers Acey Neal and Jim Arthur. Leonard Slye had been the caller at those dances. Bill's friendship with Roy led him to perform at the annual Roy Rogers Festival held in Portsmouth where he mixed with Western stars. He noticed that Iron Eyes Cody always had

Western movie personality Iron Eyes Cody sits with Bill Sanders at the Roy Rogers Festival, circa 1990s. *Photo courtesy of Bill Sanders.*

The great Western star Lash LaRue and Bill Sanders at Roy Rogers Festival. Ramada Inn, Portsmouth, Ohio early 1990s. *Photo courtesy of Bill Sanders.*

a pretty girl at his side and Lash LaRue was a hit with everyone.

In 1992, Bill and Betty went to Apple Valley, California for three months to make repairs to the house Cleda kept there. Roy was semi-retired and lived close by, so he rode his one speed Schwinn bicycle over and served as sidewalk superintendent. He dressed casually and didn't do much work but he would stand with his hands in his pockets and say, "Why are you doing that?" When he did not show up, he was often at a swap meet to "see if I could find something I don't have."

While Bill worked on Cleda's house, her son Andy Henry

Bill and Roy relax at the home of Roy's nephew Andy Henry in Apple Valley, California 1990. *Photo courtesy of Bill Sanders.*

told him about Roy's fear of flying. Roy loved to fish and hunt and had gone to Alaska bush country in a small plane. The pilot passed out and the plane lost its level. Roy shook the pilot and he recovered. But it really scared Roy. After that he always drove to jobs that were within driving distance.

Bill and Betty often visited the Rogers' home. It was fenced and the entrance had iron gates with RR on them. The climate was dry so they poured the lawn in concrete since Roy did not want a sprinkler system. There was a lobby with a pool table where you entered the house. Roy loved to shoot pool and was pretty good. He said he learned how to play back home in Ohio. The living room had a giant television and recliner chairs with vibrators and back warmers. Roy and Dale were passionate soap opera fans and talked about them as though they were real life.

Bill Sanders stands in front of the gates and concrete front yard of Roy's and Dale's home in California. *Photo courtesy of Bill Sanders.*

The Rogerses had no servants and they liked doing their own cooking. Roy was fond of his old familiar pots and pans. He cooked roasting ears in one that was bent, sometimes burning his hands. Dale would get after him.

Dale and Cleda had a cornbread competition. Made from scratch in the iron skillet, it had a tasty brown crust and was not too thick.

Each Sunday the Sanders family attended church with Roy and Dale. They sat about one fourth of the way back, Roy in a straight back chair and Dale to his left in the pew. Afterward they always went to the same restaurant for a country breakfast. They sat in the rear with church friends. To them, Roy was a regular guy—no celebrity— and they just shot the breeze. One morning a stranger came up and stuck one of those extended cameras in his face. Roy said, "I wish you wouldn't do that, it bothers me." The man persisted and Roy lost his temper. He jumped up and said, "Get that damn thing out of my face!" Dale quieted him down.

When the house repairs were done, Bill and Betty returned home but they remained in close contact with the Roy and Dale. They had Roy's phone number so he could be kept up to date on Cleda.

In 1996 when Cleda became ill, Roy and Dale flew to Cincinnati where Bill picked them up. On the way home Roy did not feel well so Bill and Dale talked. She loved Willie Nelson and they sang Willie songs together.

The floodwall mural of Roy Rogers done by muralist Robert Dafford in Portsmouth, Ohio. Dale Evans liked it very much. *Photo courtesy of John Roger Simon.*

Roy and Dale rested at Portsmouth's Ramada Inn. The next morning they went to Scioto Memorial Hospital for a good visit with Cleda where they shared fond memories.

At Roy's suggestion they had breakfast at the K&M Restaurant. Dale picked up the ticket. Then Bill drove them down Front Street where they had their first look at Portsmouth's floodwall murals so beautifully painted by Louisiana's Robert Dafford. Roy noticed that the Roy Rogers mural was close to another Duck Run boy, Branch Rickey. Dale commented that Roy's facial expression was perfect.

Though concerned about Cleda, Roy and Dale were especially pleased with their trip home.

Bill Sanders holds warm memories of those cherished experiences. He performs each year at the Roy Rogers Festival.

Mary Lou Crabtree owns the Slye homeplace. She stands in front of it. The tree was there when Leonard was. *Photo courtesy of Gary Hurn.*

The young mother was always patient in teaching little Martha correct behavior. One Sunday in church Martha looked up and tapped on her mother, indicating she wanted to say something. The mother bent over and whispered, "Why should we be quiet in church?"

Martha softly replied, "People are sleeping."

Chapter Six
MARY LOU CRABTREE

By virtue of being the daughter of Charlie and Ollie Hiles—
Charlie was Leonard Slye's best friend and next-door-neighbor
on Allen Hollow—of being granddaughter of Clell and Ethel
Hiles, of owning and living in Leonard Slye's homeplace with
her husband Ferrell Crabtree (the place where her son Gary lives
today), Mary Hiles Crabtree has seen Leonard Slye from many
angles.

Ollie Speakman, from Circleville, Ohio, and Charlie Hiles
were married and lived on Allen Hollow on land given to them
by Charlie's parents, Clell and Ethel. They were good friends
with Andy and Mattie Slye, Leonard's parents. The families have
been closely connected for a long time. Charlie and Ollie built
good relationships with their neighbors and birthed six children:
Tommy, Jerry, Benny, Josephine, Lula Belle, and Mary Lou.

Mary was born in Portsmouth in the old General Hospital. She
learned as a youngster that one of the hollow natives, Leonard
Slye, had made a name for himself outside Allen Hollow and
put their community on the map. When reference is made to
Leonard's origins, that place is usually called *Duck Run* rather
than *Allen Hollow*, or *Inskeep Road*, or *Leonard's homeplace on the*

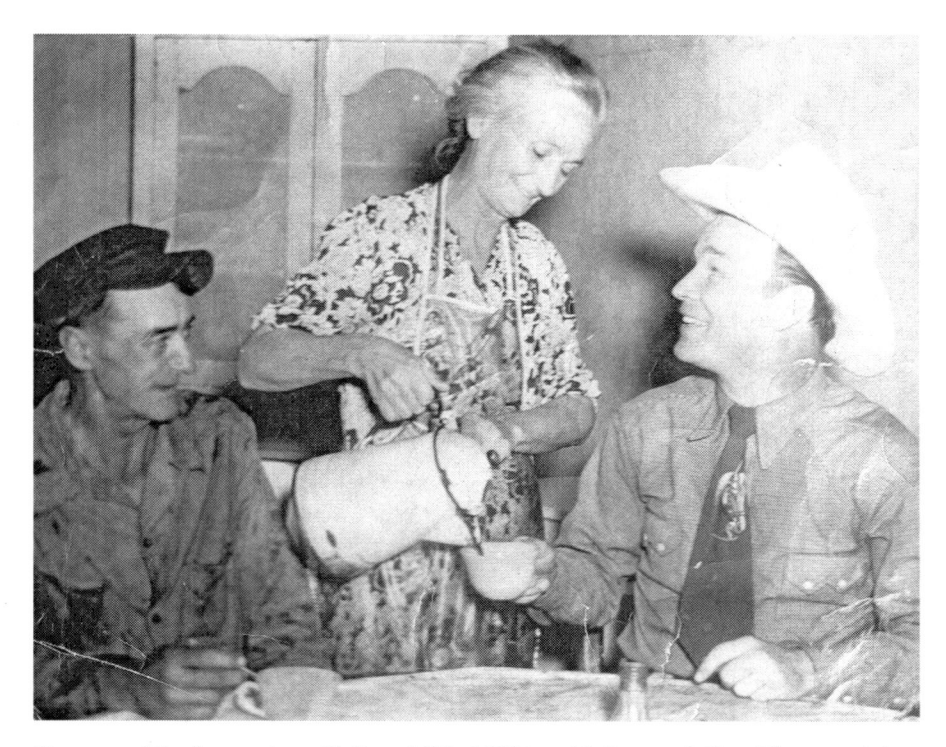

Owners of the homeplace Clell and Ethel Hiles with Leonard Slye. They are Mary Lou's grandparents and Leonard called Ethel his second mother. Note the beautiful coffee pot. *Photo courtesy of Mary Lou Crabtree.*

point. Allen Hollow is now named Sly (they took off the 'e') Road. The community consists of good, sound, country people and Mary has the benefit of having spent her life here.

Mary's dad, Charlie Hiles, and Leonard were best friends throughout their lives. Charlie called him *Len* and he called Charlie *Chuck*. Charlie and Leonard were the same age, were neighbors, were ornery, liked each other, and got in trouble together.

Grown men often enjoy telling of their childhood and Charlie often told of theirs. He also liked to recall their mischief because it's a more colorful story. He, Len, and neighborhood boys loved to explore the surrounding woods. They ran dogs, climbed trees, fought, played ball, hunted, and worked together. Many country boys become "borrowers" of chickens. That activity became a contest among the boys. Charlie and Leonard

Mary Lou Crabtree stands at the head of Allen Hollow now called Sly Road. The Slye original home was located to the left. *Photo courtesy of Gary Hurn.*

were good at it, too. They roasted the birds in a special place in the hollow. Sometimes they got real brave. They stole a chicken, cleaned it, and took it back to the owner and asked her to cook it.

Country homes at that time rarely had indoor bathrooms and even those that did usually had an outdoor toilet. The boys liked to turn them over, especially at Halloween.

Charlie's mom, Ethel Hiles, said Leonard was a crack shot. He could throw straight and handle a rifle or slingshot. He was bad to shoot birds with his slingshot and Ethel got after him for that.

Charlie and Leonard were in the same grade at Duck Run School. It was about a mile from their homes and the boys walked there together. The school was built of wood and served students from grades one through eight in one room. That building was replaced by another made of brick that had two rooms for grades one through six. It stands there today next to Duck Run Church.

Charlie said Guy Bumgarner was one of their teachers and they

Charlie Hiles and Leonard Slye sit in the floor of the homeplace for cake, coffe, and to visit. Back row Lillian Jordan, Mary Hiles Linegar, Pauline Lundy, and Ralph Jordan. Man standing in rear is unidentified. *Photo courtesy of Mary Lou Crabtree.*

learned easily from him. But that didn't stop them from taking mischief to school. Guy stood Len and Chuck in the corner and paddled them both if they needed it. One day Leonard locked the toilet door on Guy and he got a licking for that, too.

Mary's grandparents, Clell and Ethel Hiles bought the Slye homeplace and lived in it until they died. Leonard felt close to them because he had spent so much time in their home with their son, Charlie. That closeness continued throughout their lives and Leonard loved to come back and see them.

By the time Mary was a young girl, Leonard had gone away and become *Roy Rogers*. Once when he, Dale, and others were performing at the Ohio State Fair in Columbus, Roy decided to bring his troupe and visit home. Roy, Dale, Pat Brady, and the rest arrived at the homeplace. They went inside to visit Clell and Ethel and enjoy some good food—especially Ethel's beans and corn bread. She always had that in the house.

Neighbor kids were there and, after eating, Roy unloaded Trigger from the trailer. He put Mary up on Trigger's back and she rode that beautiful horse. Mary remembers sitting high in the saddle. Roy gave most of the kids a ride. Dale had Buttermilk along but did not unload her. Pat Brady had Nelly Belle on a flat bed but he didn't unload either. They had a short but special visit. (People noticed that if Dale was with Roy, they usually didn't stay long.)

Anytime Roy came home he wanted to see friends, but most of all he wanted to visit Ethel Hiles. He loved her and called her his second mom. It gave him a certain satisfaction, seeing her, being in his family home, eating her cooking, and just being comfortable. Ethel was always happy to see Roy and made him feel right at home.

Mary Lou grew up in rural Ohio and attended McDermott Elementary and High Schools. Inskeep Road runs up on one side of her homeplace and Allen Hollow, the other. Ferrell Crabtree, one of twelve children, lived on the Inskeep side, Mary on Allen Hollow. But, as Mary says, "Ferrell found me."

Ferrell was the son of Lowell Crabtree, a musical man and

Charlie Hiles and Leonard Slye were best friends for life. In front of Charlie's home on Allen Hollow 1980. *Photo courtesy of Mary Lou Crabtree.*

friend of Leonard Slye. Ferrell was musical, too. He liked to play guitar and sing George Jones' songs. He knew almost all of them and could get his voice to sound like that of George, especially on "White Lightning." Ferrell took to Mary and they were wed. He was employed in the McDermott stone industry.

Mary's grandpa, Clell, died but Ethel continued living on the homeplace until her own death. She left the property to Mary's uncle, Strauther Hiles, who lived in Cleveland. Mary and Ferrell needed a home so Strauther sold it to them. About 1975, they moved in. Strauther was pleased to keep the place in the family and for it to be owned by someone friendly with the Slyes. Mary and Ferrell lived there about twenty-five years.

When Roy visited he felt most at home when he spent time in his childhood home. Locals observed that Roy took a real liking to both Ferrell and Mary, and was comfortable in their presence. He liked to stay there, to walk over and visit with those with whom he grew up. Mary Lou saw a lot of Roy Rogers. Roy liked Ferrell. He said, "Ferrell, you're like your dad, Lowell."

Roy tried to be inconspicuous when not performing. He sometimes flew to Columbus, rented a plain looking car and

Roy came in quietly to visit Charlie Hiles. Mary Lou found them sitting on the ground eating sardines and crackers. Here Lula Belle Hiles Crabtree sits behind Roy at Charlie's. *Photo courtesy of Mary Lou Crabtree.*

drove it to Inskeep. One day Mary looked out and saw him drive by. She figured he was headed for Charlie's so she walked up to his house. There sat Roy and her dad in the yard eating sardines from a can along with saltine crackers. "Roy liked poor people's food." Roy always wanted to see Ethel and Charlie and Mary was usually involved in that. He wanted privacy and sought it at the homeplace. Most of the locals honored his wishes.

Cleda moved home from California to a place she bought in Portsmouth. Roy loved Cleda and stayed with her sometimes. One day, Cleda called and asked if Mary and Ferrell would walk up Allen Hollow with Roy and her. On that walk, Cleda and Roy recalled many memories of their move from the houseboat to that Allen Hollow house. They spoke of living in the last house in the hollow for about two years while they worked together to build the homeplace on the point. They spoke fondly of their parents and two sisters. When they reached their destination, they explored the home site. The building was gone but remnants remained. Roy said, "There're a lot of memories in this old hollow. Our cabin was right up there on the bank." They told about Manley Crabtree who lived on the opposite bank a little down from their house. He lived alone and called himself By. By hunted ginseng and slept with a pet black snake. He said, "That's By's pet." Mary Lou knows that day was really a really special one. When Roy and Cleda left, they drove around to see old friends.

Roy liked musical gatherings. When one was arranged during his local visits, they tried to keep it quiet, inviting only people Roy knew. Local musicians gathered in a barn that stood behind the homeplace. The floor was well-suited to dancing. Those involved were usually friends of Roy's or Charlie Hiles. Lowell Crabtree and Roy shared the square dance calling. Both were good at it. Others played and sang. Everyone visited and some had a nip. Mary went to those events and usually saw Ferrell's uncle, Hubert Crabtree, there. The barn sometimes filled with people while others stood out in the yard.

Roy phoned once but said he didn't have much time. He wasn't sure where everyone who he wanted to visit lived so he asked Ferrell to drive. They went in Ferrell's car from home to home. Ferrell accompanied him on each visit.

(L to R) Mary Hiles Linegar, Lillian Bond Jordan, Leonard Slye and Pauline Lundy at the homeplace. *Photo courtesy of Georgia Furr.*

They included Lowell Crabtree, Pauline Lundy, and Pat Jordan. The experience allowed Ferrell and Roy good time to talk.

Another day Roy called; he could come out only for a short while that time as well, but he wanted everyone to gather at Mary's place. Some drove over and Ferrell picked up the rest. They sat in a big circle on the floor, ate cake, drank coffee, and talked. What a special sight! The group included Pat Jordan, Roy Rogers, Mary Hiles, Pauline Lundy, Charlie Hiles, Eugene Crabtree, and Lillian Jordan. They didn't tell anyone else and had a good time. On such days Mary Lou fixed a lot of cake and coffee and got to hear some great talks. That day was typical of many she experienced with Roy.

Other times when word got out that Roy was home, lots of people showed up. In fact, the sheriff had to be called. One deputy each stood at the front and back doors to keep people out. Mary and Ferrell's son, Gary, was outside playing at one of those events

(L to R) Roy Rogers, Ferrell Crabtree, and Elmer Sword with area children at the homeplace in 1982. *Photo courtesy of Mary Lou Crabtree.*

and when he tried to go in, the sheriff wouldn't let him. Gary was able to get Mary's attention through the window. She spoke to the sheriff and Gary was allowed into his own home.

The Portsmouth Recognition Society held a small event there while Roy was inside having his visit. He looked out the window and saw one of the Society members, Elmer Sword, holding out his arms trying to keep children away from the house. Roy went out and said, "Don't do that. They are my family and friends."

After Cleda returned to Ohio, she got urges to return to California to visit Andy, her son, as well as her brother. She also wanted Mary and Ferrell to see Apple Valley. She asked them more than once to drive her car, all expenses paid. Ferrell disliked long drives and dealing with highways and cities. "We have our own Apple Valley here," was his response.

Mary's dad, Charlie, took a notion to try California. His best friend had found it suitable, so he made the journey. He stayed with Cleda's son and even worked there awhile. Roy was gone a lot and Charlie was unhappy. He soon returned to his beloved hills.

In 1983, Charlie fell ill and was hospitalized in Portsmouth.

Cleda phoned Roy and he called the hospital. Mary Lou was standing beside her dad's bed when the telephone rang. When she answered, Roy said, "Is this Mary Lou? How's Chuck?" Charlie had been despondent but

(L to R) Mary Lou Crabtree, Dale Evans, and Ferrell Crabtree stand in front of the ol' homeplace in 1984. *Photo courtesy of Mary Lou Crabtree.*

revived and talked with his friend, Len. Two days later he died.

Ferrell left the stone company and went to Mitchellace Shoe String Factory in Portsmouth where Mary had a supervisor position. When Ferrell's health failed, the couple moved into a modular home just in back of the homeplace. Ferrell died in 2003. He was a fine man and they had good years together. They raised two children, Gary and Tonya Crabtree. Gary now lives in the homeplace.

Because of life's circumstances, Mary Lou Hiles Crabtree feels a closeness to Roy Rogers. They shared the home where he was most happy in many ways. She says, "Roy was a country man, a kind man. I never heard him raise his voice. He never changed in the way he treated all of us."

Today Mary Lou owns the homeplace and lives in her house behind it. She is involved in her church, has cared for her mother, attends to the rest of her family, and has some mighty special memories.

Roy Rogers and Dale Evans are escorted by Don and Margaret Gordley in their Chrysler convertible in the Portsmouth, Ohio Roy Rogers Festival. *Photo courtesy of Margaret Gordley.*

The older I get, the better I used to be!

Chapter Seven
MARGARET GORDLEY

Margaret Gordley from Wellston, Ohio, is a graduate of Portsmouth East High School in Sciotoville, Ohio. After she worked several years in the Treasurer's Office in the Portsmouth, Ohio, Court House, Margaret was elected Scioto County Treasurer in 1984. She held the position until 2005 giving her fifty-four years in that office.

Margaret Walter married Don Gordley and they enjoyed working together on community efforts. They were Roy Rogers' fans and it felt natural to get involved when his hometown decided to honor him. In the early 1980s Elmer Sword, John Irwin, Jim Wilson, and others organized the Roy Rogers Festival. Don and Margaret soon became involved. Their purpose was to honor the accomplishment and perpetuate the legacy of the King of the Cowboys. The committee set up a scholarship through the Scioto County Area Foundation, to be awarded to a student of Shawnee State University.

The festival grew and area enthusiasts began donating Roy Rogers memorabilia. At about that time Don Gordley became Scioto County Registrar of Motor Vehicles. His office was on Fifth

Street near Washington in Portsmouth. He decided to designate space in his new workplace for the donated items and call it The Roy Rogers Museum. The museum was officially opened during the festival of 1984. Western movie star, Lash LaRue, used his bullwhip to cut the ribbon made of a roll of tickets. The museum grew and remained in Don's office for several years until his office closed. LaRue Horsley, the Portsmouth Post Master, then made a place for the display in the post office basement. A new museum opened in 2012 on Second Street in Portsmouth and the items have been moved there.

When the festival was established, a parade was held each year on Saturday morning in the streets of downtown Portsmouth. The parade marshal was Roy Rogers when he was home and he rode on the back of a Chrysler convertible owned by the Gordleys. Don drove and Margaret rode up front.

Roy spent his childhood in Duck Run and, fortunately, the homeplace is still standing. Shortly after the festivals began, the committee elected to install an historical marker at the homeplace. The unveiling of the marker, which stands at the convergence of Inskeep and Sly Roads, took place during one of the early festivals. Committee members, Georgia Furr, Nancy McDowell, and Margaret took a busload of participants there. Tables were set up and they enjoyed cookies and punch. Unfortunately, Roy was unable to attend.

Each year on Festival weekend a banquet is held on Saturday night. One year in the mid 1980s Don Gordly was committee president for the first time and served as Master of Ceremonies for the banquet. Don and Margaret sat at the head table with Georgia Furr, Lash LaRue, Nancy Horsley, Dale Evans, and Roy

Bullwhip ace and cowboy star Lash LaRue uses his whip to cut the ribbon of theater tickets held by Harold Lyons and Don Gordley in front of Don's license bureau at 714 Fifth Street. The bureau housed a hometown Roy Rogers exhibit. September 1984. *Photo courtesy of Margaret Gordley.*

Rogers. It proved a great opportunity for visiting and Roy and Dale took it in stride.

On another occasion in the late 1980s the Rogers were home and staying with Cleda. Dale asked if she could be driven around. Margaret picked up Dale and Cleda and they covered the town pretty thoroughly. Dale showed excited animation and when they descended the Sunrise Avenue area. She was taken by the beautiful trees.

Once in the mid 1980s, Don called Margaret from his office

and asked, "Want to go to lunch?" Margaret walked up the street to the registrar's office and when she stepped inside, there sat Roy Rogers. He had flown to Columbus, rented a car, and driven down by himself. He came to Don's office to visit, see the exhibit, and to sit-and-talk. Margaret feels Roy had a distinct air that was so comfortable, talking to him was like talking to a neighbor.

After they had a good visit, they went for lunch. Just up the street was the popular Town House Restaurant. Roy's lifelong friend, Homer Albrecht, owned it. They had attended Union Street School together as boys. Don called the Town House and spoke with Frank Johnson, the cash register man. Don explained the situation and asked Frank to reserve a table and to keep it quiet. Roy was dressed in street clothes—no hat or boots and he wore sunglasses. They walked over to the restaurant and were seated in the back booth. Their waitress was Patty Johnson who now works at Patsy's Inn in Portsmouth. Patty was a longtime friend of Margaret's and a Roy Rogers fan, who had worked there for years. She took Don's and Margaret's orders, unaware of the other guest's identity until Roy spoke. His voice caused her to gasp. Her mouth dropped open and she looked at Margaret. Margaret gave her the quiet sign. Patty was so taken, she was speechless and trembled as she wrote the order. The trio ate and left.

The next time Patty and Margaret met, Patty exclaimed, "I waited on Roy Rogers!"

Starting Roy Rogers...

Under Western Stars (Republic, 1938)
Billy the Kid Returns (Republic, 1938)
Come On, Rangers (Republic, 1938)
Shine On, Harvest Moon (Republic, 1938)
The Arizona Kid (Republic, 1939)
Rough Riders' Roundup (Republic, 1939)
Frontier Pony Express (Republic, 1939)
Southward Ho (Republic, 1939)
In Old Caliente (Republic, 1939)
Wall Street Cowboy (Republic, 1939)
Jeepers Creepers (Republic, 1939)
Saga of Death Valley (Republic, 1939)
Days of Jesse James (Republic, 1939)
Young Buffalo Bill (Republic, 1940)
The Dark Command (Republic, 1940)
The Carson City Kid (Republic, 1940)
The Ranger and the Lady (Republic, 1940)
Colorado (Republic, 1940)
Young Bill Hickok (Republic, 1940)
The Border Legion AKA *West of the Badlands* (Republic, 1940)
Robin Hood of the Pecos (Republic, 1941)
Arkansas Judge (Republic, 1941)
In Old Cheyenne (Republic, 1941)
Sheriff of Tombstone (Republic, 1941)
Nevada City (Republic, 1941)
Bad Man of Deadwood (Republic, 1941)
Jesse James at Bay (Republic, 1941)
Red River Valley (Republic, 1941)
Man from Cheyenne (Republic, 1942)
South of Santa Fe (Republic, 1942)
Sunset on the Desert (Republic, 1942)
Romance on the Range (Republic, 1942)
Sons of the Pioneers (Republic, 1942)
Sunset Serenade (Republic, 1942)
Heart of the Golden West (Republic, 1942)
Ridin' Down the Canyon (Republic, 1942)
Idaho (Republic, 1943)
King of the Cowboys (Republic, 1943)
Song of Texas (Republic, 1943)
Silver Spurs (Republic, 1943)
Man from Music Mountain AKA *Texas Legionnaires* (Republic, 1943)
Hands Across the Border (Republic, 1943)
The Cowboy and the Senorita (Republic, 1944)
The Yellow Rose of Texas (Republic, 1944)
Song of Nevada (Republic, 1944)
San Fernando Valley (Republic, 1944)

Lights of Old Santa Fe (Republic, 1944)
Brazil (Republic, 1944)
Lake Placid Serenade (Republic, 1944)
Hollywood Canteen (Warner Brothers, 1944)
Utah (Republic, 1945)
Bells of Rosarita (Republic, 1945)
The Man from Oklahoma (Republic, 1945)
Sunset in El Dorado (Republic, 1945)
Don't Fence Me In (Republic, 1945)
Along the Navajo Trail (Republic, 1945)
Song of Arizona (Republic, 1946)
Rainbow Over Texas (Republic, 1946)
My Pal Trigger (Republic, 1946)
Under Nevada Skies (Republic, 1946)
Roll On Texas Moon (Republic, 1946)
Home in Oklahoma (Republic, 1946)
Out California Way (Republic, 1946)
Heldorado (Republic, 1946)
Apache Rose (Republic, 1947)
Hit Parade of 1947 (Republic, 1947)
Bells of San Angelo (Republic, 1947)
Springtime in the Sierras (Republic, 1947)
On the Old Spanish Trail (Republic, 1947)
The Gay Ranchero (Republic, 1948)
Under California Stars (Republic, 1948)
Eyes of Texas (Republic, 1948)
Melody Time (RKO Radio Pictures, 1948)
Night Time in Nevada (Republic, 1948)
Grand Canyon Trail (Republic, 1948)
The Far Frontier (Republic, 1948)
Susanna Pass (Republic, 1949)
Down Dakota Way (Republic, 1949)
The Golden Stallion (Republic, 1949)
Bells of Coronado (Republic, 1950)
Twilight in the Sierras (Republic, 1950)
Trigger, Jr. (Republic, 1950)
Sunset in the West (Republic, 1950)
North of the Great Divide (Republic, 1950)
Trail of Robin Hood (Republic, 1950)
Spoilers of the Plains (Republic, 1951)
Heart of the Rockies (Republic, 1951)
In Old Amarillo (Republic, 1951)
South of Caliente (Republic, 1951)
Pals of the Golden West (Republic, 1951)
Son of Paleface (Paramount, 1952)
Alias Jesse James (United Artists, 1959)
MacKintosh and T.J. (Penland Productions, 1975)

Roy Rogers look-alike Roy Dillow and his six-year-old granddaughter, Olyvia Young. Tazwell, Virginia, 2008. *Photo courtesy of Roy Dillow.*

Hey, Bill, did you hear about those three men floating down the creek on a big flat rock? The first man was blind, the second didn't have any arms, and the third one was naked. The blind man looked down on the bottom of the creek and saw a quarter. The one without any arms reached down and picked it up, and the man with no clothes on stuck it in his pocket. —BMW

Chapter Eight
ROY DILLOW

I became aware of Roy Dillow's connection to Roy Rogers when I gave a fiddle lesson to Tom Koch at Boneyfiddle Arts Center at Second and Court Streets in Portsmouth, Ohio. A little girl and a woman came in while I was there and the girl was immediately drawn to the fiddle. A conversation developed. It turned out that ten-year-old Olyvia Dillow and her grandma, Priscilla Dillow, from Tazwell, Virginia, were in town for the annual Roy Rogers Festival. They had been down the street visiting the newly opened Roy Rogers museum. Priscilla noted that Olyvia wanted to learn the fiddle and because of the magical magnet of music, we met.

The next evening while attending the Roy Rogers banquet, I saw Olyvia and Priscilla. They introduced me to Olyvia's grandpa, Roy Dillow.

Roy Dillow was born near Tazwell, Virginia, August 18, 1941, in Dry Town near the railroad track in a one-room frame shack. His family had no electricity or telephone and used an outdoor toilet. Water was carried from a community water barrel.

At an early age Roy Dillow noticed his mother spoke often of Roy Rogers. Little Roy had never been to a movie but he heard about them and he pestered his dad to take him. His father, Roy

Sr., had found work driving a dry cleaning truck when he had returned home from World War II. He picked up and dropped off clothing for the rich people of their community. They went to the Clinch Theater in Tazwell and the first movie Roy Jr. ever saw was *Grand Canyon Trail* starring Roy Rogers. The heroine, Jane Frazee, mistook Roy Rogers for the bad guy, but after a great struggle he prevailed and she realized her mistake. Roy Dillow was in such awe of Roy Rogers and Trigger, to this day that movie remains his favorite show of all time and Roy Rogers his favorite cowboy.

There were two theaters in town, the Clinch and the Valley, and Westerns played in both on Friday and Saturday with more upscale films during the week. Roy Jr. went on weekends.

Roy Dillow's mother was quiet and did not go out much. However, she honed her son's interest in Roy Rogers shows though she never attended one with him.

In 1949, his mom had a farm accident when she stepped on a hoe and the handle came up and hit her in the head. It caused her to have headaches ever after that. A film the family did attend together was Lassie Come Home. While there, his mother had a stroke. Roy Sr. carried her out and home, but the headaches became more severe. In 1959 she died during brain surgery.

As Roy developed, Western movies grew more important in his life and he attended all sorts of them. Hoppy and Lash, Bob Steele, Red Ryder, and Johnny Mack Brown were fine but no one measured up to Roy Rogers.

Roy's passion for cowboy movies never faded. In 1972 he fulfilled his lifelong desire. He saw Roy Rogers in person at the West Virginia State Fair where Roy did six shows that weekend with Dusty and the Sons of the Pioneers. Roy Jr. spent eight hours in line to get front row seats. A fence separated Roy Rogers from the crowd but after the show as he walked by, Roy Dillow asked him for his autograph. Rogers told the guard to let him in and they went to his silver bullet trailer which was his dressing room. Roy took off his gun belt, looped it together and pitched it toward a hook on the wall about ten feet away—a perfect throw. The two Roys had a good visit.

In 1994, Roy Dillow went to Victorville, California. Roy Rogers was there and they spent more time together, talking like two old friends.

Through these many experiences Roy met Cleda and they developed a good friendship. Visits with one another followed and they often communicated by mail. Cleda sent him notes and cards and he kept them.

The time came when B Westerns were less popular. Roy made the transition to television with *The Roy Rogers Show*. Roy also appeared in TV specials and made guest appearances on programs hosted by the Osmonds, Johnny Cash, Dean Martin, Andy Williams, Perry Como, Merv Griffin, and Johnny Carson.

Portsmouth, Ohio, lies in a flood plain and had to build a strong floodwall for protection against the Ohio River. On the inside of the wall, a mural project has unfolded under the design of Lafayette, Louisiana, muralist, Robert Dafford. One of those murals shows Roy Rogers and Trigger, nicely done. On the outside of the wall is the Wall of Stars highlighting locals who have done well. In 1996, Roy Rogers was home for the Roy Rogers Festival and signed his star. Roy Dillow was there and watched the signing. When he spoke to Roy Rogers, the entertainer responded by calling his name, *Roy Dillow.*

The festival had a look-alike contest that weekend and Roy Dillow dressed as Roy Rogers. When Roy Rogers saw Roy Dillow he said, "Roy, you've been in my wardrobe."

Once, when Roy Dillow was at home working on his gun, he accidentally shot himself. He sent word that he could not come to Portsmouth that year. Roy Rogers sent him a note that read, "next time unload the gun."

The year 1997 was Roy and Dale's fiftieth wedding anniversary. They celebrated at Victorville. Roy Dillow went to wish them happy anniversary in person. Roy Rogers wasn't feeling well so he traveled about on his scooter. It was the last time he saw Roy Rogers.

The day in 1998 when Roy Rogers died was a sad one for many. Roy Dillow learned of Roy's death while driving. He pulled off the road and remained quiet.

Some who honored Roy Rogers did so by collecting. Several

Roy Dillow's "Roy Room" in Tazwell, Virginia. *Photo courtesy of Roy Dillow.*

The framed picture shows Roy Rogers and Roy Dillow among Roy's vast collection. Tazwell, Virginia. *Photo courtesy of Roy Dillow.*

years ago Portsmouth native Elmer Sword started the Roy Rogers and Dale Evans Collectors Association. Roy Dillow has collected most of his life and became the tenth member. He owns a wide variety of Roy Rogers memorabilia: comic books, lobby cards from the windows of movie houses, cap guns, chuck wagons, statues, cameras, watches, paper dolls, storybooks, lunch buckets, boots, moccasins, blue jeans, and more. He has over ten thousand photographs—some originals. Roy Rogers was second only to Walt Disney in merchandising.

Roy Dillow built a one thousand square foot room at his home in which to display his collection. It is full. He calls it *Roy's Roy Room.*

Roy Dillow reflects, "Though Roy Rogers was a hero, a star, he was a simplistic man. He loved his upbringing. He wore clothes until they were worn through with holes in his boot soles. He laughed, cried, experienced his five senses, an inspiration to many. And now my granddaughter, Olyvia, is interested."

Roy and Priscilla have been wed forty-nine years. He worked for General Instruments and for a bearing and transmission house close to home. They live in Tazwell only four miles from his origin.

Catherine, age 83, in her Florida home. *Photo courtesy Vincent Tovine, Jr.*

There was a general store way out in the country with a couple of benches on the porch for the loafers. The area neighbors heard the Church was trying to pick a new Pope. Most of them didn't know much about that but they were giving it a good talk anyhow. After a lot of discussion one of the old boys said, "Well, it seems to me like them Catholics has had it long enough. They ought to give someone else a chance."

Chapter Nine
CATHERINE MERSHON TOVINE

Charles Shaw Mershon was born on Wright's Run and was one of ten children. He loved his childhood home, especially a favorite apple tree he played in. When Charlie reached manhood, he took a girl named Myrtle as his wife. He bought land and a house on Zuefle Drive across the road from the Eugene and Ada Cattee and Ed and Bertha Graf families. It sets across from Route 73, a field, and Pond Creek. The home is still standing, has been remodeled, and is currently owned by the Bending family.

Zuefle Drive was not yet developed when Charlie bought his farm. He raised field corn on much of that area. He also raised corn in the Scioto River bottoms. It was a long way from home so he built a shack for his help and himself.

The workers shucked the standing corn by hand. They threw it into a jolt wagon pulled along at a slow pace by a team of mules. Six men, each shucking one row, walked on the right hand side of the wagon. On their left hand they wore a hand leather to protect their skin and on their right hand was either a shucking hook or peg to husk the corn. A bump board rested on the opposite side of the wagon a little higher than the low side. They bounced the ears off the bump board into the wagon.

In due time, a son was born to the Mershons and he, too, was called Charles. Charlie Sr. had the good sense to develop his musical talent and was known for his fiddling. He played at most of the dances held in the community and was soon teaching his son to play the banjo.

Charlie was fond of his neighbor, Ed Graf Sr. and often went over to his place to loaf. They'd trade ideas under the shade tree. Charlie was nicknamed Shopes and offered clever comment in conversation. When Charlie's wife died prematurely, Ed expressed his sorrow. Shopes replied, "She was the best piece of furniture in the house." Sometime later the Japanese invaded Pearl Harbor. Ed asked Charlie if he knew that the Japanese bombed Pearl Harbor and Shopes responded, "What did they want to hurt her for?"

There was a fine hole of water near the Mershon home. When neighbors went there to swim they'd often find Charlie stark naked, all lathered up having a bath. He would sometimes laugh and say that after his first bath each spring there was a ring around the creek bank.

After the death of his first wife, Charlie met Grace Beaver from Minford, Ohio. They soon married. At fifty-three he fathered his second child, Catherine, born at home on June 7, 1928. She loved Pond Creek and became playmates with Cecelia, Mary, and Paul Catlee; Ed and Clarence Graf; and her brother Charles. When the creek was down, the kids walked back and forth through the large creek culvert and when the water was up, they used the sturdy old swinging bridge to cross it. They played tag, hide and seek, the fox and the goose, anti-over, and spin the bottle. They sneaked into the corn cribs and learned to smoke, rolling corn silk in brown poke paper.

In winter they skated, made snowmen, rode homemade sleds, and had snowball battles. At Christmas they cut their own tree and made decorations for it. Most people have ice cream in the summer but country children knew winter to be ice cream time. If they wanted it quickly they mixed snow, cream, and vanilla, and had snow ice cream. Some families had a hand freezer with a gallon container in which they mixed the ingredients. They cut ice from the creek, put it in a burlap sack, and crushed it by beating a wooden mallet against the sack. They packed the crushed ice and coarse salt around the freezer container and took turns cranking until the contents turned to ice cream.

In summertime neighboring children played together. Lightning bugs were captured at night; glass jars with air holes cut in the lids became their new home. It was fun to hear tales told by the older folks. Fires were built for roasting marshmallows. They had little picnics and then the kids went to the creek to fish or swim. For fish bait, crawdad tails and worms were used.

A sad accident took place within their group. Paul Catlee was helping fix a wheel on a wagon and a wire was run through to line it up. The wire punctured his eye. After that he wore a glass eye. But Paul had spunk and after some time he devised a way to even have fun with his eye. When he, Cecelia, Mary, Ed, Clarence, Charlie, and Catherine swam he'd take out his glass eye, throw it in the swimming hole, and they all dived for it.

Catherine liked doing jobs at home to help her family. Bed bugs were a nuisance in several homes so a means was devised to control them. At the Mershons' house, a quart jar lid was placed under each bed post and coal oil poured in so the bugs would not cross. Each Sunday, it was Catherine's job to refill the lids.

Charlie Sr. traveled in a mule drawn wagon and Catherine loved to go with him. They often went up Pond Creek a couple of miles to a mill operated by the Simon family.

The Simons came here from France in the 1860s and started the mill soon after. They built a stone wall and large wooden water wheel to harness Pond Creek water. It powered the wheelbarrow factory and sawmill that had an up-and-down saw to cut the logs.

Sister Emerita Simon was a little girl when her dad, August Simon, had his eye put out by a flying piece of wood in the wheelbarrow factory. Each evening at 6:00 p.m., they rang the dinner bell at their home. Then she ran down to the mill to meet her dad and walk home with him. Dust swished between her toes from the dry dirt road.

The Simons owned a mule drawn jolt wagon with a special rack designed to haul thirty-six wheelbarrows. They were made from oak in three different sizes. Except for the wheel, they were completely wooden. The price was four dollars each. It was possible to lean a large one against a tree and take a nap in it. The wheelbarrows were sold in Ohio, Kentucky, and West Virginia. Before the Ohio River had dams, it sometimes froze solid in the winter. Ed Simon recalled crossing that frozen river with a load of wheelbarrows several times. On the east side of the wheelbarrow factory was the sawmill and there was a large sawdust pile along the creek. Logs were sawed into lumber and the off bearer stacked it on both sides of the road.

I worked that job awhile and own one of those wheelbarrows to this day.

Paul Simon's daughter, Mary Simon Dettwiller, remembers that across the road from the wheelbarrow factory sat the flour mill which was powered by a gasoline engine. There was also a gravity fed gasoline pump that pumped gas to the top where it ran down a hose into a gas tank. A corn crib was near the mill and a large scale to weigh the farmers' grain when they sold it to the mill. Inside, long belts reached between the three floors and ran the mill. It was noisy and the whole building shook. Mary's dad, Paul, worked there sometimes and he showed her the large black snake that was allowed to live upstairs because it helped control the mice. Mary's grandpa, Julius, who worked in the mills, grew very tired each day and took an hour-long nap at noon.

A small store near the mill sold items country people couldn't produce themselves such as salt, nails, sugar, coffee, candy, canned goods, and feed for animals. No one attended to the store regularly; they just put it on the books. Mary's mom, Robena, would send her to buy vinegar but Mary couldn't say it; she'd say binganeer.

Catherine Mershon was fascinated by the mill, her senses stimulated with all its power and movement and working men who were white with flour. Julius Simon always gave Catherine a sucker out of the sucker jar when she visited.

The Simons, like many other community families, held house dances. Furniture was pushed aside and one set of dancers danced in each room. Each set had its own dance caller and the musicians sat where they could be heard in all the rooms. Some of the families who held dances in their homes were headed by Eugene Cattee, Brownie Work, Ed Simon, Joe Montavon, and Ed Graf. The musicians were usually Shopes and Charlie Jr.

When Catherine was of age, she attended the Upper Pond

Creek one-room school on Route 73 above the Montavon place. She walked to school with other children and she, Alberta Montavon, and Ed Graf were in the same grade. She remembers Ed a being nice to everyone. In grades one to four, Lillian Barney was her teacher. Lillian's husband brought her to and picked her up from school except in bad weather, when she boarded with Albert and Mary Montavon. Kinney Long, later a well-known area baseball coach, was Catherine's fifth and sixth grade teacher. There were nineteen students in the entire school. When time came for high school, they rode the bus to McDermott.

Catherine's brother, Charles, was older than she so he went to McDermott before she did. Leonard Slye attended McDermott at the same time Charles was there and they both played in the McDermott band. Charles played drums. Leonard played clarinet. Because of common interests, the two country boys became friends. They both loved music as well as animals, swimming, fishing, hunting, and more. Leonard took Charlie home to Duck Run to spend the night and Charlie hosted Leonard overnight at his family's home.

The Mershons often spoke of their special memories of Leonard Slye who later became Roy Rogers.

Catherine realized that her family wasn't particularly well off so she wondered why rich people in big cars and town clothes often came to their house—if only for a brief visit. It was a different time in America and her father, like many other farmers, learned that his corn crop sold better by the quart than by the bushel. And that's why the rich people came: to buy corn liquor. They would drive their big cars in when the creek was down. If it was up, one of the family had to walk the swinging bridge to meet them. If Catherine's father wasn't home, her mother waited on the customers. The liquor was kept in jars in the creek or sometimes buried in soft earth near the house. Catherine held the lantern while her mother dug out the size jar a customer wanted. Usually visitors stayed in the car and rolled down the window. They never opened the door.

Charlie Sr. didn't trust banks. He kept his money in a container under a slab of concrete by the well. He used a pry bar to get to that little box. Charlie controlled the money in the family so if Catherine needed something, her mom sent her to town with her dad. They would catch a ride to Portsmouth out on Route 73 and then go to Bragdons on Chillicothe Street to get shoes. (She wore boys' shoes that were high top with a pocket on the side that could hold a pocket knife.) Then she'd go to George Cox's restaurant on Second Street just east of Market for lunch. It was the first place she ever saw a plate lunch. Charlie would have a few beers over on Market Street and then they'd catch a ride home.

Shopes died when Catherine was thirteen. When she was fifteen, the family moved to Route 73 to the old Lower Pond Creek one-room school across from The 73 Tavern. It was the first time they'd ever had electricity in their home. Catherine's mother, who worked at the Elks Country Club, soon retired. They moved to Dry Run and Catherine graduated from Washington High School.

Catherine had aspired to be a nurse from the time she was four-years-old. She learned that interviews were being held at Mercy Hospital for potential nursing students. Her family was not Catholic, but Catherine's mother liked Mercy's reputation.

(L to R) Victor, Vincent Joseph II, Catherine (age 60), Vincent Joseph Sr., and Deborah. *Photo courtesy of Vincent Tovine, Jr.*

With five dollars in hand, they caught a ride to Portsmouth. The board of directors was interviewing and Dr. Hermann, a member of the board, knew the family. With five whole dollars, at age seventeen and one half, Catherine was accepted into the nursing program.

At the same time, the first African American in the state of Ohio was accepted into a nursing program as well—in Catherine's class. Her name was Portia Archie. Catherine saw first-hand blatant racial discrimination aimed directly at Portia, but she was able to rise above the ignorance. At night Portia taught the other girls to dance, especially the huckle buck.

Catherine's three and one half years of study included eight months of special training at Mayo Clinic in Rochester, Minnesota. She loved all aspects of nursing and graduated from Mercy under the Sisters of Saint Francis.

She met a young Italian man, Vincent Tovine, and they married at Holy Redeemer Church. He owned a successful business, Vince's Carry Out, as well as being involved in Democratic politics. They raised two sons, Vincent and Victor, and a daughter, Deborah.

Professionally, Catherine worked at many forms of nursing, but for the last twenty-eight years she was school nurse, serving East, Harding, North Moreland, and Portsmouth City Schools.

The complexity of Catherine's life has provided her with a view of people from all directions.

And Roy Rogers stayed all night at her home!

Ray Bernard Boldman in 2014. Ray was born Oct. 2, 1916. *Photo courtesy of Rhonda Boldman Markassel.*

A fellow was in the airport with his girlfriend having breakfast. She ordered a strawberry waffle loaded with whipped cream and syrup. They finished breakfast and walked along casually. A really attractive woman passed. She had a whole lot of movement and a little shake in her walk. He looked at his girlfriend and said, "What do you think of that?"

She took a few quick steps out in front of him and gave it her best strut, looked around and asked, "And what do you think of that?"

To which he replied, "I think I just found that strawberry waffle."

Chapter Ten
RAY BOLDMAN

Ray Boldman says there are lyrics from an old song that apply to him: "I been at the hoe and I been at the plow."

At ninety-eight years of age Ray fends for himself at his home in McDermott, Ohio. Ray was born to Charles and Leona Strickland Boldman on Big Bear Creek, October 2, 1916. Similar to today, Ray was quite active. His mom used to say, "We need to put a bell on Ray because we never know where he is."

Soon after Ray's birth, the family moved near the McClay farm on Route 104 into an old two-story hotel that had catered to Ohio and Erie Canal travelers. There was a lot of scarlet fever there so the Boldmans moved again, down 104 to Pearl Overturf's place, now owned by the Emnett family.

They went to the Bannon farm for a short time before buying a one-acre piece from D. McFann which was located next to Ray's grandfather's home. Charlie Boldman built a house on it.

School time came and Ray would walk to the Duck Run wooden one-room schoolhouse. It was primer through grade eight. First grade was called primer. He had no shoes and his feet got pretty darn cold. His first teacher was Mae Massie. Others included Brian Vaneford, Guy Bumgarner, and Raymond McGlone.

Ray liked learning the rhymes Miss Massie taught her class. One he remembers:

> *Robin red breast,*
> *sitting on a bough,*
> *come get your breakfast,*
> *I'll feed you now.*

The kids recited them together and on that one, classmate Orville Ramey would say *dinner* for breakfast.

Some of the Duck Run kids were ornery and Mr. Vaneford had difficulty maintaining order in his class. Some of the boys threw blackboard erasers, pieces of wood wrapped in felt, and books around the classroom. One boy chewed tobacco in class. He put his hand over his mouth, spit on the wall, and watched it run down.

Charles Hiles, Leonard Slye, Fred Matthews, and Lawrence Wiseman built a little room of tree limbs behind the school. They met in there at recess and smoked. One day Albert Holland and the boys built a fire in the stove before school and threw a dead skunk in it. They had to turn school out that day. Fred Matthews used to provoke the teacher, then run outside and hide under the school.

It's surprising how deportment improved when Guy Bumgarner came to teach. He sang and played ball with the kids and started a 4-H club. He respected the students and they respected him.

Duck Run became overcrowded and Ray and others went to school down Duck Run Road at the Henry Springs Hotel. At one time it had been a busy place, serving many travelers but had

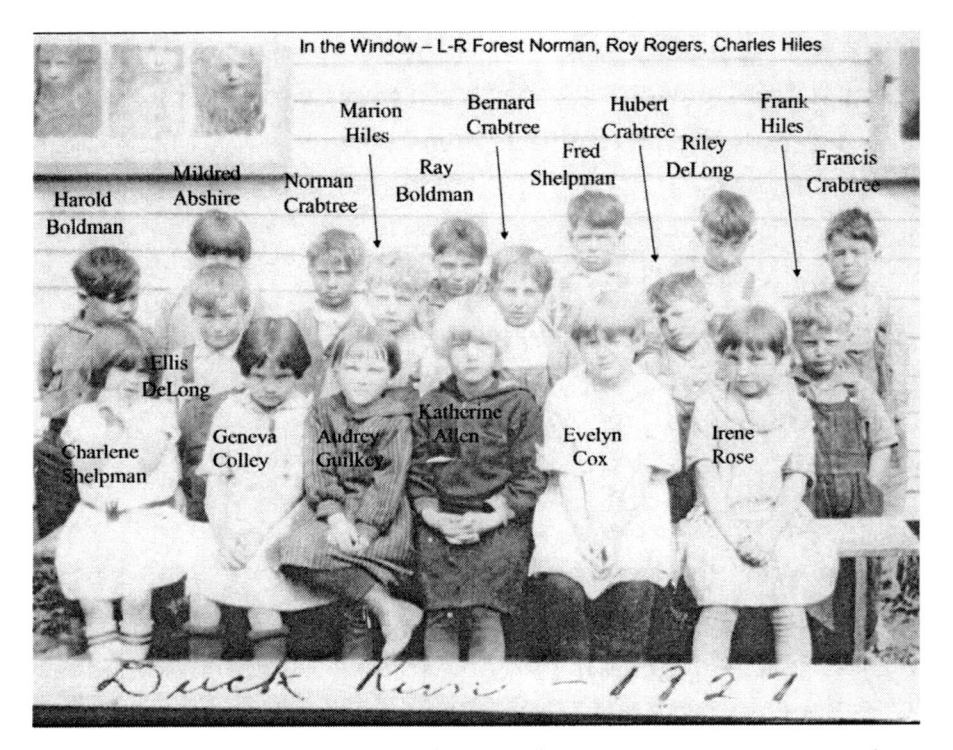

Ray Boldman and fellow students with names shown at Duck Run one room school including Leonard Slye at the window. *Photo courtesy of Ray Boldman.*

since closed except for a beer joint in one of the side rooms. A sawmill was next door. After a year, they all returned to Duck Run. The wooden one-room school was torn down and replaced with a brick two-room. Ray continued to attend for a while but quit when he got to the seventh grade because he still had no shoes.

Ray, a keen observer, noticed the older Leonard Slye and his talent. Leonard liked going to Ray's home to play guitar and sing. Ray's mother always requested the old hymn "Showers of Blessings." Ray's dad liked to take him to the school plays at Duck Run. He commented that Leonard could be the whole show, able to play any part.

When Leonard finished eighth grade, he went to McDermott

High School. Around that time, Jack Jones took an old truck and cobbled it into a school bus. He hauled country kids to McDermott. Leonard rode that bus until he quit during his sophomore year.

Ray liked to work and wanted to try his hand at that. First he helped at home, but Pearl Overturf offered him a farm job. This required him to walk or hitchhike each day to work. His first task was plowing wet ground with a team of mules in the wintertime with a breaking plow. Those rows were so long! Then he worked in the granary, shelling corn and cleaning wheat seed.

In spring he and others worked the ground and planted new hayfields, soy beans, wheat, and corn. Crops were later cultivated. Hay was cut with a horse-drawn sickle bar and raked into wind rows with a horse-drawn, rider-operated dump rake. It was doodled with a pitchfork and hauled loose to the barn. If it was soybean hay, it was dirty and heavy.

Pearl had a big barn and a hayfork that swung down out of the barn. It was connected with ropes, powered by horses, and lifted and guided to the desired place in the barn where it was then stacked by men with pitchforks. In winter the hay was tossed down from the hayloft and fed to the livestock. When the stationary wire tie baler made its appearance later, hay bales were much heavier.

Wheat was cut into sheaves with a hand cradle. They were tied and stood up into shocks for drying. Each had to be capped to keep the rain out. They were then hauled to the barn area for threshing. George and Harold Schultz had a threshing machine that went from farm to farm. It separated the wheat grain from straw, and blew the straw into a big stack for other uses. Kids played on it. Several men worked at threshing while the women were inside the house preparing glorious food. It was more than work. It was a social experience, too.

When field corn matured, it had to be shucked by hand. Open pollinated corn produced big ears. In rows of standing corn, a horse-drawn wagon walked along at a slow pace. Three men, each with a row to shuck, walked beside the wagon and threw the corn ears against a bump board on the opposite side. The board was higher than the rest of the wagon so the workers didn't have to look when they threw. Either a peg or a hook was worn on the shucking hand, the hook across the palm or the peg across the fingers. Ray used a peg. The corn was stored in narrow cribs for drying.

Some corn was cut with corn knives and then stood up in the field to form shocks. Corn stalks were tied together in the middle and armloads of other stalks leaned against it in a circular manner, forming a shock. The outside of the shock was tied with sea grass string. Later, when time allowed, it was laid on the ground and the corn was shucked. Corn was put in the crib, and fodder was stored for feed or bedding.

Farmers had to care for and clean up after livestock year round. Ray worked all the farm jobs. He was young and strong, felt well, and liked hard work. He worked ten hours a day, five days a week, for five whole dollars. On weekends he spent it.

When WWII started, Pearl Overturf was on the draft board and, initially, got a deferment for Ray but in September 1942, he was drafted into the army. He went in with Blaine Farley who later became principal of McDermott Elementary. Ray's infantry basic was at Camp Butler, North Carolina after which he was then assigned to the construction engineers.

As an aviation engineer he was sent to New Guinea where he helped lay out landing mats for planes. Cigarettes were given to those in the service along with food and toiletries. Camels, Luckys, and Raleighs were the common issue. Ray liked Lucky Strikes or Camels. You could play hits or cracks with Camels.

In boyhood, Ray's family had no well so he carried spring water about a mile to their home. That had caused a slight hernia which was further aggravated by heavy lifting on the farm and in New Guinea. He was taken to surgery in a field hospital where he remained for six weeks. Back to work at the airstrip he was not in hand-to-hand combat, but the guns of war always cracked close by. One day a Japanese soldier was found asleep in one of their hammocks. He seemed glad to be captured; he was starved.

When Ray was discharged he had a few dollars in the bank and decided he'd relax a while. In service the GIs enjoyed the night spots and there were several around home; Sum Koch's Cozy Corner, Jim McCoy's and John Shope's were all in McDermott. There were Joe Turner's in Lucasville, The Old Kentucky Home on Divide Hill, The Rendezvous on Route 104, both The 73 Tavern and Bluebird Inn on Route 73, Grant's Cabin in Cole's Park, and The Valley View Inn and George Delong's on the west side. Charlie Prose said when you bought a bushel of coal at Delong's there was a pint in the bottom of every basket. On Hill Road was a house with several slot machines. Bill and Musty Schackart frequented there. Ray knew them from his work on the farm. Ray often crossed paths at these places with others who were finding their way: Ray Irvin, Vince Montavon, Dick and Harry Strickland, Jim O'Brien, Dick Glendenning, and Charlie Mershon. Charlie could play the banjo.

Ray's dad was employed at Taylor Stone and wanted to see his son settled. When Ray's money was about gone, his dad got him work at Taylor Stone. He has been in McDermott ever since. His job was to pull cars, hard and dangerous work. He spent twenty-four years at Taylor's, eleven at Waller's, and retired on Social Security and his wife's pension.

Ray Boldman does not put on airs. A man of strong character, he lives on his own in McDermott. He still drives, and in his strong voice he spins interesting tales from his clear memory.

Ray's stepson, Roger Conley, keeps a close and healthy friendship.

Ray's daughter, Rhonda, who works at Waller's is quite gifted. As a girl she was involved in Portsmouth pageants. Jim Lovins drove her on the back of his convertible in parades. Rhonda stops to see her dad every day and, on Sunday, they go to church together.

Since they attended school together Ray got a good look at and impression of Leonard Slye, especially his artistry. It's neat to have known him. When he hears of the Slye family trip to California in the old Dodge it puts him in mind of the *Beverly Hillbillies*.

And every time Ray sees a two-wheeled, foot-powered scooter he thinks of the first one he ever saw. One day the door swung open at Duck Run School and in came Leonard on a wire-wheeled one, then ran it up and down the aisles.

Norma and Ed Graf on Pond Creek at Simon's 2013 Sorghum Festival. Behind them (L to R in background) Robert Teeters, Tom Cable, Eileen Simon Theiken, and Carol Simon Smith. *Photo courtesy of Norma Graf.*

The excited preacher railed about the fruits of alcohol. He pleaded, "If I had all the whiskey in the world I'd pour it in the river. If I had all the wine in the world, I'd pour it in the river. If I had all the beer in the world I'd pour it in the river." Exhausted, he sat down. The song leader stood and announced, "Turn to page fifty-one in your hymnals and let's all sing together, 'Shall We Gather at the River'."

Chapter Eleven
NORMA "KNUTE" HENSON GRAF

Norma Henson's mother was a Daulton. Norma grew up living and working at her Grandpa Daulton's Grocery on Second Street near Market in Portsmouth, Ohio. Helping in the store she learned the business and the people, and playing with the neighbors Norma became athletic.

Norma was a curious child. Her childhood was a safe time when a child could explore. She took great notice of her surroundings and loved to visit all the stores on that end of town.

Her dad, Herbert Henson, drove a rare Theodore Roosevelt automobile. He called it *Old Teddy*.

She began her schooling at Scudder on Fifth Street across from Saint Mary's and finished elementary school at Massie on Second Street near the US Grant Bridge.

Norma recalls the layout of the business places in that part of town. Between Second and Front on the north side, was the elegant Washington Hotel made up of sleeping rooms, a nice restaurant, and a ballroom for dancing. The place deteriorated but remained open during most of recent history. When that happened it was a time when some of the residents were down on their luck. "Funny" Porter, who ran a Sunoco station at Second and Madison, opened the Cow Shed Tavern east of the hotel. At about the same time Charlie Dixon opened The 440 tavern and dance hall on Second, a little west of the hotel. The two tavern owners were known to be honest and they held the monthly checks of the hotel guests, giving them money each day for food and necessities.

Across from the hotel, at Front and Market, was the Union Mission. It served the needs of the poor and provided them housing. Next door on Front was Simon Labold's Junk Shop. On the Market Street side were Kenrick's, Stone's Grocery, and a gas station on the corner.

Going east on Second, one could find Riley's upstairs roller rink, Westland Theater, Granger's Saloon, Jake Pfau's Bakery, Gilbert Grocers, West End Confectionary, Abbot Paint, Wyn Nye Drug Store, Simon and Kilcoyne Tavern, and Massie School. West on Second was the Hulbert Hotel over The 440, Wright's Hatchery, an ice house, a Sunoco station, Charlie and Phoebe Dickerson's grocery and tavern, Borden Milk Company, Fergie's Lunch, Pat's Café, and car barn storage for the Portsmouth streetcar line where the Bridge Carry out is today.

On the west side of Market Street, between Second and Third, were Lantz Drugs, Sam Cox barbershop, A&P Grocery, Rottingham Hardware, a narrow restaurant that introduced foot long hot dogs to the area, Counts Bakery, Geisler's Meat Market, and a Kroger store. Farmers sold their products on the Market Street esplanade. The east side of Market, from Third to Second, had Schaefer's Market, Charlie Ferrell's tavern, Charlie Cohen's Saloon (now Market Street Café), Frank Clark Barbershop, Stahler's Drugs, Jerry Distel's speakeasy, and Candyland. There were seven taverns in that area: Shorty Doerr's, Charlie Ferrell's, Charlie Cohen's, Wade and Helen's, Funny Porter's, The 440, and The Palace.

Today, the nicely restored Washington Hotel and Biggs House sit between Front and Second Streets. They are results of our government's assistance to the elderly. The senior center is there as well as Adult Day Care which serves those with Alzeheimer's Disease and other afflictions.

• • •

Major League Baseball's Branch Rickey hails from our community. In the 1930s, while affiliated with the Saint Louis Cardinals, he helped locate a Cardinals professional farm team, the Portsmouth Redbirds, in Portsmouth. Their infield consisted of George "Whitey" Kurowski at third, a fellow named Hart as shortstop, player manager Bennie Birdman at second, with Walter Alston playing first. Kurowski and several others boarded at a rooming house at Eighth and Chillicothe Streets, but Alston lived at the Washington. Norma often saw him in the area. Later, Branch Rickey switched to the Brooklyn Dodgers and Alston followed. He eventually became the Dodgers' manager. He was a school teacher in the off-season.

• • •

As Norma grew up, she graduated from Portsmouth High School, then went to Ohio State where she earned a degree in Business Administration. For a while she worked at Williams Manufacturing in the engineering department. From there she became office manager at Dayton Walther.

Her social group was sports oriented, but none of them more so than Norma. She was so devoted to Notre Dame football they called her "Knute" after the Irish Catholic coach, Knute Rockne.

Norma met Ed Graf on Pond Creek. He came from a good family and they were married in 1954 by Monsignor Casey at Holy Redeemer Catholic Church. They established a home on Pond Creek where three sons—Steve, Jim, and Bill—were born to them. Ed worked at Norfolk and Western Railroad while he and Knute raised the family.

They were handy at producing homemade foods at their annual hog butchering. Sausage, blood pudding, and head cheese were complemented by a visit to their colorful wine cellar where shelves displayed delicious looking jars of home canned goods.

Norma returned to work to help pay their sons' college costs. She spent seven years as WPAY Radio office manager and liked radio work. She continued her employment outside the home, ending with fours years in the common pleas area of the Scioto County Courthouse.

When the boys were in school at Northwest High, Norma often drove up Duck Run to the school. She thought of that boy, Leonard Slye, who roamed these parts but became known worldwide.

In childhood she thrilled at the B Western double features shown at the Laroy Theater on Saturday mornings. If under age twelve, it only cost a dime; everyone else charged a quarter. Norma would visit her aunt Otha Henson who lived near the Laroy. Her daughter, Jo Ann, was Norma's age. Aunt Otha fed the girls and they went to the show but they didn't buy anything. The three main cowboy stars were Roy Rogers, Gene Autry, and Hopalong Cassidy. Norma thought Hoppy had the most gentle smile.

She liked Roy Rogers. She appreciated that he valued his

origins but especially that he remembered and often went to visit his Duck Run school teacher Guy Bumgarner. Norma was soothed by Roy's singing and love of music. And his ranch had the neatest name, the Double R.

Norma and Ed are retired now. She remains abreast of current events, music, and sports. Their son Bill, who loves music and nature, attends carefully to the homeplace.

(L to R) Scott Mullins, Roy Rogers, and Larry Dale Mullins at the Southern Ohio Museum in Portsmouth, Ohio, September 6, 1982. *Photo courtesy of Larry Dale Mullins.*

The old fellow had passion for music and was fond of many songs but his favorite was,

"When they dropped the turtle
In Myrtle's girdle,
There was a lot less sag
In the old bag."

Chapter Twelve
LARRY DALE MULLINS

Larry's family moved to Zuefle Drive and he was in fourth grade when school began. His teacher was Ellen Travis at McDermott Elementary. He learned of his new territory and it fascinated him that one person he adored, Roy Rogers, had attended the same school and lived close by. Roy's real name was Leonard Slye and one of Larry's classmates was Andy Slye. They sat beside one another.

McDermott grade school and high school, were both made of stone quarried locally. The high school had a gym and on the front of the stage hung a big curtain embroidered *RHS* for Rush Township High School. Larry liked the school, the town, and the people. A lot of those he met knew Roy Rogers.

One of Larry's friends, Mark Teeters, lived over toward Roy's home. He knew Leonard Slye and told Larry the cowboy likes to come home to Inskeep Road and square dance, sing, play, and have fun with friends and music.

Larry, a son of Zeke and Doris Mullins, is part of a family that smiles and no wonder, he grew up in a home of entertainment. He made a radio commercial at age eighteen months for Scioto County Milk Producers when Zeke worked at Ideal Milk. Larry came on and said, "I like milk, it's good for your health."

Larry said he and his siblings had fun growing up. "If dad baby sat, we all sang together." The kids were always around show business; Zeke and Doris involved them. When Zeke went to work, it was either radio or a performance. Sometimes they were allowed to go to the radio station. It seemed magical with all those knobs, wires, and sounds. At performances the kids often played. At age eight, Larry was playing drums in the Mullins band. They never got paid but it built confidence and they grew close. "We knew our parents had such a good reputation and we wanted to live up to that."

The Mullins family did all sorts of work, store openings at Harts, Clark's, Rinks, and Ray Bob's, window fronts, fairs, and a variety of other social events.

When Larry was yet a twinkle in his father's eye, Leonard Slye had already established his career. Larry provided a DVD that documented some segments of his progress. The DVD highlighted many of Roy's accomplishments.

Because of Leonard's success he was featured on the most talked about television program in America, *This is Your Life*, hosted by Ralph Edwards on January 14, 1953. Ralph stated that world famous Roy Rogers was the most requested subject for their show in America.

Roy and Dale had been married by Oklahoma City minister, Bill Alexander. In order to get Roy to the broadcast, but to surprise him, they told him that Reverend Alexander was to be honored and Roy had been requested to speak on his behalf. It worked.

Roy's parents, Andrew and Mattie, along with sisters Mary, Cleda, and Kathleen were there. Roy and his family were touched by the moment. Mattie told that she cried at Leonard's birth he

(L to R) Ralph Edwards, Roy Rogers and his pop, Andrew Slye, with the old Dodge on *This Is Your Life* in 1953. *Photo courtesy of Larry Dale Mullins.*

Ralph Edwards, Roy Rogers and his crew on *This is Your Life,* 1953. Roy's mother, Mattie is right above her son. *Photo courtesy of Larry Dale Mullins.*

was so ugly. Roy said he, his dad, and family had built their Ohio homeplace, working together, on Inskeep Road.

Guy Bumgarner, the teacher Leonard Slye respected so, told of teaching Roy at Duck Run in seventh and eighth grade. Guy had a 4H Club there and Roy won a prize with his pet pig. He groomed it and trimmed its toe nails. Roy had a gift with animals. He had a pet ground hog that would come out when he tapped on the stump beside its hole and he fed it.

Roy's musical side was shown with the twenty dollar guitar he bought in a hock shop in Cincinnati. Even the old car they drove from Inskeep Road to Lawndale, California, made the show. In Lawndale, Leonard and his dad drove trucks, were migrant workers, and played music together.

Roy's tryout at Republic Studio in 1936 and his first movie shortly after were also covered. The members of the original Sons of the Pioneers came and they and Roy sang nicely together.

Dale Evans and their children made a special appearance along with Roy's pal, Trigger. The last guest was a little boy who had been given a fatal diagnosis at the hospital. He requested to meet Roy Rogers. Roy visited and told him if he would get well they'd be friends for life. An unexplainable recovery followed.

In 1959, Larry was an infant when a special event, Roy Rogers Day took place in Portsmouth. The DVD provided has no sound but gives some record. Wally Edwards and Leo Blackburn led a special planning group. Roy was in Ohio for a shooting match. In Scioto County he dedicated the new McDermott Post Office, and saw to the naming of the Roy Rogers Football Field at Northwest School. He appeared at the Scioto County Fair in a program managed by Fairboard Director, Dr. Walter Kline.

Others at the fair were Guy Bumgarner, Paul Doyle, and ten of Leonard's Duck Run friends. Glen Emnett presented Roy with a pet pig.

Zeke Mullins and Frank Balmert were at their broadcasting desks at WPAY and during Roy's ceremony several Portsmouth business places including Edwards Cleaners, Williams Manufacturing, Bragdons and Citizen's Bank were shown. The downtown Roy Rogers Esplanade was dedicated. Little is there today to designate that.

Larry often went with Zeke to the station and was drawn to radio work. He watched, helped, and learned. At fifteen he took a job with WPAY on what they called the God Squad. They played shows done by local ministers. Then they asked Larry to read the news but that made him uncomfortable. One day he accidentally set the waste basket on fire and thought for sure they'd fire him.

After high school Larry worked nights at WPAY. He called himself Larry Dale in order to form an on-air identity. Zeke taught Larry to be versatile. To stay employed in radio it was necessary to work different jobs. From station engineers Howard Potts and Jerry Eves he learned the technical side of radio.

Roy called Zeke once and asked him to walk down to Waller Street. Roy wanted to look at the houseboat, that used to be his family's home. The city had promised to oversee the property, but it was in disrepair. That bothered Roy and he said, "I'll never come back to Portsmouth."

Time passed and the city realized we needed Roy's goodwill, so they talked with Zeke. It was decided to place notebooks at several locations in the community that said, "We love you, Roy.

Please come home." Over 26,000 signatures were gathered and bound together in a handsome hardback book.

Zeke and Doris assembled two tour buses in April, 1982, and headed for Victorville. Don Brooks was one of the drivers. At the museum, Zeke presented the book to Roy and asked him, in person, to please come home. Roy was touched by the effort.

Roy said he had many roots in California—as well as 550 restaurants in America. Zeke told him we'd like to have a Roy Rogers restaurant at our new university. Roy also told Zeke that he loved to visit old friends at home, but found it hard to do so.

Teenager Lisa Mullins accompanied her parents to California, but her focus while there was Roy's dog, a black Labrador, that yodeled. When Roy sang and yodeled, the dog did, too. Lisa told Roy she'd like to film that, so Roy did it again and the dog joined in. Lisa noted that anytime she saw Roy Rogers he was attentive to children and animals.

In Portsmouth, the leaders began working with Roy on a date to come home. Elmer Sword of the Portsmouth Recognition Society learned that Roy and his three sisters had not been here together for years. He worked out a time suitable to all of them and Roy agreed. It would be during Portsmouth River Days.

September 6, 1982, was set as Recognition Day. Larry and his brother, Scott, were asked to follow Roy and video the events. Roy was helpful and patient through rides about town, speeches, and conveyance of honors. Roy even put his feet in wet concrete at Harold's Restaurant to be displayed later on the esplanade.

Larry and Scott followed Roy in a pickup provided by Glockner's for the three days of activities. The equipment was heavy. At the Southern Ohio Museum Roy said, "Everyone has had their picture made with me. How about you fellows?"

At the end of the third day Roy was at the Rosemount Holiday Inn with society members. Larry went there and Roy said he wanted to see the film so Larry rewound it, handed it to Roy, and headed for work after three most unusual days. Larry was twenty-three. After working with Roy Rogers those three days he said, "I never saw a man so accommodating."

That experience honed Larry's interest in the career of Roy Rogers. Each year he meets people involved in the annual festival. Famous Indian Iron Eyes Cody quipped "I've played an Indian my entire life but I'm really Italian." At a press conference another day, some participants got into a heated argument. It became tense. Lash LaRue took the microphone and recited an old western adage saying life is short. It defused the situation.

Larry also provided documentation of Roy signing the Portsmouth flood wall Collection of Stars on June 3, 1994. It was one of his last local appearances.

Larry has spent time with several stars in his work. Marty Robbins had an ease with people that compared with Roy's manner. Roy's body language revealed his genuineness. He never lost his Appalachian skills. Roy could fix a car, drive truck, work golf greens, understand animals, ride horses, be a migrant worker, musician, singer, yodeler, and dance caller. He never lost his love of real country people.

Today Larry Mullins attends to his family, does some radio work and serves as director of our county bus service, Access Scioto County, a job he's held for thirteen years.

Cleda Willoughby (center) and Bea Hollback (far right) follow the fiddle playing of John Hollback at the Hollback home in South Webster, Ohio. *Photo courtesy of Bea Hollback.*

Once I knew a girl so bashful she went in the closet to change her mind, and so innocent that when she went to confession she had to make up sins.

Chapter Thirteen
BEA THEIKEN HOLLBACK

Bea's dad, Ed Theiken, was a hard working and talented man, as well as being an excellent farmer and fiddler. He traveled from his home on Lick Run Lyra Road to Pond Creek in order to win the favor of Magdeline Montavon who lived on Cave Lick. Cave Lick is also known to have produced good corn whiskey. Ed and Magdeline attended dances where they did round dance, fox trot, one-step, waltz, and square dancing.

Soon they married and built a healthy home of ten children. Bea was number six and born in the back bedroom. It is written that middle children in large families are usually well adjusted. Her siblings are Francis, Mary, Lawrence, Anna, Mildred, Michael, Joseph, Bernadette, and Monica.

Older family members were not farmed out. Her Grandpa and Grandma Theiken lived with them as did Grandma Montavon who slept on a straw mattress. Bea combed Grandma Theiken's hair and pinned it up in a bun. Grandpa carried Bea on his shoulders; she could see everything from up there. He shooed flies and gnats with a small tree limb while smoking his pipe and he liked to use the mowing scythe.

Boredom was not practiced in this family. They had so much

to do with work and play. They enjoyed their life and they liked each other. Some of their games were tag, hide and seek, capture the flag, red light green light, tappy on the icebox, mumble peg, and kick the can. They played ball with a ball made of rags. Bats were made from flat boards. They whittled out the handles with a hatchet. They made and shot sling shots. Gravel, corn, and beans served as ammunition.

Other games they played were button-button, telephone, Chinese checkers, jacks, and cards. The girls jumped rope and played hopscotch. In the evening, they listened on the car battery operated radio to *The Lone Ranger, The Green Hornet, Jack Armstrong the All American Boy, The Shadow, Just Plain Bill,* and *The Romance of Helen Trent.* Morning favorites were *Cadel Tabernacle,* stock market reports, and the weather. Lawrence operated the radio system.

The musical Theikens made whistles from elder stems. They played their instruments in harmony together. Family imagination was always at play. The baby buggy became a jitney bus in which Mike and younger ones were pushed down imaginary highways. It had also been used in the garden to gather heads of cabbage and other vegetables. A play market was set up under the butternut tree where play vegetables were sold. Mike, Joe, Bernie, and Monica liked that. Brother Francis brought home a signal book from the Navy so they made flags and did fun work through signals.

Most food was grown on the farm. Mom and the family made and canned catsup, sorghum, jelly, jam, vegetables, and fruits. They drank homemade grape juice. Sandwiches at picnics were mustard, sorghum, apple butter, jelly, catsup, or jelly and mustard together.

Hay was cut with a horse drawn mowing machine, raked with a horse drawn dump rake, doodled by hand with pitchforks when dry, and hauled to the barn. There it was unloaded with a horse drawn hayfork controlled by ropes and dropped in the desired place in the barn with a hand held trip rope, where it was stored until it was fed to horses and cattle. The kids were so fascinated by all of it, so, Lawrence set up a play hayfork operation in the grape arbor.

The creek was damned up for swimming and fishing. Seines were made from tomato stakes and burlap sacks to catch fish, crawdads, and sometimes a turtle. Dad dressed the turtles and they made good eating. The most fun was cleaning and frying crawdad tails in Mom's big iron skillet.

Saturday was bath day in the smoke house. In winter they washed in Mom and Dad's bedroom. Three or four bathed before the water was changed in the old washtub.

When cousins Fred and Joe Hock came over they brought special items such as bubble gum and candy. Their dad was a professional baseball player and they gave Bea's family a real bat and ball.

On special Saturday nights, they had house square dances. Dad played fiddle, Gilbert Gifford played guitar and Bernard Schwamburger seconded on piano. The braided rugs were picked up, furniture was pushed to the side, and one set of dancers danced in the dining room while another set danced in the front room.

Winters were colder with more snow and they seemed long. The Theikens had homemade sleighs but the Hocks had a store-bought one. The kids rode three or four at a time until they were worn out. They ice skated in four buckle artics, had snowball battles, and played fox and geese in the snow, too.

Butter was made in a wooden churn. Ice cream was made in winter for it was the only time there was ice. They had their own cream from milking.

Hogs were butchered in cold weather. Water was heated in iron kettles to scald the hogs so hair could be scraped from their hides. The animals were gutted and cut into fat for lard, and lean for sausage, sides, hams, backbone, tenderloin, pork chops, spare ribs, and shoulder. They used heads, feet, and all. Monica used to carry a pig's eye around in her hand all day.

Lard was rendered by cooking the fat in big kettles, then squeezing it through a lard press. They ate the cracklings. Small lean chunks were ground into sausage and canned. Some was seasoned and put into links with the press. Casings to hold both liver and meat sausage links were made from the intestines which were carefully cleaned by hand. The hams, sides, and shoulders were rubbed with a mixture of coarse salt, pepper, and brown sugar, then smoked with hickory and sassafrass wood to complete the seasoning. The family ate a lot of pork and chicken but the men hunted so there was rabbit at Thanksgiving and Christmas.

The cows and horses ate hay and corn. Milking was done twice a day but Bea didn't have "the pull" for that. Chickens ate corn and scratched. Pigs ate corn and slop and potatoes, when available. Bea was in charge of cooking the potatoes in the big kettles. She loved to sit at the fence and watch the pigs eat. When they ate potatoes, they smacked their jaws together and potato pieces fell out of both sides of their mouth. Eggs were gathered and sometimes there was a snake in the nest. Wood and kindling had to be fetched each day and put in the wood box and coal in the coal bucket.

The Theikens were a truck gardening family. They started plants in the hot bed to later be set in the garden and then harvested. Selling tomatoes, cabbage, mangoes, and other produce was how Dad made a living. They worked hard to have early, fresh, clean, and healthy items so stores would buy from them. Their clientele included Midland Grocery, Massie's, Schaefer's, Schoonovers, and other farther away customers.

Bea's favorite job was picking up potatoes and they raised a lot of them. They were poured into a hand operated potato grader that sorted them by size.

Wheat crops were reaped. The sheaves were put into shocks and capped, nine sheaves at a time, and then threshed by the big machine that separated straw from the grain, and wheat from the chaff. Fine meals were prepared for the men by the women.

When berry season came, they picked loads of blackberries and raspberries—and got lots of chiggers, ticks, and scratches. The berries were sold or canned. They also canned green beans, tomatoes, corn, pickles, sauerkraut, grape juice, strawberries, peaches, sausage, and beef.

The farm was flush with daisies. So they gathered, tied, and sold them to Massie's at Memorial Day.

Mil and Bea got to mow all the grass with an old-fashioned push mower—hard work.

With all those people in the home, washday was a big one. Water was heated on the wood stove and the washing was done in a Maytag ringer washer. The clothes were dried on clotheslines in summer, and they were hung in the house in winter. What a sight!

In fall, they gathered persimmons, hickory nuts, butternuts, and walnuts to eat and to season the food.

In October the family's sugar supply was secured by making sorghum. The cane was cut, topped, and stripped. Then the juice squeezed from the stock was evaporated until it became sweet syrup. It could then be used as any kind of sugar. It was sure good in taffy, popcorn balls, baked beans, gingerbread, and so many other foods.

Magdeline dried the sorghum seed and popped it in a hot skillet.

Christmas was a time of giving, not taking. The Theikens went to church, had a good meal, and sang together. Mom made feed sack dresses and lots of homemade fudge, divinity, and other kinds of candy.

Amidst all of Mom's other work she was a quilter. Sleeping was often hot in the summer—no electric fans—but cold in the winter. The family was glad to be able to pile on blankets and handmade quilts. Crawling out from under the covers on a freezing night for a dreaded trip to the outdoor toilet was memorable to say the least.

There were lots of pets when they were growing up: crows, squirrels, ground hogs, and rabbits. They kept the kids busy.

The house was lit with coal oil lamps and shoes were shined once a week for Sunday Mass. If they needed repair, Dad did that.

By 1948, electricity was made accessible and life was changed forever. Also, the older ones began leaving home. Lessons learned from growing up in a good family were in place, though. Ed and Magdeline aged and eventually stopped truck farming.

After high school, Bea did bookkeeping in banks and a variety of secretarial work. Her musical interests continued. She met John Hollback at the Pond Creek square dance. They married and eventually built a home in South Webster, where she lives today.

Music was a major part of John's life. He learned to fiddle from his father. Bea sang more and played guitar, piano, organ, dulcimer, auto harp, and even the hand saw. She became a noted step dancer and then John took up the bass fiddle. Bea wanted to learn it, too, but not loud or with runs or decoration. She developed her style and John paid attention. Bea and John gained confidence playing in traditional music bands at square dances and other musical gatherings.

When Cleda Willoughby returned to the Portsmouth community, she was drawn to music. She attended square dances, enrolled in music classes at Shawnee State University, and became part of Sunday gatherings at the Simon farm. It was under a sweet gum tree there that Bea met Cleda. John and Bea played the kind of music Cleda grew up on and their personalities blended. Bea and Cleda had similar backgrounds with knowledge gained from growing up in the country. Cleda liked to sing and strum her small Martin guitar that had such a nice tone. Bea and John visited her home and they socialized toether.

Both Cleda and Bea grew up in homes where taffy pulling was a regular event, but Cleda spoke of double pulling and Bea didn't know that one. So one day Cleda, Bea, John, and I gathered at Bea's home to learn. One person took a large portion and began to pull. They then handed one end to another person, and the two of them pulled together handing it back and forth. Cleda was a small woman but had strikingly strong arms.

After the taffy was pulled, cut, and stored, the music came

Cleda had strong arms. In the kitchen of John and Bea Hollback, Cleda and John Roger Simon "double-pull" taffy, a skill Cleda's mother taught her. Circa 1990s. *Photo courtesy of Bea Hollback.*

out and the four made music the rest of the day. John and Bea renewed special memories for Cleda. She always said she'd like her brother to get together with them and others for music.

John's death came after forty plus years of marriage. Bea is retired from South Webster Schools. She maintains their home, helps with her family, cooks good food, feeds wild game, sings in church, travels, makes music, and plays the bass her way. She is also a world champion sorghum skimmer.

Roger Strickland is comfortable on the porch of his home. *Photo courtesy of John Roger Simon.*

The fellow had a strong weakness for early apples, especially the Yellow Transparent variety. He and his wife were out for a ride and were down in Kentucky a good piece when they grew tired. They pulled off to rest a little while and sure enough there was one of those apple trees. It was late spring and the apples were beginning to turn color but were still pretty green. Well, he couldn't resist and he got a bait of them. He got in the car and headed up the road. Before too long he looked over at his wife and said, "We'd better look for a place that has a privy." Luckily a country store came into sight. They pulled off and he hurried in. There was a woman working inside and the man asked, "Ma'am would you have a toilet?"

She said, "Yes, we do, but it's out around the building in the back." He went at a fast pace out and around the building toward the back. He no more than got out of sight when she remembered, "My goodness, I forgot to tell him about that clothes line." She rushed out the door and around the building and there lay the man on his back. She hurried up to him, looked down and said, "Oh sir, I forgot to tell you about the clothes line." He looked up at her and replied, "That's all right, ma'am, I don't think I'd have made it anyway."

Chapter Fourteen
ROGER STRICKLAND

The Strickland place is down Inskeep Road a short piece from the Slye home. Orville Strickland raised his family there. He was a close friend to Leonard Slye.

Anita Strickland Adams lives at the Strickland homeplace today in the former apple barn. She is a granddaughter of Orville; her dad was Harry Strickland. Anita is a cement finisher. She says, "I can do men's work." Anita, a woman who likes to decorate has improved the property. She recalls family stories of how Orville and Leonard spent time together.

That is where Roger Strickland grew up. His parents, Orville and Carrie Carver Strickland, birthed ten children there: four girls (Helen Hurst, Betty Jenkins, Jean

Anita Strickland Adams, daughter of Harry Strickland and granddaughter of Orville Strickland stands in front of the Strickland homeplace, now her home on Inskeep Road. April 2012. *Photo courtesy of Gary Hurn.*

Phipps, and Shirley Ralstin) and six boys (Charles "Bunt", Dick, Harry, Roger, Ted, and Tommy).

Orville believed in the virtue of hard work. He went to work in the steel mill while in his teens. He also held strongly to honoring union membership. That belief has been kept alive in the family and is held firmly today. By virtue of Ab Carver, Roger became a cement finisher. So did brothers Dick and Harry, niece Anita, and nephews Dickie, Tim, and Donnie. They all served apprenticeships and worked construction. It is hard work but pays well.

Roger remembers their original house there on the place. A martin box stood beside it. While Roger was a boy, that home burned one night. Everyone got out alive but all their possessions were lost. A fair sized chicken house stood across the road near the bank. It was twelve feet wide and pretty long so they fixed it up for sleeping. They put cardboard on the walls and a row of beds down each side. They all slept in there. Close-by was a smoke house with a cellar underneath. The smokehouse was fixed up and the family stayed in there during the days and ate their meals there.

An apple orchard grew on the bank, so the family sold apples. Their barn housed a cow and a mule but was mainly used for apple storage. Orville decided to fix the barn, transforming it into a house. The family worked together and the barn became their home. Anita lives in that home today.

The Stricklands attended McDermott schools. Roger graduated from there in 1957. He remembers the galvanized tub in which they all washed their face before school each day. Whether they continued their education or not, Orville believed his children

Roger Strickland stands in front of the Strickland homeplace, where he and his brother Governor Ted Strickland grew up. *Photo courtesy of John Roger Simon.*

should go to work at age sixteen. As cement finishers, they learned hard work.

Roger met his love, Rosemary Burton, at a Lucasville drive-in restaurant. They married and now have a home on McDaniels Road near McDermott, Ohio. She worked as a wife, mother, and school cook.

After several years of cement finishing Roger went to work for the Job Corps. As an instructor he taught concrete work. He also built buildings, parking lots—most everything. While finishing concrete for those projects, he taught his students how to do it, too. He served as instructor and coordinator for years and was a supervisor for seven centers for vocational students. He retired after twenty one years with Job Corps.

By the time Roger's brother, Ted, came along, Orville began to understand the value of education and encouraged the younger Strickland toward schooling. Ted trained in psychology but was drawn to politics. Ted had idealistic aspirations and felt he could carry them out in the political field. He was further stimulated when Watergate unfolded.

When Ted was elected into Congress the first time, his dad and Roger's son, Mark, flew to Washington. It was Orville's first airplane ride. They attended the swearing in. One of the reporters asked Orville if he was proud of Ted. He replied, "I'm proud of all my children."

Orville flew to Washington with Mark and returned home with George Bush, a Democrat from Hillsboro, Ohio.

Because they lived close to one another, Ted and Leonard Slye knew one another. Ted was campaigning for Congress one day and found himself in the same town in Ohio as Roy. He asked Roy to make an endorsement for him. It was a year Ronald Reagan was running for president. Roy responded, "My friend, Ronnie, asked me to do one for him the other day and I told him what I have to tell you, I don't get into politics anymore."

After serving several terms as Sixth District Congressman in Ohio, Ted chose to run for Governor. He was nominated and elected as the sixty-eighth Governor of Ohio on the Democratic ticket. His opponent, Ken Blackwell, had made remarks about Ted living in a chicken house. Ted **had** lived in a chicken house—a crowded one! Ted was a very good governor, a fair minded man who represented everyone, especially common people.

Residents of our area take pride in the fact that three rural boys, growing up nearly within a stone's throw of one another, made exceptional accomplishments in their professions. Those boys were Leonard Slye, Ted Strickland, and Branch Rickey.

One of the friends of the Slye and Strickland families who is originally from this area is fiddler Gordon Payne. He worked hard for Ted Strickland and played for Roy Rogers. Rodney Teeters called him one evening and asked if he'd play for a square dance at the home place. Roy was there and happy to have a fiddler.

Noted fiddler, Gordon Payne and his friend Ohio Governor Ted Strickland in front of a 1953 Willys pickup truck at the Simon's Sorghum Festival, Pond Creek, Ohio 2012. *Photo courtesy of Gordon Payne.*

Roy asked, "What are you going to play?" Gordon answered, 'Bile Them Cabbage Down," Roy exclaimed, "Bile 'em!"

Roger Strickland and Rosemary have three children, Lisa Holsinger, Gay Lynn Strickland, and Mark Strickland.

Lisa has a special interest in the life of Leonard Slye. Her passion for horses helped prompt that. She recognized the uniqueness of Trigger and the relationship between Roy and Trigger. She has a soft spot for Palominos. Lisa took to Roy's neatness, his hat, fancy silver tipped cowboy boots, and his wristwatch adorned with a gold and silver saddle.

One day Roger and Lisa were at Dick Strickland's home where Tim and Brenda Strickland live now. Roy was visiting at his homeplace. The Stricklands went to see their old friend. A group had gathered and they were making music in the barn. Roy walked down to his rental car to get something for someone. Roger asked him if Lisa could have his autograph. Roger took a piece of paper from his wallet and Roy signed it.

Since Roy was a man from the neighborhood it was common to see him there, usually with his chums. Roger saw his dad, Charlie Hiles, and Roy Rogers get in a car one day and head for Porstmouth. He wondered of their destination and what it was like to ride around with the famous singing cowboy.

Roger Strickland has lived a most complex life. Being involved in Ted's political efforts added to that. Because Roger loves his brother and feels strongly about the merit of being a Democrat, he helped Ted from the beginning. And learned a lot through the Congressional campaigns.

Ted and his wife, Frances, showed sound judgment in getting Roger involved. He became a familiar figure in his handsome

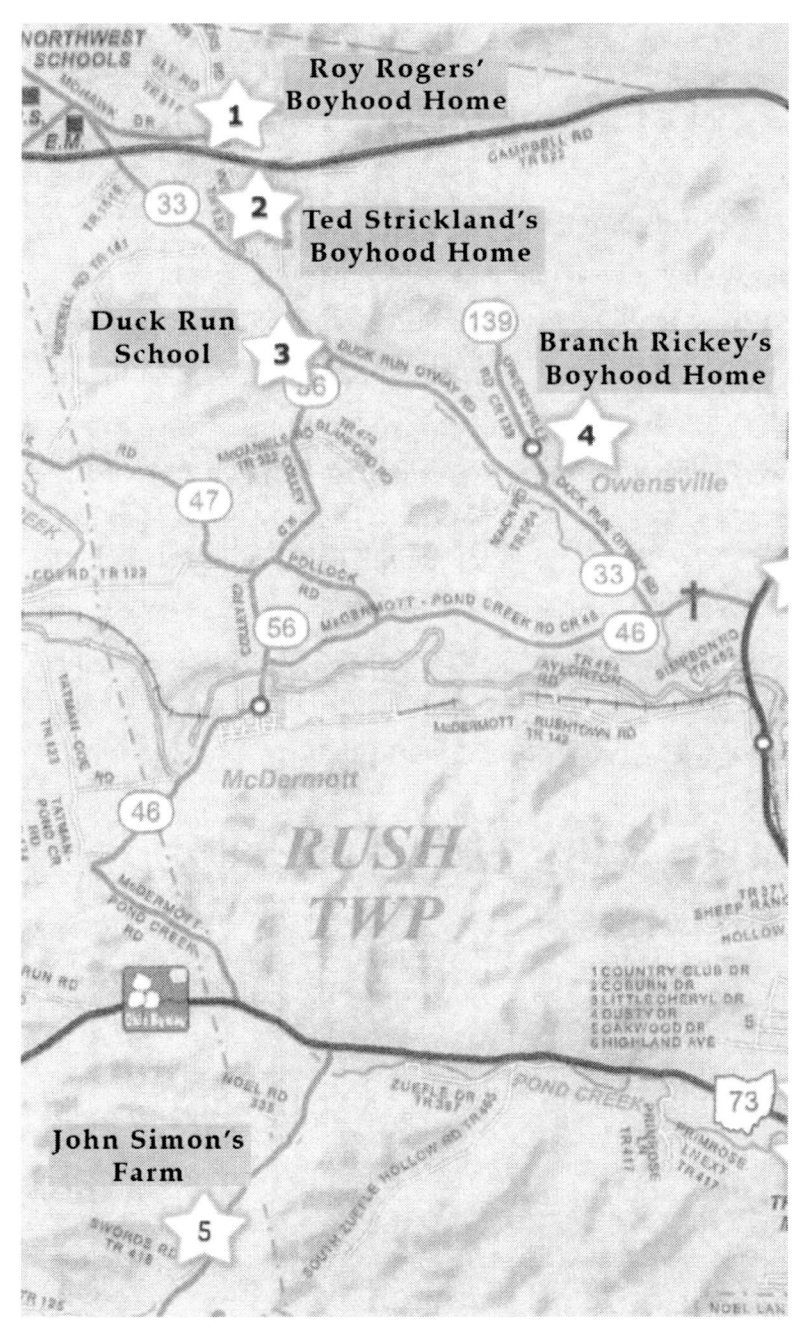

Used with permission of the Scenic Scioto Heritage Trail, Inc.; P. O. Box 536; Portsmouth, OH 45662; www.scenicsciotoheritagetrail.com.

white hat. He looks right at you, offers straight talk, and is a hard worker.

When Ted decided to run for Governor, Roger's work life was tapering down. Ted and Frances got Roger and Pat Day to wrap an RV motor home in Strickland signs and travel to Democratic dinners, rallies, union hall meetings, and other functions throughout the entire state. They were given a schedule to follow but came home when possible. They traveled thousands of miles and had a most colorful experience.

The Strickland family was happy when Ted became Governor!

Roger Strickland is a contented man. He and Rosemary are retired and live in their McDaniels Road home. They are close to their children. They own land on the Ohio River at Buena Vista. Roger goes there often to maintain the property and to care for his dog, Dumper, and his cat, Stranger. They were both dropped off there and Roger says, "We're the best of buddies."

Historic marker that sits in front of the Branch Rickey home on Duck Run Road. *Photo courtesy of John Roger Simon.*

Branch Rickey mural painted by Robert Dafford on Front Street in Portsmouth, Ohio. *Photo courtesy of John Roger Simon.*

Ruth Adkins at her homeplace in Lucasville, Ohio. Ruth provided valuable materials and memories for this story. *Photo courtesy of John Roger Simon.*

What did the corn stalk say to the farmer?
"Stop pulling my ears!"

Chapter Fifteen
RUTH SCHULTZ ADKINS

Ruth Schultz Adkins is kin to the Lucas family, founders of Lucasville, Ohio. A soft spoken woman with twinkling eyes, Ruth worked twenty-five years with children in schools. She lives next door to her dear friend, Alice Barker. They look out for one another.

Ruth had occasion to share experiences with Roy Rogers, one of them in the 1940s. When Leonard Slye attended Duck Run School, Guy Bumgarner was his teacher and 4-H advisor, and Leonard had a championship pig. Guy then became science and agriculture teacher and 4-H advisor at Lucasville School. When Ruth was old enough, she joined Guy's 4-H club. She lived on a farm on Cook Road and her first fair project was a Jersey heifer with those well-known Jersey eyes. Guy taught her how to care for and show that heifer at the Scioto County fair. Guy and his family lived in Lucasville near the Farm Bureau and Brant's General Store. Four-H meetings were held at their home and one day during their meeting, Roy Rogers walked in. There were about ten children there and he mingled right with them. A program was held, refreshments served. Guy had bought some of those old-fashioned firecrackers so everyone went outside and set them

Nell and Guy Bumgarner in front of the Lucasville Ohio Farm Bureau in 1969. *Photo courtesy of Alice Barker.*

off. "We blew up some tin cans and Roy was setting them off too."

Ruth thought she understood why Roy was so popular with children. He had such a sweet, common manner, no one was in awe of him. He was just a quiet, pleasant man.

Time passed and in 1969 Lucasville held its sesquicentennial which was blessed with large crowds. Ruth was married to Millard Adkins and they lived on a farm owned by Methodist Bishop McConnell who had married Eva Thomas, a Lucasville girl. The McConnells resided in New York but had come home for the big event. Neither of them could drive so they hired Ruth to escort them.

Activities held at the Lucasville Fairgrounds included beard growing contests, old fashioned dress and swimsuit contests, plays about local history, caravans, beauty pageants, parades, the champion Lucasville basketball team, and several good meals. Governor James Rhodes was on hand and Roy Rogers and his son, Dusty, were very involved.

All dignitaries were seated on a reviewing stand. The McConnells and Ruth were included. Roy Rogers sat directly in front of Ruth. He was relaxed and appeared to have a really good time. He showed special joy when friends from his boyhood showed up.

Because of her quiet, inquisitive manner, Ruth learned greatly from the experiences.

Ruth has held a lifelong interest in Roy and, based on her early close interaction with him, she feels Hollywood left him unscathed. Today Ruth lives in Lucasville. She and her sons, David and Tom, work hard for the historical society and several other community organizations.

Guy Bumgarner and Roy Rogers, long standing friends. *Photo courtesy of Ruth Adkins.*

(L to R, front row) Leonard Slye, unidentified, Homer Albrecht, Dick Finney, Dick Marting, Dick Taylor, Miles Smith, unidentified; (second row) Margaret Briggs, unidentified, unidentified, Jean Leach, unidentified, Virginia World, Madeline Knost, Mary Jane Sprecher, Bev Horr; (third row) Jack Davis, unidentified, Pauline Esselborn, Mary Lib Hall, unidentified, Helen Gilbert, unidentified, Merle Beekman, unidentified; (fourth row) unidentified, Ira Martin, Sam Kenyon, Edward Gibbs, unidentified, Arthur Rigrish, unidentified, unidentified. *Newspaper clipping courtesy of Georgia Furr.*

The little girl lived far out in the country and had never been to town. Her relatives came and picked her up for her first trip there. In town there were all sorts of new sights. She'd never been in a hotel. They went in and there stood a full length mirror. She'd never seen one so she went over to look and commented, "My goodness, little girl! You don't look well. I have a sweet potato in the car. I'll get it and that will help you feel better." Upon returning she walked over to the mirror, held out the sweet potato, but then exclaimed, "You already have one! I'll eat this one myself."

Chapter Sixteen
JEFF ALBRECHT

Jeff Albrecht is an adept Portsmouth, Ohio, businessman, involved in job creation and business growth in his local area.

Jeff's dad, Homer Albrecht, was the same age as Leonard Slye and lived close to his family when the Slyes lived on the houseboat. They were in the same grade at Union Street School and remained friends for life.

Homer, also a local businessman, owned The Town House, a restaurant on Fifth Street in Portsmouth. It was a good place to eat real home cooking. After Leonard Slye became Roy Rogers and came home to visit from California, he liked to eat there. That gave him the opportunity to enjoy a satisfying meal and visit with his old friend. They had extended talks in the back booth.

Jeff Albrecht owned the Ramada Inn on Second Street in Portsmouth for years. He recently had it remodeled and changed the franchise to Holiday Inn. It is a pleasant place to stay, has good food, and is appropriate for special gatherings. The annual Roy Rogers Festival has been held there for years.

Roy and Dale usually stayed at the Ramada and they and Jeff became familiar. Roy had come from this area. He knew the locals, enjoyed their easy going manner and liked visiting

The landmark Union Street School where the Slye children attended while living on their houseboat home on the Ohio River. Built in 1877, it stood at the northwest corner of Fourth and Union Streets in Portsmouth, Ohio. It was destroyed by fire caused by an arsonist in 1929. At the time of the fire, there were 600 kindergarten through eight grade students enrolled and sixteen teachers employed. *Photo courtesy of Georgia Furr.*

with them. Dale, who was less inclined to socialize, liked being punctual wherever she went and Roy's visiting often made them late. One day Jeff was standing in the hotel lobby in front of the elevator. The doors opened and there stood Dale and Roy. Dale was explaining to Roy that his visiting downtown with old friends was again making them late. Roy never said a word. When she finished, Roy, who always tried to stay relaxed and comfortable, stepped off the elevator, smiled at Jeff, and said, "How you doing?"

Since Jeff owned the Ramada he spent his workday there. He and Roy sometimes talked about the hotel business or Roy's movie life. Roy compared present day conditions with those of the 1930s when he became Roy Rogers. The cowboy movies of Roy's time were called "B Westerns." Filmed on a tight budget, Roy said he was paid $3,500, for each movie he made at Republic Studio. He was like Cowboy Copas, another local boy who rose to fame on the *Grand Ole Opry*. They were much like many other stars of their generation: very rural, poor, and formally uneducated, not prepared to deal with the business world of the city. Once they learned to claim royalties, conditions improved.

The years when Roy came home for the annual festival alone,

An autographed photo from Roy Rogers and The Sons of the Pioneers, inscribed to (Lloyd) Pop Copas, better known as *Grand Ole Opry* star Cowboy Copas. Leonard Slye and Lloyd Copas were childhood friends. (L to R) The Farr Brothers, Tim Spencer, Roy Rogers, and Bob Nolan. It is not known why they called Copas "Pop." *Photo courtesy of Mike Copas.*

he stayed at the home of his sister, Cleda, on Williams Street. That gave him time with her and allowed him to sometimes slip out to Lucasville or Duck Run to do what he really liked, visit with his childhood chums.

Jeff believed he also did that to allow attention from fans to be given to the other stars there for the festival. Jeff learned that Roy was not one to steal the show.

Roy was modest. Each year a large breakfast gathering took place that included a sizable Western show of rope tricks, shoot-outs, re-enactments, look-a-like contests, singing, movies, and all-star introductions. Roy always arrived late. They introduced him and he congratulated all the visiting stars.

Other Western movie personalities attended the festival. Native American star and environmental activist, Iron Eyes Cody, with his fine lady on his arm, was well-liked. Tall, handsome Sunset Carson with a pleasant voice and twinkling eyes had a concession every year. So did bullwhip master, Lash LaRue, the man in black. He was the favorite of many and always the life of the party. So many fans saw these and other stars in movie houses across America and locals enjoyed them at the Eastland, Westland, Pan, Empress, Lyric, and Garden theaters. What satisfaction to see them in person and be able to look into their eyes.

One morning after breakfast with the stars, the hotel manager came running to Jeff's office and exclaimed, "You have to come with me to the pool." When they arrived, employees were cleaning up the area, preparing to close the pool. A woman sat in one of the chairs and refused to leave. Jeff told her the area had to be closed but first it needed to be cleaned up but no amount of persuasion would move her. She explained, "Roy Rogers sat in this chair and

I'm not getting up until you sell it to me." Finally, Jeff asked the manager to check the price of the chair. The manager returned and saying it cost $139.00. He relayed that to the seated woman, she forked over the money and, quite pleased with herself, proudly walked away carrying her Roy Rogers' chair.

Jeff Albrecht has owned the hotel for a long time. He got to know Roy Rogers pretty well. Jeff found him to be "a person just like you and me, same emotions and frustrations. He wanted to be at ease, to avoid tension. A kind man, fame and fortune did not affect him."

Russell and Alma Euton Hoffer on the porch at their home in Henley, Ohio, 2013. *Photo courtesy of John Roger Simon.*

The young man who lived near town was out in the country visiting his cousin. He was telling his cousin that near town where he lived, he could get all sorts of new things that those who lived in the country didn't even know about. He held out a cylindrical object and said, "Look, here is an example. This is a new invention."

The country fellow said, "I never saw anything that looked like that before. What is it?"

"A thermos bottle," the town man replied.

"What do you do with it?"

"It's to keep hot things hot and cold things cold."

"So what do you have in there right now?"

"Iced tea and chili."

Chapter Seventeen
RUSSELL HOFFER

Russell Hoffer was born and raised in the village of Rarden, Ohio. This gentle, efficient man is the result of growing up in a quiet family who practiced the Golden Rule, and liked to fix things and fix them right.

His father, Cloice, owned a garage in Rarden which served as the local John Deere dealership. They handled all John Deere products. That speaks of the sort of businessman Cloice was. Today John Deere dealerships are located only in more densely populated places and require a million dollar investment on the part of the dealer.

Russ was drawn to mechanics from the beginning. As he figured out later it serves three of his strong needs: to meet people, to evaluate problems, and to make machines better. He had a comfortable relationship with his dad and spent all his spare time at the shop. Cloice was an efficient teacher. He hired good help. They included Russell who worked on everything he could. As he worked, he learned.

At age fourteen, Russ quit his formal education while a sophomore at Rarden High School and went to work full-time at the garage. There was plenty to do and Russ loved it. When

World War II came, there weren't as many men available in the workforce and that required Russ becoming more involved.

While developing his mechanical skills, Russ naturally wanted his own car to work on. Don Mason, a Rarden farmer, had a 1932 black Chevy two-door sedan sitting out in a field. It wouldn't run. Russ gave fifty dollars for the Chevy. Rusty and neglected, a lot of repair was needed but, typical of Russ, he got it going.

Russ had taken a shine to "the girls" so the old Chevy came in handy. He met Alma Euton and they hit it off. When Russ was eighteen, he and Alma "jumped the broom."

The young couple liked attending movies together. Movies were new to Russ for his mother did not approve of going to the show. One of the cowboys Russ and Alma particularly liked was Roy Rogers. His movies were good and Roy was handy with horses. Russ knew Roy came from nearby, but had not paid it much mind.

Russ and Alma lived in the east end of Rarden. A favorite pastime was taking Sunday drives together. One day in 1949 they were in the Hanging Rock area and saw a sign at the raceway. That day they attended their first stock car race. Any kind of car could be used. To qualify as a stock car, it had to have the same engine and parts as when it was made. Russ is not one with a need for domination, but the aura of all those cars drew him in. He wanted to see what he could do racing cars and he told Alma, "I'd like to do that." She didn't like the idea because the cars were required to have roll bars and seat belts, obvious indications there were safety hazards.

That winter he built his first racer, a 1940 Ford V-8 coupe. A flat head Ford limits what you can do without a lot of money.

Regulations allowed that an additional car part could be used if it is original. Russ got a 1938 Chevy coupe with overhead valves, a six-cylinder. He won with it.

His first race was at Portsmouth Speedway at Friendship, Ohio. Though he did not place first that first year, it proved a good learning experience. In his second year he did begin to win. He raced against some of the better local drivers such as Red Coleman, Chet Hackworth, Jack Stockholm, Tony Montavon, Junior and Paul Spencer, Gene Comstock, Carrol Speck, and others. He also raced against big time visiting racers.

Home life for Russ was interrupted when he was called into the army during the 1950s. G. Sam Piatt wrote in the *Portsmouth Daily Times* about the Korean War era veteran. Russ was tested and though he had many skills, he had not learned to be a good reader. Having no false pretenses, he went to reading school. Eight weeks of basic training was done at Fort Knox, Kentucky. Twenty-two weeks were spent in truck and tank mechanic school at Fort Aberdeen Proving Grounds, Maryland. He then spent a few days at Fort Dix, New Jersey before he was moved to the Brooklyn Naval Yards. There he boarded a battleship that had been used in WWII, the *George W. Gothels*. The ship carried 1,800 soldiers and 1,800 civilians. The Atlantic Ocean was turbulent and soldiers were housed up front where the ride was the roughest.

Russ hails from southern Ohio where the speech reflects the culture. Pronunciation and use of words is done "our way." For example, some call a sack, a *poke*. Soon after sailing, each person on board the *G.W. Goethels* was issued a sack in case of sea sickness. Russ asked, "I wonder what we're supposed to do with these pokes?" His buddies laughed and asked what a poke was. From then on, even in Europe the boys all called him *Poke*.

The ship landed in Bremerhaven, Germany, and Russ was stationed at Swibruchen. Later he moved to Saint John De Angeles ordinance depot in France where he rebuilt army trucks and Jeeps.

In France, Russ had an experience that impacted his life greatly. He loved racing and had four good years of racing experience before he entered the Army. Alma was opposed to it, but Russ intended to return to racing when discharged. One day he went to a big race in Lemone, France, and a tragic accident happened. An axle broke and the wreckage went up through the audience. One hundred and twenty-eight people were killed. The accident made a deep impression and he resolved not to race again but to go home and be a good mechanic.

Russ was discharged and tickled to be home. He and Alma returned to Sunday drives and attending cowboy Westerns. There were theater houses in both Peebles and Portsmouth that showed Westerns and Roy Rogers was still riding the range.

Russ went back to work with his father; the Rarden garage looked good to him. Paul Koch also worked for Cloice then. He had been a classmate of Leonard Slye's at Duck Run and told stories of that time. Leonard had learned guitar and played at school. He rode his horse to school some days and tied it outside. All that made Leonard seem special, even though he had been a poor kid from Inskeep Road.

As Cloice aged, business slowed. He gave up the John Deere dealership in 1961. The garage operated until 1967 but then closed.

Russ went to Dayton, Ohio, and worked part-time as a welder at Pyper Construction Company. He didn't like it very well so he returned home. The owner of the Pyper Construction Company drove to Rarden and asked Russ to return and work full-time. Russ accepted the offer, worked there twenty-one years, then retired.

Soon after Russ had returned to Dayton, the shop boss was fired and Russ was put in his position. He didn't care for it much but worked as boss until they hired another, Joe Wheeler. Joe was a good guy and all he talked about was Roy Rogers. When Joe was growing up, he often wore a Roy Rogers cowboy suit, Roy Rogers guns, boots, belt, and hat. He still carried his Roy Rogers dinner bucket to work. When he learned that Russ came from Roy's home community, he really got excited.

Another local man, Conway Kratzer, worked at Pyper's. Conway grew up close to Russ out on Thompson Hill near Otway. Conway, a personable man, got a great kick out of Joe and his antics. He even called him *Roy*. Conway drove a Ute, a large earthmover, for Pyper's. One day the Ute broke down. Usually it was Joe who went out and fixed Utes, but that day Russ was sent. Conway said, "Where's Roy?"

Russ' wife, Alma, was sometimes employed by Georgia Furr at the annual Roy Rogers Festival. She helped with everything, especially food preparation and clean up, and arranging the pool area.

Alma and Russ lived in the Northwest School District. When the new high school was dedicated, Roy Rogers was the speaker for the large crowd who attended the event. Alma was there. The school sits near Roy's homeplace and close to Duck Run.

Russ and Alma have a son Mark Hoffer, a well respected worker who learned greatly from Russ. Mark was an avid bicycle rider. One day he rode the bike from home over Route

Mark Hoffer with the 1918 Fairbanks-Morris stationary engine at the Simon Farm in 2013. *Photo courtesy of Gary Hurn.*

73 to Union School on the flats and from there up Arion road to crossroads on Pleasant Hill. He went to see Blake Travis and Blake was at his grandparents John and Mildred Miller. She was known as "Bobe" and after attending school with Leonard Slye they remained lifelong friends. He often walked in anannounced always on the search for some of her good pie.

On this day they were in the living room and Leonard walked in asking for a certain kind of pie. Bobe didn't have that flavor so they all sat down together and ate the kind she had, a spontaneous experience with Roy Rogers.

Today, Russ and Alma enjoy retirement together. Russ is past eighty-years-old but works everyday, always busy. He is sought by neighbors and area farmers to care for their equipment. "If it won't start, get Russ." Two signs hang on their kitchen door:

One nice person and one old grump live here

and

If Mama's not happy, nobody's happy.

Frank Waller at his Waller Stone Company office in McDermott, Ohio, April 2014. *Photo courtesy of Rhonda Boldman Markassel.*

My Bonnie leaned over the gas tank
The contents therein to see
She lighted a match to assist her,
Oh bring back my Bonnie to me.

Chapter Eighteen
FRANK WALLER

This story was researched with the help of the Waller Brothers' production manager, Connie Scott, and Rhonda Boldman Markassel, the Wallers' secretary for the past forty years. Rhonda, a piano player, was a student in my sixth grade class at McDermott School in 1965, my first year teaching.

Frank Waller and Leonard Slye grew up in the community of McDermott, Ohio. Frank developed a vast knowledge of area sandstone while Leonard honed the skills necessary to star in the movies so popular in their day—B Westerns. They were of such quality and consistent story line, former *Grand Ole Opry* manager Dee Kilpatrick commented it took only seven days to make that kind of film.

Brothers named McDermott were also interested in the area's stone. They saw potential in the Brush Creek stone ledges and their stone business. As the nearby town was laid, it was named after them—McDermott.

Near that time Lafayette Taylor came to Rarden, Ohio, in pursuit of timber. As his timber industry developed, he noticed stone ledges in the area and thought he could harvest those, too. He ran an article in a trade magazine seeking someone to quarry stone so he would be able to mill it. The Waller Brothers— Francis,

Clark, and Charles—of Lancaster, Ohio, answered the ad. About 1885 a deal was struck and they established their quarry at Rarden.

Mr. Taylor settled in Rarden and built a swell home that stands today. As his knowledge of stone grew, however, he felt that the supply and quality of rock was better in McDermott. Soon after 1900, Taylor bought the McDermott stone business from a Mr. Smith. He moved there after closing his Rarden venture.

He bought the two-story hotel built of stone in downtown McDermott, added a third floor, and made that his home. He built a museum next door to house the big game trophies he hunted and preserved. Both buildings are still standing and his home is now Rest Haven Nursing Home.

The Wallers closed their Rarden quarry, moving to McDermott in order to continue to supply Taylor with stone. It was a mutually beneficial arrangement until about 1915 when Taylor told the Wallers he had another way to get stone. But the Wallers had bought land that occupied a semi-circular area around where their office is located today. They quarried and milled stone there and continued to buy other area land rich in sandstone. The Waller stone business was in need of ready funds and was advanced financially by the Williams and Selby Shoe companies.

Stone layers were formed during the Ice Age by glacial pressure. Stone type and quality is determined by sedimentation and the amount of pressure it has received. Each layer is separated by shale. If the ground cover is too deep, stone is sometimes quarried underground. The Wallers had intended to quarry an underground section between McDermott and Pond Creek, but that effort was abandoned. They did some surface quarry work on the Simon place on Pond Creek, however.

The quarrying of stone and the growth of McDermott town

puts one in mind of coal camp development in Appalachia. A company store once stood where the quarry office is today. Part of it remains. Employees' families bought food and supplies there and the cost was deducted from their pay. Company houses were homes for employees. Shanties were built behind the company store for bachelors.

The town grew but times were slower. Four passenger trains ran to Portsmouth everyday. The whistle blew for work time, lunchtime, and quitting time. Some packed their lunch; some walked home. In town you could get a large-scoop ice cream cone for a nickel at Joe Mope's store, or choose to shop at Jack McNeal's, Bill White's, or Helen Higgins' clothing store.

Employees had a quiet, but strong bond. They worked hard together and yielded good products—some in the quarry, others in the mill. Mark Crawford worked there. So did Leroy Montgomery, Mick Gillette, Red Euton, Joe Prose, Ray Boldman, and Friday Miller. Frank recalls the men drinking from a spring behind the store. He often carried a three gallon bucket of the spring water to the men and they drank from a dipper.

Building stones were in demand and the Waller Brothers Stone Company grew. They produced a variety of products such as bridge stones, liners for steel mill pickling tanks, burial vaults, and jail cell blocks. Some area buildings made of stone were the Portsmouth Post Office, the Library, Manley Methodist Church, and several schools including McDermott Elementary and Secondary.

In the 1950s a new product was developed as a result of interesting circumstances. The Quaker Oats Company made bran cereals that gave off an acidic byproduct. They wanted to find a use for it. The Kewaunee Institute, makers of chemical laboratory furniture, was asked to help. The Wallers found sandstone could be impregnated with the chemical byproduct. It grew stronger, did not break, and worked better than any other stone product in America. The material took three weeks of processing and was called Kemrock.

Kewaunee, a name from Native Americans located in the current-day Wisconsin area, worked with Wallers to build a local plant where they could manufacture the new high quality lab tables. Wallers furnished the land, supplies, equipment, and manpower. Kewaunee marketed Kemrock and paid Wallers a royalty. For about fifty years there was little competition to the product and it complemented the Wallers' business nicely. Less expensive, similar products manufactured today have since cut into sales.

Presently, the Waller Brothers Stone Company has three managing partners: third generation Frank Waller is general manager, Lowell Shope, and C.D. Scott. They make Scioto County sandstone products.

Leonard Slye daydreamed and may have wondered if he would work in the quarry. His homeplace is now owned by Mary Crabtree. Mary's husband, Ferrell, worked at Waller's. In later years Charlie Hiles sold land on Allen Hollow to the Wallers. Others on Allen and Inskeep did, too. When that area was quarried, Roy Rogers felt uneasy about the land usage but held no ill will toward the Waller family.

Frank Waller's Aunt Catherine, his dad's youngest sister, was born in 1915. She and Leonard Slye met in McDermott. They dated and she liked Leonard. She often shared positive memories of him with her family.

In childhood Frank and his chums often took the morning train to Portsmouth and returned home on an evening one. They loved to go to the show, especially Westerns at the Lyric. The shows were exciting and had good music. They saw Hopalong Cassidy, the Lone Ranger, Gene Autry, and Roy Rogers. They thought it was great that Roy was from around home. Frank liked the Palamino, Trigger, and the silver on Roy's saddle. Inspired, Frank bought a metal Roy Rogers dinner bucket, toted it to school, and has it yet today. When Frank went to college, his friends wanted to hear about Roy and the community.

Scioto County has one of the best county fairs in Ohio and Roy liked to come home for it. Frank's family attended McDermott Methodist Church and the church had a booth at the fair with a reputation for good food. Frank's mother, Gay Waller, worked the booth. Waller's built special stone tubs to hold ice and bottles of pop. Frank's job was to select the right flavor and open it for patrons. Roy came to their booth to see old friends and to eat— especially pie which was his favorite. When Frank knew Roy was coming to the fair, he'd arrive early. Roy talked, laughed, and shook hands with everyone.

Roy Rogers came to McDermott to speak at the dedication of the new post office in 1959. The old one was part of Denver Duncan's Store and the new one was near it. Cotton Thompson, the postmaster, had married a Duncan. Roy was friends with the Duncan family and agreed to be the speaker. Frank went with some teenage friends. The town was packed. It seemed everybody was there and nearly all of them, including Frank, shook hands with Roy. He stayed a long time, walking about and "mixing." He knew so many who were there and he appeared filled with joy.

Today Frank Waller enjoys his family and stays involved in the community. He supports Ohio State University sports and still markets the quality stone that put McDermott on the map.

Roy Rogers visits with Dr. Richard Brunner at his dentist office in Portsmouth, Ohio. 1990s. *Photo courtesy of Dr. Richard Brunner.*

Why did the Amish woman divorce her husband?
He was driving her buggy.

Chapter Nineteen
DR. RICHARD BRUNNER

When Doctor Richard Brunner attended an appearance by Roy Rogers in downtown Portsmouth, Ohio, as a part of the largest crowd he had ever seen in that city, he hardly dreamed that one day Roy would sit in his dental chair.

Richard Brunner worked hard to attain his dream of practicing dentistry. The United States Navy paid his way through dental school at Ohio State University where he graduated in June 1945, in the B12 Navy Program. In return he was obliged to work as a naval dentist for two years.

His first assignment from June 1945 until April 1946 was Hunter's Point Naval Shipyard in San Francisco, California, near present day Candlestick Park. In April 1946 he received orders to the Fleet Marine Force at Pearl Harbor, but was soon transferred to Tien Sien, China, and attached to the Seventh Service Regiment of the First Marine Division who had been given orders to repatriate Japanese citizens from China to Japan. In May 1947 Dr. Brunner was sent to Mare Island for discharge.

Having fulfilled his Naval obligation, Dr. Brunner returned

to Portsmouth. Williams Manufacturing Company had opened a clinic for its employees and he was hired as clinic dentist. After 1955 Dr. Brunner worked for a while with Dr. Coburn. Then he held his own practice for several years in the National Bank Building of Portsmouth.

In 1981 Cleda Willoughby, whose brother was Roy Rogers, retired from her work with the Roy Rogers Museum at Victorville and came home to Portsmouth. Roy Rogers' former teacher and mentor, Guy Bumgarner, and his wife, Nell, were patients of Dr. Brunner and friends of Cleda. When Cleda needed a dentist they suggested the good doctor.

Dr. Brunner was a great Roy Rogers fan.

One day in the 1990s Cleda left a phone message for Dr. Brunner. When he returned the call, a man answered and said that Cleda could not come to the phone but explained, "This is her brother, Roy, and she'll call you."

When Cleda phoned she related that her niece was there visiting and she needed dental attention. She asked Dr. Brunner if he could work her into his schedule. He replied, "Sure I can work her in if you let Roy bring her to the office."

Cleda asked Roy to take their niece to the dental office. When they arrived, Lindsey Hedrick, head of Ohio Power Company, was in the dental chair. His care was soon completed. Then introductions were made and everyone visited a while. Roy made everyone comfortable. Pictures were taken of Mr. Hedrick, Dr. Brunner's chairside dental assistant Emma Phipps, another office girl, Dr. Brunner, Cleda's niece, and Roy Rogers sitting in Dr. Brunner's dental chair.

The girl's dental needs were attended to and a most unusual workday was completed.

Dr. Brunner and Cleda maintained their friendship until her death. Today he is enjoying an active retirement in his Portsmouth home.

Zeke served during World War II in Ireland. When the war was over he made his way toward the sea to board a ship for home. At the dock he stopped because of a woman standing there, her body heaving as she wept. Zeke was so touched he went to her, lay his hand on her shoulder, and asked, "Why are you weeping?"

She told him that during the war her boy had sailed for America but that he never wrote and she was worried sick about him. Then she asked Zeke, "Do you suppose you could find him?"

Zeke inquired, What's your boy's name?"

She replied, "Dunne. And he lives in a little brown shack on a bank in West Virginia."

Zeke knew he'd have to pass through West Virginia on his way back home to Kentucky, so he agreed. He crossed the sea and after a few stops someone told him the next stop would be West Virginia. The ship docked and Zeke got off. He walked into a nearby store and asked the clerk if he knew where there was a little brown shack on a bank. The fellow replied that there was a shack like that out back. Zeke approached the shack and knocked on the door. A man came out and Zeke asked, "Are you Dunne?"

The man answered, "Yes, I'm done," and Zeke said, "Why don't you write your poor old mother in Ireland? She's worried sick about you!"

Chapter Twenty
SAM McKIBBEN

Sam McKibben was born in Youngstown, Ohio, into a family of steelworkers. His people had come there from County Antrim, Ireland. When he flashes his mischevious smile, it may be a sign that one of his ditties is on the way:

> I once knew a man they
> called Moon.
> Haven't seen him since
> way past June.
> Even then he couldn't
> carry a tune,
> That rascal, Harry Moon.

Sam McKibben in his early career days. *Photo courtesy of Sam McKibben.*

Sam and his sister Carol are the two children of Raymond J. and Martha Cash McKibben. After their dad attended Ohio State University law school, he went to work for Elliott Ness in the Bureau of Alcohol, Tobacco and Firearms in pursuit of illegal whiskey during Prohibition before the 18th Amendment was repealed.

Sam's family moved to Portsmouth in 1944 where Sam was schooled at Lincoln Elementary and Portsmouth High School, both good experiences. He likes learning.

Sam's colorful manner is ever present but he found the order of military life suitable, too. In 1956 he began a long and varied military component of his life. It included active duty Air Force service until 1960, Air Force Reserve from 1969 through 1976, and the Naval Reserve until 1985. At that time he went active until 1989, reaching the rank of chief petty officer. He settled back into the reserves from 1989 through 1998 and reached the rank of Lieutenant. Sam looks dearly on his thirty-two military years and would do it all again.

Sam is well known locally for another lifelong interest, being an announcer on radio. It began in 1959 while stationed in Lake Charles, Louisiana. He became staff announcer on the local station and then came home to WPAY to serve in the same capacity. In 1962 he moved to WNXT as an on air announcer. In 1967 he learned something about himself when he took a job at WSAZ TV in Huntington, West Virginia, on the midnight-to-six AM shift. He was not cut out for the shift or the drive.

Sam returned to WNXT in 1968 and also married Jeanette Burnette, his girl for life, from the Big Run community. She was a very supportive wife and they were completely comfortable with one another.

A deadly tornado hit northern Kentucky and Wheelersburg, Ohio, in 1968. It took seven lives and caused mass destruction.

Sam and Bill Dawson went to Wheelersburg and interviewed survivors first hand.

In 1972 Sam began attending college and moved to Athens where he also worked at WATH. After earning a degree in radio and TV communication, he moved to WIMA in Lima, Ohio, and got into the news business.

In 1973 he came home to WPAY as news director, but then went to WOSU radio in Columbus. He explored other interests, too, and became a nursing home administratror in 1990. After a return to radio, he tried his hand as director of a local transportation company, Access Scioto County. He taught for a while—K through twelve— in public schools, and was also an instructor of communications at Shawnee State University.

In the past several years Sam has been news director and public affairs director at WNXT. Local listeners like him. In such a life he has met interesting and famous people, Roy Rogers included.

Sam read a story about a *Wall Street Journal* writer who visited California. While there he went to speak with Roy. He asked Roy if they could go over to Victorville for the interview. As Roy was putting his hat on, he said to his wife, "Dale, I'm going over to the museum to play Roy Rogers." The man took special notice of Roy's and Dale's stuffed animals on display. Of their beloved dog, Biscuit, Roy said, "We have a taxidermist friend here and he preserved our dog". Next they came upon Dale's horse, Buttermilk, of whom Roy explained they felt the same way, so they had her stuffed as well. When Trigger came into view Roy said, "And you know how I loved Trigger."

The journalist looked at Roy and commented, "Don't get me wrong, Roy, but for Dale's sake, I hope you die first."

At home Sam once spent a good evening in Harold's Restaurant attending a dinner recognizing Dale Evans, put on by the Portsmouth Area Chamber of Commerce. Dale, a big band singer and movie star, worked nicely with the crowd and was gracious.

And Sam had a personal experience with Roy Rogers that probably no one else has had. He was working at WPAY in the late '70s on the 5 A.M. shift. It was pouring rain. He parked his car at Selby Shoes and walked around the building toward 1009 Gallia Street, the WPAY entrance. It was pitch dark, the door was locked, and a man stood at the door in a heavy black raincoat and hat. Sam didn't recognize the man and felt alarmed, but he spoke. Sam saw his face and then recognized Roy's voice. Roy seemed shorter than usual without his cowboy hat and boots. Sam opened the door and they talked as they ascended the steps to the studio. Roy and Zeke Mullins were great friends and Roy sometimes came to visit. Zeke was another local radio celebrity and already on the job that morning. They visited for ninety minutes or so. Sam even heard singing and guitar coming from Zeke's room.

In Sam's life of radio, some of those with whom he worked were Bob Wagner, Bill Dawson, Jim Hufferd, Mary Ellen Thuma, Frank Balmert, Roy Vastine, Jim Rowland, Bill Warnock, Sandy Dresback, Steve Hayes, Zeke Mullins, Jan Morton, and Norma Graf.

When asked why he chose radio as a profession Sam recalled, "My generation heard radio. I was taken by it as a child. I sat glued in front of ours when F.D.R. had fireside chats. It was amazing to hear that voice come out of there. I wrote essays in school about broadcasting and some of us boys hung around

WPAY. D.J. Don Ferris liked kids and let them read the baseball scores." Sam has talents suited for his work. He is interested in others, has a good memory, and can spin an interesting story with an exceptional voice. He also has Irish eyes that "twinkle rather than glare."

Today Sam works at WNXT and is mentor to younger radio persons. He cares for his home and his beloved cat, Midnight, attends the life center, and enjoys varied acquaintenances. He is often heard as the featured speaker at local military events.

And Sam can claim a special experience early one rainy morning with the King of the Cowboys who came to WPAY in a long black raincoat.

At Doris' request, Zeke picked up a whole chicken for her to cook. Soon he heard her in the kitchen struggling over it. Doris told Zeke she was able to get it plucked and the pin feathers out, but she'd tried everything and just couldn't get the hair off.

Zeke studied a bit, then went into the other room and got his safety razor. He used that on the chicken and the hair came right off. After finishing, Zeke went in the other room and composed a letter to the Schick Razor Company. He told them he and his wife had used everything but hadn't been able to get the hair off their chicken until they resorted to his Schick safety razor — and it took the hair right off!

A couple off weeks later Zeke received a letter from the president of the Schick Company. The letter read: "Dear Mr. Mullins, Our board of directors and I carefully considered your letter and as a result of it, next year our company will produce a new line of razors. We'll have the women's Schick, the men's Schick, and the chicken Schick."

Chapter Twenty-One
SHARON MUSSER SCOTT

Sharon Scott was born to parents who lived near the New Boston and Portsmouth city line. Her dad, Ernest Musser, came to Ohio from Greenup County, Kentucky, with his family. He attended New Boston schools and played football so he would be able to use the showers. During the Great Panic he made the adventuresome decision to quit school and become a hobo along with his chum, Clay Harmon. When he returned home he went to work in the electrical department of Detroit Steel Corporation.

Professor of Nursing, Sharon Musser Scott at Shawnee State University in Portsmouth, Ohio. *Photo courtesy of Sharon Musser Scott.*

Sharon's mother, Romona Chapman, was a Lewis County, Kentucky, girl. She came to Ohio to be caretaker of the John and Minnie Fisher family. The Fishers and Mussers were related. Ernest and Romona met, married, and lived in the three thousand block of Gallia Street in Portsmouth. There they raised three children, Betty, Sharon, and Eula (Teeny). Romona was a housewife and great cook and worked at Williams Shoe Factory. An enterprising woman, she bought the Cotton Montel Lunch Room. She later married Roy Thompson and they renamed it Thompson's Bar and Grill.

Betty managed telephone transmissions for her employer in Cincinnati. Teeny took over the running of Thompson's. She decorated the place in a beautiful and rustic manner.

Sharon's neighborhood was blessed with children and because of movies, comic books, and TV, the old west played into a lot of their activities. A favorite game was the wagon train. It ran on the south side of Gallia Street toward the Norfolk and Western railroad terminals, the round house, and the historic Y.M.C.A. where Blind Ed Haley played the fiddle. Their train was made up of bicycles, wagons, tricycles, and kids riding stick horses. They fancied it to be straight out of the old west, a product of the aura cast by Roy Rogers, Dale Evans, and similar stars. Most of them went to the B Westerns at the Ohio and the Pan theaters and could do a recognizable imitation of the characters.

The gang included the Willis kids, Carlos Collingsworth and his sisters, the Sizemores, the Cowlings, the Spears, the Askews, the Coles, the Ishmails, Sharon, Betty, and Teeny. One day a Willis boy was up in a tree out of sight with his lasso. As the train passed beneath, he roped Sharon. Then he came down the tree and removed the rope—from around her neck.

Sharon's sister, Betty, was her main playmate. Their parents often gave them money for a show, candy, and bus fare home. Sharon always blew her bus money on candy and walked home.

Betty loved horses and sometimes agreed to walk home with Sharon if she would agree to ride stick horses home. Sharon didn't mind the deal. All this was inspired by Betty's favorite horse, Trigger.

Sharon has another reason to feel connected to Roy and Dale. She distracted herself with play and fantasy because her mother was confined to a tuberculosis sanitarium for some time.

Eula and Howard Marcum lived across Gallia Street from the Mussers. Eula liked kids and was good to Sharon, so she visited Eula often. Eula bought Dale's book, *Angel Unaware*, and read it to Sharon. It told of Roy and Dale losing their daughter at a young age. The book expressed Dale's love of her child, her sorrow in her death, and how her faith soothed her. It expressed her feelings in a heartfelt and genuine way.

Sharon attended Garfield and McKinley Elementary Schools, and graduated from Portsmouth High School. She married Ralph Scott and had two children, Ralph and Carol Dawn, at a young age. Ralph is a businessman and a long distance truck driver. Dawn operates a funeral home.

Aspiring to be a nurse, Sharon attended the Ohio University School of Nursing. She worked as a nurse at Scioto Memorial Hospital and at Goodyear. In 1978 she began a long and interesting career as an instructor of nursing at Shawnee State University. While working full time, she earned two Master's Degrees, one in Higher Education from Ohio University, and a Master's of Science in nursing at Bellarmine University.

A lifelong fan of Roy Rogers and Dale Evans, Sharon had a special experience in meeting Cleda Willoughby through local, traditional music circles. She and Cleda took part in a bus trip to Norris, Tennessee, with Art and Patty Murphy, hosted by Georgia

Cleda Willoughby speaks with Grandpa Jones on the main stage of the Museum of Appalachian's Tennesse Fall Homecoming in Norris, Tennessee, mid 1990s. *Photo courtesy of Earlene Woten.*

Furr. The Museum of Appalachia, located in Norris, holds the largest Appalachian festival in America. Loyal Jones, Director of the Appalachian Center in Berea, Kentucky, met Cleda and immediately got the attention of John Rice Irwin who operates the event. John Rice took Cleda to the main stage and interviewed her in front of the entire crowd. The first thing John said was, "You're Roy Rogers' sister," to which she quietly but assertively replied, "No. Roy Rogers is my brother." Cleda was invited to perform at the 1996 festival along with other local musicians but that was not to be. In 1996 Cleda became ill.

Sharon's profession allowed a memorable experience for her. As a nursing instructor she lectured some days and had practical clinical experiences for the student nurses at the hospital other days. On clinical days Sharon arrived at the hospital before 7 A.M. in order to evaluate and select patients relevant to her students' present course of study. She learned one morning that Cleda Slye Willoughby was a patient on her floor and that her brother, Roy, was home to visit. Sharon's thoughts went back to her Garfield school days and the Roy Rogers and Dale Evans Double R Bar

Ranch thermos she carried to school. Sharon selected Cleda as a patient.

Each clinical consisted of nine students. This group had eight females and one male, Jason Martin. Sharon asked the group if any of them had ever fancied themselves cowboys or cowgirls. Jason spoke up that he had. Sharon selected Jason, a capable student, and said, "I'd like you to care for Cleda Willoughby. Her brother is Roy Rogers." She discussed particulars of Cleda's care and told him that Roy was in her room. Jason, a Minford High School graduate, is a son of Tom and Jan Martin. They are great Roy Rogers fans. Jason and his wife, Jill, live in Proctorville, Ohio. Jason was introduced to Cleda, Roy, and Dale, and he worked in and out of the room all day. He was involved in conversation with each of them and knows today how special that was.

After the shift began, Sharon went into the room to talk to Cleda and Jason and to check the status of care. She knew Roy was there for she'd seen him in the hall earlier. When she met Roy and saw Dale sitting beside him, her knees buckled. That scene, after having Dale's book read to her, and knowing the impact the couple had on America, was incredible. Roy and Dale stayed much of the day, and Sharon was able to visit with all of them. That day added special color to her career.

With Dale and Roy she had a warm, personal experience. And to be sure, Sharon treasures her Roy Rogers and Dale Evans Double R Bar Ranch thermos bottle!

Sharon is retired and lives on the beautiful Ohio River. She built much of her home herself. She loves her dogs and cats, and special time with her grandson and several other family members. Sharon reads and is an avid quilter.

Les Leverett and his sweetheart and wife Dorothy Vandiver Leverett. *Photo courtesy of Les Leverett.*

Is it true that roosters lay those double yolk eggs?

Chapter Twenty-Two
LES LEVERETT

One of the most talented and honored American photographers is Les Leverett. He was born in Montgomery, Alabama, in 1927 to William and Hassie Mae Leverett and was raised in a home with two sisters. When his father, a Baptist evangelist, died, Les continued his formal education but went to work as well at a young age. In tenth grade, however, he quit school and began working full time as a welder at Alabama Dry Dock and Shipbuilding Company in Mobile, Alabama.

At age eighteen, Les was drafted into the Army in 1945. Trained in Denver, he was then assigned to a troop ship, the Haverford Victory, carrying replacement troops to Europe and returning with war weary men. After the war, he developed an interest in photography that began with experiments with his dad's Civil War binoculars. He used them to project self drawn images on the bedroom shades.

In February 1949, Les married Dorothy Vandiver, the girl he still calls his sweetheart. They have two sons, John and Gary, and a daughter, Leslie Elizabeth.

Dorothy's work at the National Life and Accident Insurance Company took them to Nashville. In 1960, Les was invited by

National Life to start a photography department. He worked for National Life but more interesting to him, also took pictures for the *Opry* radio station WSM (We Shield Millions) and *The Grand Ole*

(L to R) Hank Snow, Roy Rogers, and Dale Evans on *The Grand Ole Opry*. *Photo courtesy of Les Leverett.*

Roy Rogers performs on *The Grand Ole Opry* accompanied by the group Riders in the Sky. (L to R) Roy Rogers, Too Slim (Fred LaBour), Ranger Doug (Douglas B. Green), Woody Paul (Paul Chrisman), and *Opry* staff fiddler Joe Edwards. August 30, 1979. *Photo courtesy of Les Leverett.*

(L to R) *Grand Old Opry* step dancer Ben Smathers, Roy Roger's manager Art Rush, Roy Rogers, and *Opry* stage manager, Vito Pellettieri. May 16, 1970. *Photo courtesy of Les Leverett.*

Roy Rogers and Dale Evans perform on *The Grand Ole Opry*. Country music star Hank Snow stands in the shadows to the right. May 16, 1970. *Photo courtesy of Les Leverett.*

Opry. His tenure as *Opry* photographer continued for thirty-two years until his retirement in 1992.

His work has been shown on hundreds of albums, books, magazines, newspapers, videos, and other places. On a personal note, a Les Leverett photo is the cover image on my book, *Cowboy Copas and the Golden Age of Country Music.* A perfect picture, it shows Copas playing "Alabam" onstage of the Ryman Auditorium. Through the contact in acquiring the photo for my book, Les and I formed a warm friendship.

Les, who loves a good laugh, pays close attention to those who inspire humor. Grandpa Jones was one of his favorites. They often roomed together on duck hunting trips. They were in a hotel lobby and a man excitedly ran up to Grandpa and said, "Grandpa, I met you on an elevator one day," to which Grandpa replied, "Was it going up or down?" He often made reference to the weather. In a dry time he might say, "It's been so dry the old cow is giving that powder milk."

The job Les held included work at the great *Hee Haw* program. That made Les laugh. When Roy Rogers and Dale Evans were

(L to R) On the *Hee Haw* set, producer Sam Lovullo, Buck Owens, Dale Evans, Roy Rogers, director Bob Boatman, and Roy Clark. October 27, 1976. *Photo courtesy of Les Leverett.*

Dale Evans and Roy Rogers in their bib overalls and straw hats on the set of the television show *Hee Haw*. *Photo courtesy of Les Leverett.*

guests, they could ham it up with the best of them, taking part in various segments in straw hats. It was reminiscent of Leonard Slye being the ham in plays while a student at Duck Run one-room school.

Roy and Dale were popular guests of the *Grand Ole Opry*, too. On one such visit, Les was asked to film Roy and Dale arriving at Berry Field, the old Nashville airport. Les was accompanied by excellent *Opry* step dancers Ben and Margaret Smathers. They had worked with Roy and Dale on several state fair jobs.

Roy and Dale were coming in from two different places and Dale arrived first. Les, Margaret, Ben, and Tammy Wynette's husband met her. Dale sat in the car with them and had a great talk before Roy got there. When Roy pulled in, they all met and visited on the tarmac. Roy was in his full "Roy Rogers" clothing. Roy's manager, Art Rush, was along and Ben Smathers asked Les to take Art to supper. They went to a steak and biscuit place and "hit were good!" Art told Les he had managed Roy for years even though they never had a written contract. They worked only on handshakes.

When Roy was Leonard Slye, he loved to fish in the many creeks near his Inskeep Road home and, as Roy Rogers, he still wanted to fish. In Nashville, Bill Forshee, a friend to Les, took Roy fishing.

The popular couple fared well at the *Opry*. Sometimes Dale played piano and Roy sang. Les had many photo opportunities. The Ryman dressing rooms were few and a bit congested so the girls usually dressed in the girl's bathroom. When Roy learned this, he chose to do likewise. One night, Les and Dot were standing outside that restroom when Roy came out. It gave Dot and Roy a chance to get acquainted!

Les worked with and visited Roy Rogers several times during Roy's career. Les says, "I am convinced he was a real person, a star without being glittering. Though he was often surrounded by people, he seemed to find time for everyone."

Les Leverett can never retire as he is so vital in country music history, a living resource.

A friendly, pleasant, direct, and helpful man he draws out the character when he meets one.

Roy Rogers with *Grand Ole Opry* square dancers Margaret and Ben Smathers at the Nashville Airport May 16, 1970. *Photo courtesy of Les Leverett.*

Les lives happily at their Goodlettsville, Tennessee, home. He holds abundant awards and continues to earn more. He is soon to be flown to Los Angeles by Annenburg Space for Photography. He is one of thirteen (five living) country music photographers to receive this national honor. Their work will be hung first in Los Angeles, then it will spend time in the Smithsonian exhibit before going to the Country Music Hall of Fame.

Les Leverett is a stimulating man to know, a real friend.

David Bauer on the job at Market Street Hardware, Portsmouth, April 2014. *Photo courtesy of John Roger Simon.*

As the cow said to the farmer, "Thanks for a warm hand on a cool morning."

Chapter Twenty-Three
DAVID BAUER

David Bauer is a Portsmouth, Ohio, native and a 1971 graduate of Notre Dame High School. He is retired after working thirty years in grounds maintenance at Shawnee State Park in historic Roosevelt Game Preserve, the largest forest in Ohio.

Dave's father, Gilbert Bauer, was employed by Sears and Roebuck and traveled to different stores each week. Once he knew his schedule for the following week he would rush an envelope containing that schedule to the local train depot and hand carry it to the porter who would see that its destination was reached quickly. Inside that envelope was his schedule for visiting the various stores that week. Dave often went along with his dad on those depot trips and was impressed by the entire scene. That prompted him to become a model train buff, an interest he holds today.

Another influence in Dave's life was his Uncle Orville Mower who served at Christmas time as a helper of Santa Claus. Dave saw the happiness and helpfulness given by Santa to others and wanted to try it himself. He secured a Santa Claus suit and wore it the first time at a Wheelersburg, Ohio, retirement home. As he walked down the hall a woman came to he door and said, "Santa, come in here. There's a man under the bed."

Santa knelt, looked under the bed, and replied, "Yes, there is a man under here, What do you want me to do?"

She said, "Make him go away," and she went down the hallway.

When she returned Santa said, "Now look under the bed."

She knelt, looked under the bed, and said, "Oh, thank you, Santa."

When Dave was seven-years-old he was already a Roy Rogers fan. In October 1959, Roy had come home to Portsmouth for a visit. A new post office in McDermott, Ohio, was going to hold their opening ceremony and the featured speaker was Roy Rogers. He had grown up close by and had attended two years of high school and played in the band at McDermott School. Dave's mother, Vera Bauer, and his aunt, Juanita Mower, took him to the dedication. It was a warm, October day and Dave was wearing a pair of shorts, no shirt. There was a big crowd, the sun was shining bright, and Dave was lost in the shuffle. B.R. Scholl, an Ohio State highway patrolman was standing nearby. He lifted Dave up and held him so he could better see and hear the ceremony. Dave recalls the patrolman was wearing his winter uniform and the wool scratched his skin but together they witnessed that special event. Their picture was displayed in the Columbus Dispatch magazine section the following Sunday, October 4, 1959. Today, a photo of Roy Rogers hangs inside the McDermott Post Office.

Dave currently works at Market Street Hardware in Portsmouth, which displays a nice Roy Rogers' exhibit. That display prompts customers to tell stories about Roy. One woman told Dave recently of an experience she had in the late 1930s, soon after Roy became a famous cowboy. At the time many locals still called Roy, Leonard.

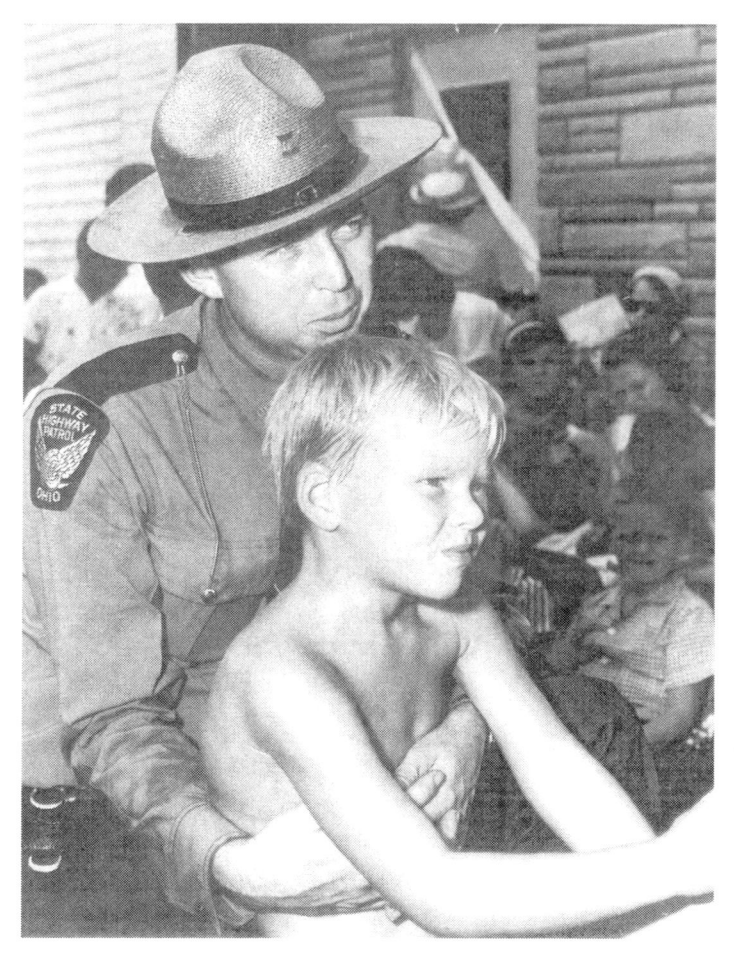

Ohio State Patrolman B.R. Scholl helps seven-year-old David Bauer see his hero Roy Rogers at the Post Office dedication ceremony in McDermott, Ohio, October 1959. *Photo courtesy of David Bauer and The Columbus Dispatch.*

The woman was sitting in a local theater, The Lyric, watching a Roy Rogers Western. Sitting close to her was an elderly woman. It may have been her first time in a movie theater. The film grew more exciting as an outlaw came slipping up on Roy behind a huge rock cliff. The woman jumped up and shouted, "Look out Leonard, they're going to bushwhack you!"

Barbara Pratt stands in front of the Port City Cafe and Pub on Chillicothe Street, Portsmouth, 2013. *Photo courtesy of John Roger Simon.*

"What's fer Supper, Grandma?"
New potatoes and butter beans,
Home cured side that's not too lean,
Sorghum syrup that'll stand the test,
and Barbara Pratt can have the rest.

Chapter Twenty-Four
BARBARA PRATT

Floyd and Janie Clark raised one child, Barbara. She was so special they never had another.

In the 1940s they left Greenfield, Ohio, and came to Portsmouth so Floyd could take work at our thriving Detroit Steel plant. Janie was employed at Selby Shoes. When Selby's closed, she went to work at Consolidated Components in the basement of the Fowler Building. They made military helmets.

As with so many steel working families, the Clarks lived in New Boston, so Barb got her twelve years of schooling there. She liked the school and the town itself. Barb played first clarinet in the band but changed to trombone because of that cute guy, Dennis Day, who played trombone, too.

Barb took her higher education in Richmond at Eastern Kentucky University in the study of recreational therapy. It suited her. She trained at Shriner's Hospital in Lexington, Kentucky, as part of her internship.

Employment began for Barb at Portsmouth Receiving Hospital as an activity therapist. She became director of the department, then moved to public relations and was the director of volunteer services. She worked in client advocacy until retirement.

Barb has two children. Her son, Joseph Clark, married a Bennington from South Webster, Ohio. Joseph graduated from Capitol University and coached football for a time at Kent State. He now teaches in Bowling Green, Kentucky. Barb's daughter, Brooke, is a counselor in Lexington and her husband is an athletic trainer at the University of Kentucky.

After retirement Barb worked as volunteer services and blood services coordinator for the Red Cross for five years. She then became coordinator of the Golden Bears, a senior group who supports Shawnee State University sports. In that capacity, she has met many interesting older residents of our area.

One day in a conversation with Misty Cook, Steve Hayes, and Rick Mayne, Barb suggested they should start a program with a person on the street who interviews people and highlights special events of the area. It was about that time when popular radio personality Zeke Mullins retired. Misty took Barb to the Ramada and held a mock interview in which Barb interviewed Misty. Afterward Misty said, "Barb, you can do it." Barb had been trying sales, but it just didn't fit her personality. The radio management asked her to take Zeke's place and discuss community events with local residents. Barb agreed to try. She set her own format and Cory Maillit ran the board. Eventually Barb managed the program. She learned as she went.

She has been on the job now about seven years. The program focuses on residents of our area and promotes a positive image. It's a boost in self esteem to be on the *Barb Pratt Show*.

Barb's favorite program experience, her morning with Mary Ellen Thuma, was arranged by Debbie Daniels. Mary Ellen had done a similar radio program herself. They celebrated her birthday and Mary Ellen told really interesting stories.

Another highlight was her morning with Frances Strickland, the wife of the Governor of Ohio. Her husband, Ted, grew up on Inskeep Road in the Duck Run area. Frances has a special ability to tell stories. Her secret service people stood outside the door.

Barb has given many people a chance to be on radio for the first time, such as the talented Russell Hoffer. Most are nervous before the show, but glad they did it after it's over.

Barb has met lots of special people, but to meet Roy Rogers was an extra thrill. She had been such a fan of his and had read Dale's books. Barb had a job as local volunteer coordinator. She and a group were on their way to have dinner at the Ramada. When they went in, there sitting on a little raised wall in the lobby were Roy Rogers and Dale Evans. They were waiting for someone to pick them up and take them to Cleda's. Being the outgoing person she is, Barb led the group right over and they introduced themselves. Mrs. Vern Riffe was there. Her husband was Ohio's Speaker of the House of Representatives. Roy and Vern knew one another. Barb's mother, Mrs. Riffe, and Cleda went to church together at First United Methodist. They all visited comfortably and Roy was animated in conversation. Dale was a little less patient and suggested she and Roy could have waited up in their room. Barb noticed Roy's casual demeanor as he let Dale's comment slide off. Barb and the volunteers thanked Roy and Dale for the visit, then went to eat their meal.

(L to R) Roy Rogers, Guy Bumgarner, Dusty Rogers neighborhood boys at Lucasville, Ohio celebration. 1969. *Photo courtesy of Alice Moulton Barker.*

On Barb's radio show, she has interviewed Western stars who came to our town for the Roy Rogers Festival. Roy's son, Dusty, who looks so much like his dad, is one of them. Another is the lady who runs the local Roy Rogers museum. She spoke with a Rogers family member who is an airline stewardess and sings "Happy Trails" with passengers on flights. A man who made a special impression with his stimulating personality was Western star Lash LaRue.

The family member Barb knows best is Dodie Rogers. She's as "genuine as you can get." They met on the show and now are

Facebook friends. Dodie and her husband bring their puppets to Barb's program each year.

There is a new local magazine called Portsmouth Metro. *It features Portsmouth people and events. Harriet Carlson is one of the writers. The first article in the first issue highlights local favorite Barb Pratt and discusses her love of another local favorite, sorghum syrup, and the ways she eats it—warmed up as she sops her biscuit.*

(L to R) Wilma Montavon Brooks, Dale Evans, Roy Rogers, and Don Brooks in Victorville, California 1981. *Photo courtesy of Don Brooks.*

The old fellow up Bear Creek invented a new drink, whiskey and carrot juice. When he drinks it, he feels sort of rough the next day, but he can see a lot better.

Chapter Twenty-Five
DON and WILMA BROOKS

In Don's early life he was a "town boy" and attended Grant School, grades one through three. His family moved and life got better. He got to live in the country. They moved to the Little Bear Creek area near the busy general store owned by August and Lucy Redoutey. Lots of folks got together there and loafed, and August made them welcome as long as they carried in wood for the stove. John and Ed Diehlman sometimes arrived in their A Model Ford. Don loved to listen to everyone's tales. Windy Thompson, Jim O'Brien, Bill Joyce, several Jewetts and other Thompsons—and of course August and Lucy were always there.

Don was a student at Union Elementary, grades four through eight, out on the Flats. He then became a Redbird and graduated from Otway High School. He remembers that two local residents, Rose Ann Joyce and Estle Stall, were among his classmates.

Don's wife, Wilma, grew up on Pond Creek. She was one of a large family raised by Alfred and Alice Staten Montavon. She graduated from McDermott schools. Her mother was also a McDermott graduate and played in the school band with Leonard Slye. Her instrument was the trumpet and his, the clarinet.

Growing up, Don worked on local farms and, later, farmed

(Row one, second from right) Alice Staten holds her trumpet. She is the mother of Wilma Montavon Brooks. (Second row, third from right) Leonard Slye holding the clarinet. *Photo courtesy of Don Brooks, Ed Montavon, and Dave Montavon.*

for himself before being involved in other enterprises. His main occupation in life has been that of a Greyhound bus driver and that has afforded him extraordinary experiences including the opportunity to meet many interesting people. His job covered

The 1926 McDermott High School Band. *Photo courtesy of Don Brooks, Ed Montavon, and Dave Montavon.*

a wide territory. One night in 1960, while Don was asleep in Charleston, West Virginia, the phone rang. Wilma answered and the dispatcher asked, "Is Don a Democrat or a Republican?"

Don said, "Tell him I'm a strong Democrat."

When Don took the phone, the dispatcher said, "Good, you are driving Hubert H. Humphrey." He was to pick up his passenger at six a.m.

Senator Humphrey was a well-known and popular Minnesota Democrat and was being challenged in the West Virginia presidential primary by a gregarious but little known senator from Massachusetts named John F. Kennedy. The J.F.K. organization felt that if he, a wealthy, eastern Irish Catholic, could convince the residents of rural, impoverished, and Protestant West Virginia to vote for him, it would go a long way toward winning the presidency.

Don went to work driving and the entire group stayed at the same hotel. On the second day out, Senator Humphrey asked him if he would stay on as his driver. Don told him that request had to be made directly to Greyhound. Humphrey did and Don stayed on.

The senator was natural and likable. One evening in Charlestown, he asked Don if he'd been to supper. The two of them ate together, which was a pleasant privilege. After the meal, Senator Humphrey flew to Charleston while Don drove the bus.

Don had a friend, Dan Maroney, who was also a bus driver. He was the driver union's president and later served as international president of the Amalgamated Transit Union. He was Irish Catholic and had been chosen to drive the J.F.K. group.

One night at the Charleston garage, someone put H.H.H. stickers all over J.F.K.'s bus. Dan got so upset he had to go to confession.

Humphrey and Kennedy put great energy into that primary. The two buses met one day on the road and it was on national television. The candidates got off, shook hands, and had a friendly visit. They liked each other. Sometimes Jackie was with Jack, working the crowds. Two of President Franklin Roosevelt's sons came in support of Senator Humphrey.

It was May in 1960. On election night the candidates and their staffs were all at their headquarters in the hotel. J.F.K. was ahead. Bob Kennedy came to Humphrey headquarters and offered good wishes. A wonderful experience it was. One good man won and another good man lost.

Before the fall election, the Humphreys invited Don and his family to Washington, D.C. Don was tied up with work but Wilma and their son, Donnie, went and spent several days. They saw the city and got to visit with the Humphreys and their children.

Don and Wilma grew up in Scioto County during the era of cowboy Westerns. One of the stars of those shows grew up in Scioto County, too. In 1955, Don was running a store and it was his custom to pick up supplies from the train in McDermott. When he arrived, word was out that Roy Rogers was coming to town. Don drove his old station wagon back to the store and picked up every neighbor child he could get inside. Some were Wilma's brothers and sisters and Larry Strickland was in the crowd.

Roy had been to the Ohio State Fair in Columbus, Ohio, and decided to make a spontaneous stop at his home on Inskeep Road. He wanted to show McDermott to his family. Pat Brady a movie sidekick, was along. Larry Strickland went over to Pat and asked, "Where's Nelly Belle?" (Nelly Belle was Pat's famous Jeep.) Several residents were there as well. Roy walked around and talked and had lots of pictures taken.

Don was involved in various activities. He liked the idea of running square dances so he rented an upstairs hall on Second Street in Portsmouth from a Mrs. Meisel. He hired a good band made up of Hoad Copas, Charlie Mershon, Ray Sargent, and Fred Evans. It was an enjoyable experience, but didn't last long.

Don was driving for Greyhound when Zeke and Doris Mullins were running tour buses. The Brooks and Mullins families lived on Zuefle Drive, Don in the sixth house up on the left. Zeke rented tour buses from Greyhound and asked Don if he'd like to help him get a charter operation started in the '70s. When Zeke needed Don to drive, he just knocked off work at Greyhound.

In both 1981 and 1982, Don drove Zeke's bus to Victorville, California. On one of those trips, Roy Rogers took the group to his Apple Valley home, which was a short distance from the museum. It was two-stories and shaped like a horseshoe. Don hauled everyone to Roy's house where they stayed outside, talked, and shot pictures.

Don Brooks, Roy Rogers and the old Dodge. Victorville, California 1981. *Photo courtesy of Don Brooks.*

Roy's favorite motorcycle brand was Indian. He had two of them on display at his museum. It was pleasing to Roy when Zeke came. He liked Zeke and he always brought people Roy knew.

On another trip they went to the museum but Roy was nowhere to be found. Don began browsing around and found him working on something behind the building. On that trip Roy talked with Wilma Brooks for quite a while. She told him that her mother had played in the McDermott band with him. A band picture was on display and Wilma asked Roy if he could pick her out. Roy walked over and, after all those years, he pointed to her and said, "That's Alice Staten." Then Roy said to Wilma, "I'm going to take you on a special personal tour." She was able to ask him anything she wanted and he explained everything.

Don said, "It was just like seeing him in McDermott."

Back home Alice watched a lot of Roy Rogers programs on

(L to R) Don Brooks, Roy Rogers, and Zeke Mullins on one of the bus trips to see Roy in Victorville, California 1981. Don was the driver. *Photo courtesy of Don Brooks.*

television. She'd exclaim, "I can't believe it! He was so shy he wouldn't look at a girl."

Don added, "Roy was one of the best. I really liked him. He gave of his time happily." To this day, Don is heartened that such successful men as Hubert Humphrey and Roy Rogers were so genuine.

Don and Wilma are retired in Florida. He drove thirty-three years for Greyhound and, after moving to Florida, he did eleven more years for East Coast Lines. They raised five children — three girls and two boys — and are now quite involved with the Lions Club giving help to the blind.

Mark Harris and Ron Ripenhoff at Mark's place of business, Market Street Hardware in Portsmouth, Ohio. A portion of Mark's Roy Rogers collection is shown in the display cabinet, 2012. *Photo courtesy of Gary Hurn.*

After many years of yearning to play the violin, the woman bought one. Determined, she practiced every day but found it difficult. Months and years passed before she finally mustered the courage to arrange a concert. On the special day, many from her community were in attendance. Nervously she took the violin from the case and started to play. An older woman in the back of the room began to weep. The violinist made her way slowly to the back, reached out, and said softly, "I've touched you." To which the weeping woman replied, "No, I'm a musician."

Chapter Twenty-Six
MARK HARRIS

Mark Harris is the hardworking and musical owner of Market Street Hardware and Toy Town on Market Street in Portsmouth, Ohio. Employed there are Ron Riepenhoff, Richard Brown, Howard Morgan, Jr., and David Bauer.

When Mark was a sophomore at Clay High School, he went to work at True Value in New Boston, Ohio, for Ray and Ferne Belcher. Much of his day was spent repairing tires from all sizes of vehicles that were owned by the town of New Boston. It was hard, dirty, dangerous work. In 1970 he moved to Toy Town and concentrated on selling bicycles. He could sell six hundred a year. In 1980 Mark became Toy Town manager, and in 1988 Toy Town and True Value consolidated.

The Belchers sold the business to Mark in 1998. At the time all was well but after the events that occurred on 9/11, the American consumer has become more cautious. The business moved to Market Street right on the esplanade in 2000 into an area known as Boneyfiddle home of the historic Corn Carnival. Mark finds the west end of town friendly, helpful, and steeped with memory.

Mark is a musician. He has three pianos in his store and loves to play. At age fifteen he took some lessons for one year from

Musical friends Roy Rogers and Orville "Pappy" Harris (standing next to Roy). Others are unidentified. *Photo courtesy of Mark Harris.*

Imogene Darling. After that he learned by ear. He can hear a tune and bring that melody from a piano in a most spirited manner. His grandpa, Wilfred Sheridan, a fantastic pianist who kept a grand piano in his home, encouraged Mark. He helped Mark and often took him along to the New Boston Methodist Church where he was the organist.

Mark respects his uncle, Orville, who was known as "Pappy" Harris and loved his piano playing. That playing has quite a history. Orville was captured by the Japanese at Corregidor Island during WWII. He gained fame as a piano player while he was confined. He formed a prisoner band and entertained both his captors and the prisoners, which lifted morale. He also survived the Bataan Death March. After the war he came home and provided musical entertainment in local dance halls and other venues.

Mark has a Roy Rogers exhibit in his store with a unique picture of Roy and Orville Harris on the wall. Orville sparked Mark's lifelong fascination with the King of the Cowboys. Orville was a noted local musician and music is the thread that ties Mark, Roy, and Orville. At one of the Harris family reunions Orville told how he and Roy had met, formed a close friendship, and how he gave Roy tips in music.

Today Mark attends to his business, coordinates local model train enthusiasts, plays his piano, and helps those in need.

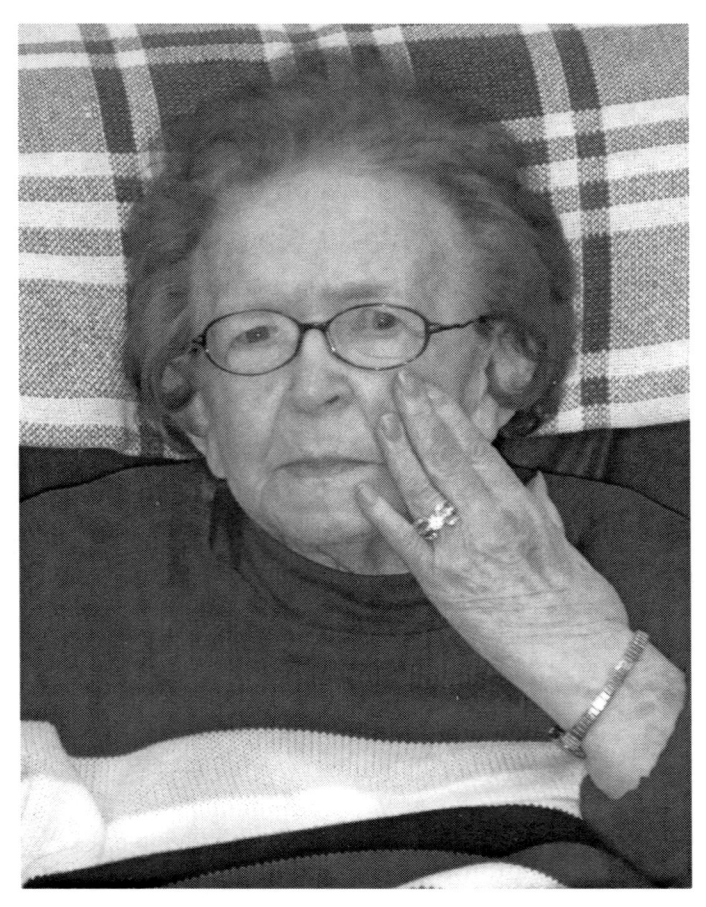

Dorothy "Dot" Wilkerson in 2012. Dot once ate pie with Leonard Slye and Guy Bumgarner. *Photo courtesy of Jamie Williams.*

Way out in the country the fellow ran into his neighbor, Charlie. He said, "Hello, Charlie. I saw you and your wife going up the road the other day. You were on a mule and she was walking?"
   "She ain't got a mule."

Chapter Twenty-Seven
DOROTHY MORITZ WILKERSON

Dot Moritz was a farm girl who grew up on Maple-Benner Road in Lucasville, Ohio. Her parents, Arthur and Blanche Moritz, had lots of kids who helped them harvest their produce and attend to the chickens and dairy cattle. Dot helped clean out the stables and be part of a farm family working together.

Country people worked hard but also had a need to be social. They satisfied some of that need through working together with neighbors or family: making hay, stringing beans, shucking corn, butchering livestock, or making sorghum. They also shared meals together. The Moritz family often ate with Guy, Nell, and Laura Bumgarner. Guy was a teacher and had taught several of the Moritz children. His wife, Nell, and their daughter, Laura, were nice, and they all enjoyed the visits and good food. Before coming to Lucasville School, Guy taught at Duck Run where one of his students was Leonard Slye.

Leonard had since gone to California and become Roy Rogers, but he liked to come home and visit when possible. He sometimes unexpectedly showed up at one home or the other.

Dot recalls one such day when Roy appeared at the Moritz

family home. Blanche, as usual, had cooked a big meal and made six pies. The Bumgarners were there and supper was almost on the table. When Roy walked in, Blanche hurriedly cleaned up a spot for him in the parlor to make him special. Dot remembers thinking, "What's he doing here with the poor people?" But he just acted like one of the family.

Roy got up from his place in the parlor and went to the kitchen. He said, "I'm kind of hungry and I want to be here with the kids and the pie." Roy had a special weakness for pie and homemade pumpkin was his favorite. Blanche handed him a tablespoon. He picked up a pumpkin pie, sat on the bench with the kids, and ate the whole dessert. Roy visited with everybody for a good while and when he left, he took a pie with him. It seemed funny to Dot for a movie star to be so natural.

Dot learned how to work on the farm and when she grew up, she became a cook and baker at her brother's truck stop in Ironton, Ohio. She was also a cook for some time at Clay School as well as selling Stanley Home Products with such success, she won trips to Las Vegas and Hawaii.

Dot married Dave Wilkerson and often speaks of her deceased husband. Their favorite song was "Peg o' My Heart." When Dave was traveling, he would find it on a jukebox, call Dot, and they listened to it together over the phone.

For several years Dot has been in the care of her children as well as Jamie Williams and the excellent staff of Adult Daily Living in Portsmouth, Ohio. Mixed in with Dot's quips they sing "Peg o' My Heart" at most every gathering there.

The former Duck Run Baptist Church and congregation. It stood near the Duck Run school. A new church stands there today. *Photo courtesy of Keith Crabtree and Hubert Crabtree.*

"Excuse me, buddy, could I borrow a dollar 'til my humpbacked uncle gets straightened up?"

Chapter Twenty-Eight
KEITH CRABTREE

Keith Crabtree is the youngest child of Hubert and Tharlene Crabtree. He grew up on Inskeep Road right across from the homeplace of Roy Rogers. Keith had the benefit of his dad's many stories about Leonard Slye, that boy who came from right across the road but gained such fame. Hubert was a bit younger than Leonard, but since there were not usually many kids in each neighborhood the two ran together. Their age difference did not matter. The young ones learned from the older ones.

The Roy Rogers homeplace stands where Allen Hollow and Inskeep Road meet. Allen Hollow was named after a man who lived on that road, Bullskin Allen. He was a patron of nearby taverns and rode his mule back and forth. If Bullskin got a snoot full he counted on his mule to get him safely home. He had to cross a couple of creeks on the trip. One winter night he didn't show up at home so his boys went looking for him. They found him in a creek bed, passed out, his hair frozen to the ice, but still alive. They got his hair free from the ice, took him to the house, and thawed him out; he pulled through.

Inskeep Road is now blacktop surface but was once a dirt road. The dust or mud would squish up between your toes. Inskeep is so named because an Inn once stood on that road to keep the weary traveler. Legend holds that Frank and Jesse James slept there. That was before Hubert's time but he knows the stories. He told Keith that if someone died at the Inn they were buried in a cemetery closeby which is up behind Quinn Crabtree's place on Inskeep.

Keith now lives close to the home where he grew up. Some changes have been made. The upper part of Inskeep Road is now Roy Rogers Road, and Allen Hollow is Sly Road. When those changes were made official, the media came. Keith was a barefoot boy and played amongst all the dignitaries. That evening his family watched the evening news on WSAZ-TV, from Huntington, West Virginia. Keith saw himself running all around with no shoes.

Leonard Slye and his playmates grew up in rural America during a time when people entertained themselves and music was much a part of that. Leonard's father, Andrew, was a musician and so was Keith's father, Hubert. They played music together. So many in that community played, sang, and danced. One of the especially talented ones was Lowell Crabtree, Keith's uncle.

When Leonard went to Hollywood, it was the singing cowboy era and it was nearly a requirement to know how to yodel. When he tried out for a movie role at Republic Studio he told Hubert they specifically asked him to yodel and call a dance. They had plans for their upcoming movies. Those skills came naturally to Leonard because of Lowell and others and because of Leonard's musical development in his home community.

As the lives of the Inskeep boys moved along, several of them went away for work. That included Hubert and Leonard. Hubert and most of the others returned home to live in their beloved hill country, but Roy Rogers could only come home for visits. Hubert told Keith that some of them worked in Cleveland for a while. Around that time, Roy came to town with a rodeo. After the show one evening he went to the workers' boarding house. Hubert was asleep and Roy took hold of his foot and dragged him out of bed.

Roy came home whenever he got a chance. If he could get to the homeplace without notice, the visits would be quiet and to his liking. If word got out he was home, swarms of people came to the little hollow. On one such occasion when Keith was a boy, he came home from school and Roy was there and people were everywhere. Keith had to make his way through all of them just to get to his house.

Keith feels that Roy's home community influences made him the person he came to be. The fact that Roy wanted to come home and stay all night on Inskeep really struck him.

Keith is a surveyor, has a family, and is a member of the Northwest District Board of Education. He is an advocate for those in need. When Northwest School was built, smaller schools were closed—a community loss. They were McDermott, Otway, Rarden, Morgan, and Union. Keith's project is to secure stones from each of those schools and assemble them in a display at Northwest.

• • •

Keith has been quite helpful in gathering material for this book effort and has acquired and cleaned up many pictures, especially the back cover photograph,

Simon's Sorghum, made annually at John R. Simon's Sorghum Festival. Elizabeth Marie Fleming Perkins knew the author as "The Sorghum Man."

We were so poor that for breakfast we had a big bowl of popcorn. For lunch we drank water. And for supper we just swelled up.

Chapter Twenty-Nine
ELIZABETH MARIE FLEMING PERKINS

It was Christmas time 2011 and while making some rounds with guitar in hand at Heartland of Portsmouth nursing home, I was passing room 306 when a voice rang out, "Music!" With that I was drawn into her room and she exclaimed, "The sorghum man." A special friendship resulted with a ninety-year-old, classy lady, Elizabeth Marie Perkins. We made conversation and, along with her roommate, ninety-six-year-old Carmen Collins, sang "Silver Bells." Elizabeth, who liked to go by Marie, was born in Siloam, Kentucky. She made her way to Portsmouth, Ohio, and at age seventeen married Thomas Perkins. They lived in a nicely kept home on Lincoln Street.

Marie secured a job at The Beverly Shop on Chillicothe Street. The store specialized in women's clothes and complemented her interest in fashion and desire to be sharply dressed.

Marie said she was "always terribly drawn to music." She did not play an instrument but listened, and dancing and singing were her musical instruments. She found her way to places that satisfied her musical needs. One such place was Kobacker's

Department Store on Chillicothe Street. Local music and radio personality Zeke Mullins had a daily, early morning show there in the windows. Several attended.

Marie's husband, Tom, was called to military service in the Fiji Islands during WWII. She, like so many others, became a "war widow." Several of these women loved to attend square dances where you could waltz, sing, and step dance the night away. Marie's brother, Shelby Perkins, worked in the Baltimore shipyards but often came home on weekends and went with them to the dances. Their favorite was down on Second Street. It had a wooden floor, sweet music, good caller, and lots of dance partners. Marie proclaimed that she "likes a good do-si-do, to change partners, and get a whack at all of them." The musicians on Second Street were excellent; Blue Creek fiddle champion Fred Evans with Sam Cox on banjo and Zeke Mullins on guitar. The dances were attended by good people from Ohio, Kentucky, and surrounding rural areas.

Marie and three other war widows often went out for supper. They especially enjoyed The Manhattan Bar and Grill on Gallia Street. The Manhattan offered a nice atmosphere, good food, two dance floors, and usually had bands both afternoon and evening. One late afternoon the girls were eating there when Roy Rogers and two other men walked in. Roy was wearing one of those flashy plaid jackets that was in vogue at the time. They looked at the room, the dance floor, music stand, and P.A. system, and then sat down to talk a while before leaving. It was learned that Roy was to make an appearance there and was getting acquainted with the set-up.

The girls finished their supper and went home. Marie stayed over with her girlfriend, Helen White. They talked late into the night about their unusual experience of meeting Roy Rogers face to face.

Johnny Crabtree, the left handed guitar player at Ross County, Ohio Fair. John is a popular entertainer at Tom Cable's Southern Ohio Opry, 2008. *Photo courtesy of Johnny Crabtree.*

Friend said his wife was like an old pair of shoes...everything was worn but her tongue.

Chapter 30
JOHNNY CRABTREE

Johnny was born to Lowell and Grace Benson Crabtree in the old Smith and Everett Hospital. He was one of twelve children, three girls and nine boys. Their home was on Inskeep Road close to the Leonard Slye homeplace. Lowell was a little older then Leonard. He attended Duck Run school before Leonard did, and they ran together as boys.

There were a lot of square dances in the area and Lowell took special interest in calling. Leonard danced and learned calling from Lowell. After Leonard became Roy Rogers, there was often a dance in the barn on the homeplace when he came to visit.

When Johnny was growing up, he

Roy Rogers, Johnny Crabtree's mother Grace Crabtree, and Johnny's brother Paul Crabtree, who died in an accident at Waller Stone. A birthday party for Roy at his homeplace. *Photo courtesy of Johnny Crabtree.*

(L to R) One of the Slye girls, Mary or Kathleen, Lowell Crabtree, unidentified, Leonard Slye, and Cleda Slye Willoughby at the homeplace. *Photo courtesy of Johnny Crabtree.*

wondered why people were always talking about Roy Rogers. As he and the other children played and rode their bikes, they would stop and ask directions and lots of questions about Roy.

One day Roy and Trigger pulled in and Roy had his daughter, Dodie, along. Johnny, Quinn Crabtree, and Dodie spent most of that day playing together.

Several families lived nearby and they held daily games of pitching horseshoes and playing softball. The ball field was up Allen Hollow before it was quarried. Charlie Hiles' wife, Olie, was an adult at the time but she always got in the ball games and she was good.

Johnny attended McDermott schools, and in McDermott they played fast pitch softball. Johnny and his five brothers, Paul, Claude, Larry, Ferrell, and Jerry, played on one team. Paul was later killed in a Taylor Stone accident.

John built a house on Inskeep Road next to his dad's. One day, he looked out and saw Roy Rogers was over there. John went down, sat on the porch with them, and listened to them tell their memories. As boys Lowell and Leonard liked to hunt rabbits but

Roy Rogers and Johnny Crabtree's pony Chance at Johnny's dad, Lowell Crabtree's place on Inskeep Road. *Photo courtesy of Johnny Crabtree.*

had to go up to Lowell's old home to fix them. They had hidden so Charlie Hiles couldn't find them. He would've eaten all the rabbit. They didn't need a dog to hunt because Lowell could bark like a beagle and did so. Johnny had a colt named Chance that he'd bought from Don Strickland. Roy and Chance posed together for pictures that day.

John's dad loved to sing but did not play the guitar so his lines sort of ran together. He sang a lot of babies to sleep as they bounced on his knee. His songs were old standards and he had a special one called "The Counties." Instead of saying Ohio's eighty-eight counties he sang them. He was a spiritual man and if a bleeding child was taken to Lowell he silently recited a special Bible verse and stopped the blood.

Roy was home once and they had a dance up in the barn. Roy and Lowell were calling and Ferrell sang. Roy mixed with everyone. He pulled a twenty out of his billfold, gave it to Ferrell and asked him to go get refreshments.

On another occasion, Roy stopped on his way from Columbus. It was his birthday so a party was thrown in the homeplace. John stayed in the kitchen where Roy was and experienced all the excitement of family and neighbors.

The musical environment of family and neighborhood had its way with John. John did not play an instrument then, but began using his voice instrument; he sang. John is left-handed and musical instruments are right-handed friendly. However, Pat Goodson got him started on electric bass and then he learned guitar. Paul and Marilyn Cox had a music building in Otway where John built his confidence. Closer to home he joined Wayne Vastine on guitar, Jim Goodson on bass, Rodney Teeters on banjo, and Pat Goodson on lead guitar. He also teamed with fiddler Don Hancock and lead guitarist Red Ruggles.

John has developed as a singer, and is respected among his peers. He writes songs and sings favorites from George Jones, Stonewall Jackson, Conway Twitty, Merle Haggard, and Pedro, Ohio native, Bobby Bare.

Local promoter Tom Cable has a great passion for music and has established a very popular Saturday night show, The Southern Ohio Opry. John, who has played there for ten years, has been on the program with Charlie Louvin and Leona Williams. He has also teamed with Georgette Jones on such songs as "White Lightening."

John says Inskeep was a great place to grow up but no big

Charlie Louvin, of the great *Grand Ole Opry* duo The Louvin Brothers (Ira and Charlie), and Johnny Crabtree at Tom Cable's Southern Ohio Opry located on State Route 348 and Henley Deemer Road, McDermott, Ohio. Circa 2009. *Photo courtesy of Johnny Crabtree.*

deal, really. He respects Roy Rogers because Roy appeared as an old country fellow who was really happy to be at home among friends.

John works in maintenance at Southern Ohio Medical Center. He has two daughters and two stepdaughters, one of whom he's teaching to play guitar. And it is a big deal that both he and Roy Rogers are products of that special musical community.

Alice Moulton Barker at her grand old home in Lucasville, Ohio, 2013.
Photo courtesy of John Roger Simon.

By the time I got to greener pastures,
I couldn't climb the fence

Chapter Thirty-One
ALICE MOULTON BARKER

Alice Moulton Barker has a very interesting life. She turned ninety-five on December 15, 2013. She commented at the end of one of our interviews when asked if she was getting worn out, "When you're ninety-five you're already worn out."

Alice was born in Lucasville, Ohio, and has lived her entire life there. Her feeling for that community is reflected in a small sign on her beautiful screened-in porch, "I love Lucasville." Her home is sturdy and warm, built by Mr. Apple of Brandt and Apple Hardware. The house was once home to two funeral parlors.

She was born to Arthur and Bertha Rockwell Moulton and grew into an independent and assertive woman. Those qualities were cultivated by her mother who worked hard for women's rights. At the time, E.O. McCowen was County School Superintendent. He believed strongly in Republican politics and wanted the teachers on his staff to follow suit. That created unrest. Alice's mother led a group who worked there to get politics out of Scioto County Schools. They later started a push to run beer out of Lucasville. Alice's mother allowed her to wear slacks to school when that "just was not done." Alice learned from her mother to think independently and she developed self respect.

Alice's dad, Arthur Moulton, ran a successful Ford dealership in Lucasville. Father Clemet Borchers, the Catholic priest at Otway, bought his cars and had them serviced there. Father Borchers saw that one of the mechanics, Crip Spriggs, was always singing, so he asked him about it. Crip replied, "I either sing or cuss. When you're here I sing."

Alice was schooled locally and enjoyed attending the Lucasville system. She got involved in sports in high school and especially liked basketball. Her team played schools such as McDermott, Rarden, and Otway. She has a friend, Rose O'Brien, who played for Otway. Duck Spriggs drove them to their games. Later, girls' basketball was outlawed on the pretense it wasn't proper.

In 1934 Lucasville and Portsmouth High Schools combined to take students on a train trip to Washington, D.C. Famous Kentucky author Jesse Stuart who taught at Portsmouth was along. He was quite a spirited character. Alice had an interest in his book, *Taps for Private Tussie*.

After high school Alice attended Ohio State University for two years majoring in Home Economics. The country was in the grip of the Great Depression but Alice managed. While at O.S.U. she went to watch the Columbus Redbirds baseball team and Branch Rickey was sometimes there.

Branch eventually became part of her family. Born in Stockdale, Ohio, his family bought a place on Duck Run. When time came for high school, the Rickey family moved to Lucasville so Branch could be educated there.

Alice Moulton's father had a sister, Jenny. She and Branch met at Lucasville High School and took a shine to one another. Jenny's father, Chandler Moulton, thought Branch wasn't good

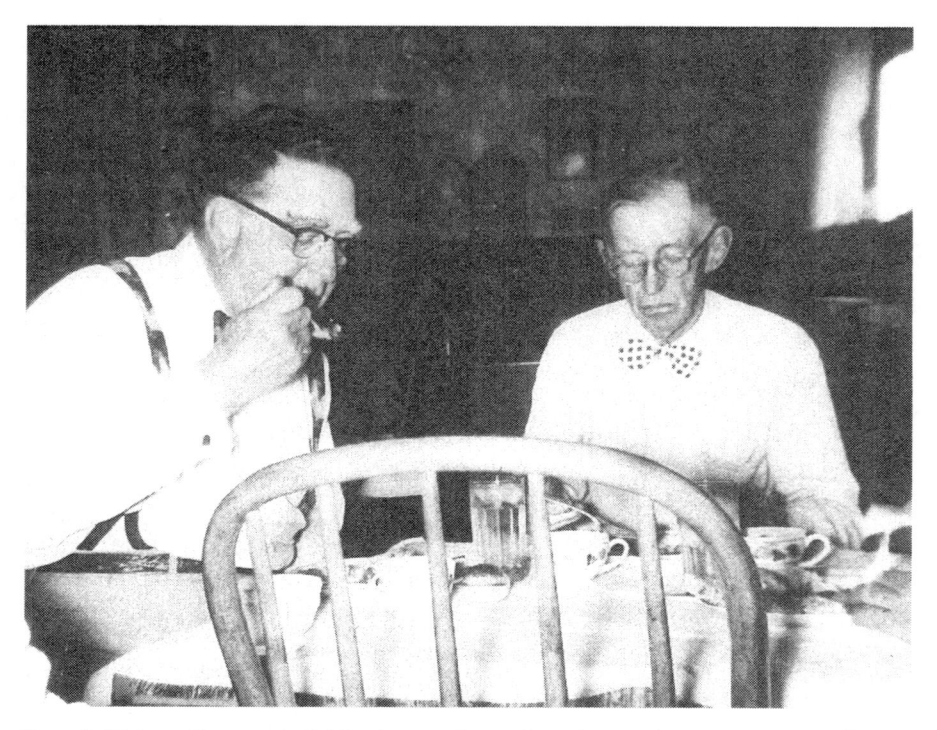

Branch Rickey, (he married Alice's aunt Jenny Moulton so he is Alice's uncle), and John Moulton eat supper at the Moulton house. *Photo courtesy of Alice Moulton Barker.*

enough for Jenny but she would have no other. They married and parented a swell family. Jenny called herself Jane then.

As their family grew, so did Branch's reputation as a sound baseball man. He took control of the Saint Louis Cardinals after moving up through the ranks.

As they raised their family, Jane traveled with Branch. Jane's sister, Mabel, stayed with the children in Saint Louis. In summer, Jane and the children came home to Lucasville and lived in the Moulton home. Mabel came with them.

When Branch traveled to Lucasville, he was driven by a chauffeur and usually stayed overnight. He was the type of person who made every moment count. Alice often saw him play bridge

HOMETOWN ECHOES--- By C. Kessler

·MEMOIRS·
ONE OF BRANCH RICKEY'S BOY-
HOOD PASTIMES, BACK IN LUCASVILLE,
OHIO, WAS SWINGING ON JANE
MOULTON'S FRONT GATE.

Clipping of September 29, 1945, "Hometown Echoes" using the subject of Alice's uncle, Branch Rickey, and aunt, Jenny (Jane) Moulton. *Photo courtesy of Alice Moulton Barker.*

and talk on the phone at the same time. Branch chewed on a cigar and if the subject of Communism came up he got riled. He was a strong man with a course voice and dynamic personality. Alice says, "He was good at telling you what to do."

Alice was able to spend a lot of time with the Rickey children because of their frequent visits.

Another fellow with strong Lucasville ties was Roy Rogers. He liked to come home and visit and, when on the road, he kept an eye out for home folks. Uel Underwood, a Lucasville teacher, told that when he served in the military out on the west coast, Roy came to entertain the troops. As he walked by, Uel simply said, "Scioto County." Roy said, "Don't let that man get away." They had a good visit.

Uel, too, was a good friend of Guy Bumgarner, Roy's former teacher. Guy was well-liked and respected by the majority of his pupils and their parents. He had a way that allowed people to feel comfortable with themselves. That kind of environment encourages artistic tendencies. Good examples of Guy's influence were the exceptional local artist, George Little, and the talented Leonard Slye.

When Lucasville held their sesquicentennial in 1969, Guy invited Roy to participate. Roy accepted and they got to spend two or three days together. Roy stayed the nights at Guy's and Nell's home.

During the sesquicentennial, men were required to wear a beard and, if caught without one, could be tried in court and sentenced to shackles and

Roy Rogers on the telephone at the home of Guy and Nelle Bumgarner in Lucasville, Ohio 1969. *Photo courtesy of Alice Moulton Barker.*

head stocks. Contests were held and dignitaries honored. Roy and his son, Dusty attended the three-day celebration. One evening a storm hit, the electric went out, and the horses were spooked. The festivities were all moved inside with nearly everyone in the community involved.

Roy attended the official events but during the rest of the time he mingled and visited. He wanted no fanfare; he just wanted to be able to talk to all sorts of people who he knew were there. He sometimes borrowed a car and made off to the home place. Ohio governor James Rhodes was there. When the official parade took place, Roy rode

Guy Bumgarner and Alice Barker at 1969 Lucasville, Ohio, "court proceedings" at their sesquicentenial. Alice in her 1890s style catalina swimsuit. Alice says, "How would you like to go in the water wearing that?" *Photo courtesy of Alice Barker.*

(L to R) John Artis, unidentified, Roy Rogers, and Dusty Rogers at the Lucasville Fair Grounds, 1969. *Photo courtesy of Alice Barker.*

on a float. Governor Rhodes was provided a float but he said, "No, thanks. This is Roy's day. I'll walk."

Alice entered the bathing suit contest in her 1890s-style Catalina swimsuit. Alice later commented, "Can you imagine going in the water in that?"

After graduating from O.S.U. in the '40s, Alice went to work in Portsmouth at Atlas Fashions, a store where women shopped for nice clothing. Atlas was owned by William Atlas. His father had been a pack peddler. Pack peddlers worked out of a home store, and carried merchandise through the country on foot, selling it door to door. William cultivated a successful business and depended greatly on Alice. Most of her career was spent there.

There was bus service from Lucasville to Portsmouth but not

POSTLUDE--BY ROY ROGERS

Guy Bumgarner came to our country school in Duck Run, Ohio when I was in the 6th grade. He took over the teaching from a very unpleasant teacher, who favored some children and was quite tough on others. He was always beating on the boys, but seldom disciplined the girls in the same harsh manner. Finally, he was replaced by a mild-mannered, wonderfully fair teacher named *Guy Bumgarner.* Guy was the most important and inspirational man in my young life. He started the 4-H Club, the basketball and baseball teams.

Within two months, Guy Bumgarner had us literally "eating out of his hand"! Because of his support of me in the 4-H Club, I won First Prize of the Scioto County Fair--for the best pig in the county. The prize was an all-expenses-paid trip to our State Capital, Columbus, Ohio...indeed, a great thrill for a twelve-year-old boy.

Under Guy's fine teaching and fairness, all the students came to love him. He encouraged us to be the best we could with our talents and in the programs we chose. He gave me a wonderful, new and positive outlook on life, which I believe contributed to my success in show business. Years later, I was featured on the "This Is Your Life" television program by Ralph Edwards. The biggest thrill of the evening for me was when they introduced Guy Bumgarner and he walked out on the stage to greet me after many long years. It seems like yesterday. I shall always be grateful to Guy Bumgarner.

Roy Rogers

Page from the Bumgarner family history written by Guy Bumgarner's daughter. Courtesy of Ruth Adkins.

at the right time to accommodate Alice's work schedule. Her independent, industrious nature didn't let that stop her—she hitch hiked. Either the milkman, ice man, Ohio Power man, or state highway patrolman usually gave her a lift to Portsmouth each morning. In the evening she hitch hiked home. Her work life was enhanced each day by conversations with various souls who were willing to be helpful by giving her a ride.

Alice lives in her own home in her hometown. Her daughter lives close by. Alice stays physically active. Each day she and friends go to the local Double R.D. restaurant that was named for owner Berthie Hannah's grandchildren. There Alice gets all the news—and passes some along. Alice is a resource for local history and much else. In her kitchen are signs that read "You Have To Decide, Even To Hesitate" and "Grant Me the Senility to Forget People I Never Liked, The Good Fortune to Run Into The Ones I Do Like, The Eyesight To Tell The Difference."

The fellow from way out in the country bragged, "I have a level headed girlfriend. Tobacco juice runs out of both sides of her mouth at the same time."

Chapter Thirty-Two
THOMAS OWEN

The story of Thomas Owen was made possible through his friend, Maynardsville, Tennessee, disc jockey James A. Perry. James is an advocate for traditional music and had helped greatly in honoring the legacies of both Cowboy Copas and Roy Rogers. James knows Thomas to love music; he will perform at the drop of a hat and that characteristic led Thomas to meet Roy Rogers. That's why he suggested I contact Thomas for inclusion in this book.

Thomas grew up in Tazwell, Tennessee, and it was there his skills in music were developed. He entered military service as a young fellow and, along with military duties, he became leader of a musical group. They played most weekends for their fellow troops as well as civilians.

Thomas is left handed and has found stringed instruments are more friendly if you are right handed. In those days he played bass, lead guitar, banjo, but he loved most to play his Martin D-28 electrified guitar. Thomas served twelve years before he developed lung problems and had to take an early release.

Back home his marriage was in trouble which led to his wife and he divorcing. That was upsetting so Thomas decided to relocate. He was skilled at nearly all mechanical and maintenance work. His good friend, Jam Up Gulley, worked in California. There were jobs there and pay was better. Thomas left Tazwell for Hollywood, California, with Jam Up. A second friend had a service station and another, Kenneth Peore, did maintenance work. He went to work with both of them.

Kenneth and Thomas were called one day to the CBS television recording studio in Hollywood, to do some work. Soon after that, the job of maintenance supervisor became available. Thomas applied and was hired to take care of the entire CBS operation there. CBS recorded the shows of stars such as the Smothers Brothers, Mickey Rooney, Danny Kaye, Roy Rogers, and many others. According to Thomas, Roy was the only nice one of the bunch, but he often "tightened up" when The Boss—Dale—came around. She liked a person to "snap to."

CBS had a revolving stage and one scene required Roy Rogers to call for Trigger. The moving stage made Trigger nervous and the horse moved in such a way that it caused the stage to click as it turned. Dale would not film anymore until the click was fixed. Thomas removed a panel on the side of the stage and crawled in to repair the flaw. The space was filled with spiders and he got spider webs all over him. After he finished his work he crawled back out and began to replace the panel. Someone behind him began wiping him off with his hands. Thomas turned to see Roy Rogers. Roy said, "Young fellow, you may have a black widow in there." Thomas was shocked when he saw who it was.

He said, "Hello, Mr. Rogers. How are you? Thank you for helping me." Roy asked Thomas who he was and where he came from. When Thomas told Roy he had come from Tennessee looking for work, Roy told him, "I came from Ohio to California looking for a job too."

Roy's unassuming manner came across clearly causing Thomas to reflect on the fact that even as famous as Roy was, he had remained such a modest man. They talked awhile and Dale called Roy back to the stage.

They next day Thomas was in the cafeteria, sitting alone, having a hamburger. Roy came in and got a hot dog. Instead of sitting with the cast, he sat down with Thomas. Roy remembered him from the day before and called him by name. Roy said he had to eat the hot dog fast before Dale got there because "she would take it away from me…says they are not good for me. She serves as my disciplinarian."

As they talked, Thomas learned that he and Roy had a lot in common: their rural backgrounds, a deep interest in music, and a love of shooting pool as well as riding horses. Roy spoke a lot about Trigger and asked Thomas to come to the ranch so they could ride horses and shoot some pool.

Roy filmed at the CBS studio for over a week. He made a good impression on everyone. On Roy's last day Thomas was working in his office. Roy knocked on the door, came in, and sat down. He told Thomas he had enjoyed their time together and that the invitation stood to come to the ranch. Thomas hated to see Roy leave.

From his work at CBS, Thomas found Roy to be a most unusual star—a plain man in a fancy suit, a good fellow from the farm. He was pleasant and always good to everyone.

Thomas thought Roy had a wonderful life.

Why was Roy so pleased to find Thomas Owen? Roy was on

a movie set surrounded by those not of his culture. Many of them appeared uncomfortable with themselves and others. In Thomas he found the "real ticket," a capable and genuine person—rare in Roy's world. They shared a similar Appalachian background. Roy came from the hills of southern Ohio; Thomas from the hills of Tennessee. Many of their ancestors arrived from Europe and settled those hills. They loved their simple way of life. When they had to leave it for work, they sought others who were like the people they knew when they were growing up: quiet, musical, nature- and home-loving, who honored God and family and even spoke in a similar manner.

Thomas' people, especially, lived in a region of Appalachia where speech is very identifiable. They made no effort to change it to be like others. They hung on to their identity. For example, they still put the "h" sound in front of words such as ain't (pronounced hain't) and it (pronounced hit) and their accent remains distinctive.

Roy saw that familiar strength in Thomas and clung to the satisfaction of being in his company for the days they were together.

Roy Rogers' fame never took away his need for someone like Thomas Owen.

The old fellow had never been married but when he was in military service, he got engaged to a hula dancer.
   She wiggled out of it.

Chapter Thirty-Three
EULA CRABTREE ADKINS

Eula Crabtree, daughter of Hubert and Tharlene Swords Crabtree, grew up near the confluence of Allen Hollow and Inskeep Road in sight of the family of Leonard Slye, who is now Roy Rogers. She knew that her father had been a chum of Leonard's in boyhood and that their friendship held firm through their lives. Her parents shared memories with her of their experiences with Leonard—mostly good ones.

Eula is a member of a large family; her siblings are successful people. None of her older brothers or sisters had gone to college, but Eula was a bookworm and wanted to pursue higher education. The study of law seemed appealing, but so did nursing. Carl Austin was her counselor at Northwest School. His wife, Karen, was a nurse and had attended the school of nursing at Holzer Hospital in Gallipolis, Ohio. Eula's family

Eula Crabtree Adkins in 1973. *Photo courtesy of Eula Crabtree Adkins*

Eula Crabtree Adkins in the Bahamas 1981. *Photo courtesy of Eula Crabtree Adkins.*

was so supportive of her becoming a nurse, she enrolled at Holzer.

She worked hard for years at the Holzer minimal care for diagnostic studies and became head nurse of that unit. Eula worked in every area of Holzer, including obstetrics and the nursery. She also spent a short time at Holzer's Jackson Clinic.

In 2002, Eula moved to Portsmouth's Southern Ohio Medical Center (SOMC). It was close to home and she worked in the monitor care unit, a step down from intensive care. When Hospice opened a local branch, she was interested. Hospice is an organization that cares for the terminally ill. Eula liked Hospice's mission, which includes healthcare without machinery and patients making their own ultimate decisions with dignity, so she began nursing there.

Over the years Eula was aware of the coming and goings of Roy Rogers. When he came home, he always hoped he could visit quietly without crowds knowing he was there. On one visit, concrete was being poured behind the Slye homeplace and Roy put his handprints in it. Eula said that even though Roy was such a talented and handsome man, he was able to talk to everyone no matter what their age or social status. "If I had been in his age group I'd have gone out with him."

Roy loved to square dance and he could call the dances, too. They would usually get up a dance when he was home. They were held in the barn near the homeplace on Allen Hollow. One night Eula attended. She did not dance that evening but loved the spontaneous excitement created by the setting. Several locals were there and a few younger folks. Roy got up to call. Some dancers were right in step but the younger ones were not able to pick it up. After a while, Roy observed, "This isn't working so well." He went over and took a seat. Eventually the dance proceeded nicely and Eula now realizes how special that experience was.

Today Eula continues to work in Hospice nursing. She looks out for her children, reads, raises a garden, and treats friends with her famous zucchini relish.

Clara Walsh Simon, the author's mother. *Photo courtesy of John Roger Simon*

The author's father and sister, Edward Louis Simon and Mary Kathleen Simon. *Photo courtesy of John Roger Simon*

About the Author
JOHN ROGER SIMON, Ph.D.

My piano-playing mom, Clara Walsh Simon, came from a musical Irish family. She liked people and was a swell cook, so our home was a hub of family activity. She played tunes on the piano as I (learned and) seconded on banjo. Ed Simon, my dad, was of French descent. He was honest and hard working and he supported the music and Irish ways.

Mom's sister, Rose Walsh, an exceptional piano player, taught me the beauty of the fiddle as we listened to Herman Crook on the *Saturday Night Opry*.

A joy of my life has been playing acoustic, traditional music

John Roger Simon and Cleda Willoughby at the home of John and Bea Hollback. *Photo courtesy of John Roger Simon*

The author attended lots of cowboy Westerns at The Garden movie theater in Portsmouth as a child. *Photo courtesy of Bill Glockner.*

with talented friends such as Aaron Wolfe, Tommi Stanley, Myrtle Euton, Grover Mustard, Roy Hill, Charley Kinney, and so many others. After locating our Irish and French kin in Europe, I went there and lived and learned with each.

My work life has included farms, sawmills, construction, eight years in the local steel mill, and three in the United States Army. Going to college much of this time, I earned degrees from Ohio University and put them to use teaching at several levels. Most of my university teaching at Shawnee State, Ohio University, and Rio Grande was in the area of psychology and Appalachian music, culture, and history.

It is satisfying to live here on The Simon Farm on Pond Creek. Larry Miller of our local Amish community said it is the prettiest valley he's ever seen. I was raised here and I loved it from the beginning. Built with hard work by my people, I've been allowed to spend my life caring for it and enjoying it.

Over the years, I have arranged and participated in numerous musical occasions and founded the Sorghum Festival at our family farm to honor Appalachian artistry. With the help of friends it continues today.

A new, musical education has resulted from writing books on two, southern Ohio men, Cowboy Copas and Leonard Slye. Both men's families welcomed me and helped greatly in my fact gathering. Their knowledge was supplemented by many interesting local people who provided their own stories and friendship.

It has been a pleasure and honor to record these histories!

The author has written one book on Lloyd Estel Copas,* who became known as Cowboy Copas, and this book on Leonard Slye, who became known as Roy Rogers. The two of them met as young men and played music and attended Western movies together. Each of these southern Ohio boys became stars, Cowboy Copas in country music and *The Grand Ole Opry,* and Roy Rogers in the movies and on television. *Photo courtesy of John Roger Simon.*

* *Cowboy Copas and the Golden Age of Country Music*

Index

CPSIA information can be obtained at www.ICGtesting.com
Printed in the USA
LVOW11*0405090714

393481LV00003B/3/P